PERGAMON INSTITUTE OF ENGLISH (NEW YORK)

Language Teaching Methodology Series

PRINCIPLES AND PRACTICE
IN
SECOND LANGUAGE ACQUISITION

Other titles in this series include:

ALTMAN, Howard B. and C. Vaughan James
Foreign Language Teaching: meeting individual needs

BRUMFIT, Christopher J.
Problems and Principles in English Teaching

CARROLL, Brendan J.
Testing Communicative Performance: an interim study

DUFF, Alan
The Third Language: recurrent problems in translation into English

FISIAK, Jacek (ed.)
Contrastive Linguistics and the Language Teacher

FREUDENSTEIN, Reinhold
Teaching Foreign Languages to the Very Young

FREUDENSTEIN, BENEKE; PONISCH (eds.)
Language Incorporated: teaching foreign languages in industry

JOHNSON, Keith
Notional Syllabuses and Communicative Language Teaching

KELLERMAN, Marcelle
The Forgotten Third Skill: reading a foreign language

KRASHEN, STEPHEN
Second Language Acquisition and Second Language Learning

LEONTIEV, Aleksei A.
Psychology and the Language Learning Process

LEWIS, Glyn
Bilingualism and Bilingual Education

NEWMARK, Peter P.
Approaches to Translation

ROBINSON, Pauline C.
ESP (English for Specific Purposes)

SHARP, Derrick W. H.
English at School: The Wood and the Trees

STREVENS, Peter
Teaching English as an International Language

TOSI, Arturo
Immigration and Bilingual Education

See also SYSTEM: *the International Journal of Education Technology and Language Learning Systems* (Sample copy available on request)

PRINCIPLES AND PRACTICE
IN
SECOND LANGUAGE ACQUISITION

STEPHEN D. KRASHEN
University of Southern California

PERGAMON PRESS
Oxford · New York · Toronto · Sydney · Paris · Frankfurt

U.K.	Pergamon Press Ltd., Headington Hill Hall, Oxford OX3 0BW, England
U.S.A.	Pergamon Press Inc., Maxwell House, Fairview Park, Elmsford, New York 10523, U.S.A.
CANADA	Pergamon Press Canada Ltd., Suite 104, 150 Consumers Road, Willowdale, Ontario M2J 1P9, Canada
AUSTRALIA	Pergamon Press (Aust.) Pty. Ltd., P.O. Box 544, Potts Point, N.S.W. 2011, Australia
FRANCE	Pergamon Press SARL, 24 rue des Ecoles, 75240 Paris, Cedex 05, France
FEDERAL REPUBLIC OF GERMANY	Pergamon Press GmbH, Hammerweg 6, D-6242 Kronberg-Taunus, Federal Republic of Germany

First edition 1982
Reprinted 1983, 1984

Library of Congress Cataloging in Publication Data
Krashen, Stephen D.
Principles and practice in second language
acquisition (Language teaching methodology series)
1. Language and languages—Study and teaching.
2. Language acquisition. I. Title. II. Series.
P53.K73   1981   407   81-13909   AACR2

British Library Cataloguing in Publication Data
Krashen, Stephen D.
Principles and practice in second language
acquisition.—(Language teaching methodology
series)
1. Language and languages—Study and teaching
I. Title   II. Series
401'.9   P53
ISBN 0-08-028628-3

*Printed in Great Britain by
A. Wheaton & Co. Ltd., Exeter*

Acknowledgments

I am indebted to many people who have helped me both directly and indirectly. I can only mention a few of them here. Earl Stevick and Robin Scarcella kindly provided me with detailed comments on nearly every aspect of the manuscript. I have also received a great deal of useful feedback from John Schumann, John Oller, Adrian Palmer, Tracy Terrell, Andrew Cohen, Steven Sternfeld, and Batyia Elbaum. I am sure this book would be much stronger if I had followed all their advice. The task of writing this volume was made much easier by the support and understanding of my family, my wife Eula, my children Deborah and Daniel, and my parents Leo and Julia Krashen. I would also like to thank my colleagues in the Linguistics Department at USC for their intellectual stimulation and encouragement. I especially thank Larry Hyman, Edward Finegan, Eugene Briere, Elaine Andersen, Elinor Ochs, Edward Purcell, John Hawkins, and Bernard Comrie.

Contents

Chapter I

Introduction: The Relationship of Theory to Practice

The purpose of this book is to take a new look at an old question: the relationship between second language teaching practice and what is known about the process of second language acquisition. The usual way to do this is to discuss some research results first, outline a possible theory, and then list some implications. I will, to some extent, follow this plan. A significant portion of this book is, in fact, devoted to summarizing the current state of second language acquisition theory as I see it. Following this, I will draw some general conclusions about application to methods and materials, and eventually describe what characteristics effective materials should have.

Before going through this exercise, however, it is important to state in advance that "theory" and "theoretical research" should not be the only input into deciding on methodology and materials. While my emphasis here is on theory and its implications, it is dangerous to rely only on theory. There are at least three different ways of arriving at answers in methodology and materials, and we must consider all of them. I will devote the remainder of this introduction to a brief description of these three areas, and a discussion of how they interrelate with each other. We will then see what each has to say about method in second and foreign language teaching. My view, for those who like the punch line early, is that all three ways arrive at precisely the same answer. The solution to our problems in language teaching lies not in expensive equipment, exotic methods, sophisticated linguistic analyses, or new laboratories, but in full utilization of what we already have, speakers of the languages using them for real communication. I will also conclude that the best methods might also be the most pleasant, and that, strange as it seems, language acquisition occurs when language is used for what it was designed for, communication.

1

A. Three Approaches to Method

1. THEORY OF SECOND LANGUAGE ACQUISITION

The first area we will discuss will be the central focus of this volume, second language acquisition theory. As developed today, second language acquisition theory can be viewed as a part of "theoretical linguistics", i.e. it can be studied and developed without regard to practical application. As is the case with any scientific theory, it consists of a set of *hypotheses*, or generalizations, that are consistent with experimental data. These hypotheses can be arrived at using any of a variety of means (a brilliant insight, a dream, etc.). They must, however, be able to predict new data. In other words, hypotheses are not summaries or categories for previously existing data and observations, but must pass the test of accounting for new data. If our current hypotheses are able to predict new events, they survive. If they fail, even once, they must be altered. If these alterations cause fundamental changes in the original generalizations, the hypotheses may have to be totally abandoned.

Note that according to this way of doing science, we can never really prove anything! We can only look for "supporting evidence". When we do not find supporting evidence, or when we find counter-evidence, our hypothesis is in trouble. Even when we do find supporting evidence, when the hypothesis makes the correct prediction, a critic can always say that we have not found "enough". Thus, a scientist, professionally speaking, is never able to state that anything has been "proven". All the scientist can do is have a current hypothesis that he or she is interested in testing.

Later in this book I will present a series of hypotheses that make up a coherent theory of second language acquisition. According to the rules of scientific method, it will always be "just theory" and never be "definitely proven". The hypotheses I will present have, however, been found to be consistent with a significant amount of data, experimental and otherwise, and have not yet been confronted with serious counterexamples, in my view. They make up, collectively, my "position". This does not mean that I necessarily "believe" them. What it does mean is that these hypotheses are consistent enough with existing data to be worthy of consideration, and that they appear to capture the data better than other existing generalizations.

Theory is abstract, and does not attempt to be practical. I hope to convince the reader, however, that in the case of second language teaching, there is nothing as practical as a good theory!

2. APPLIED LINGUISTICS RESEARCH

A great deal of research goes on in linguistics that is not aimed at supporting or attacking any coherent theory. This research, rather, is aimed at solving practical, real problems that confront society. A few examples will hopefully make this category clear.

An example that will be important to us in our discussion of language teaching consists of experiments that compare teaching methods. Quite simply, a group of students is taught a foreign language using method A (e.g. audio-lingual), and another group is taught the same language using method B (e.g. grammar-translation). The results of such an experiment would certainly be of interest to theoreticians, since a particular theory might predict that students studying using one method would do better than students using another. The experiment itself, however, is designed for practical ends, i.e. to decide which method we should use in our schools.

The research literature contains many applied linguistics experiments examining other questions of very practical relevance, e.g.:

Will instruction in a second language make children more intelligent? (or less intelligent?)

Should non-English speaking children in American Bilingual Education begin to read in their first language or in English?

3. IDEAS AND INTUITIONS FROM EXPERIENCE

A third approach to method does not rely on experimentation at all. It relies, rather, on the insights and observations of experienced language teachers and students of foreign languages. It consists of "ideas that work" (the name of a column in the *TESOL Newsletter* edited by Darlene Larson, consisting of pedagogical techniques sent in by teachers), introspections by language students (e.g. "diary studies"), and other informal observations. While results of research are regularly presented in professional journals, teachers' insights are not easily accessed and shared. Language teaching organizations often arrange meetings so that experienced teachers can share their techniques and insights with others (e.g. the highly successful "mini-conferences" organized by the California TESOL organization). Empirical support for new techniques is neither expected nor presented; rather, the word of the teacher is sufficient evidence, often, for a new idea to be at least tried out in different classes.

B. Interactions Among Approaches to Practice

Before discussing what each approach has to say about methods and materials, I would like to make a modest proposal: the three approaches should influence and help each other. It seems obvious, first of all, that researchers would be interested in the results of applied research, since such experiments can provide potential confirming and counter evidence for theories of second language acquisition. Similarly, it stands to reason that applied linguistics researchers should pay some attention to strictly theoretical research, since a successful theory might give researchers deeper insight into the results of their studies.

It also seems reasonable to suggest that researchers in both theoretical and applied linguistics would benefit by both teaching and studying languages, in order to get more insight into the language acquisition process. Similarly, one might expect practitioners to be interested in the results of research, and one might also expect researchers to be very interested in the opinions of both teachers and language students.

Figure 1.1 illustrates this ideal world, with information flowing between all three areas that influence language teaching methodology. Figure 1.2 is, however, much closer to the actual state of affairs: there is, today, very little interaction between and among the three areas.

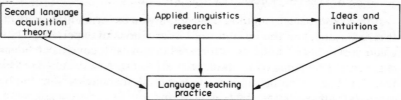

Fig. 1.1. Ideal relationship between theory, applied linguistics research, ideas and intuitions and language teaching practice.

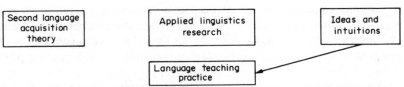

Fig. 1.2. Actual relationship between theory, applied linguistics research, ideas and intuitions and language teaching practice.

In reality, many researchers are no longer involved in language teaching and language acquisition, and do not interact with teachers. There is also far too little interaction between theoretical and applied research; those who search for the best method are often too little concerned with the underlying theory. What is perhaps most evident is that teachers and materials developers pay little attention to research and theorizing of any sort.

There is good reason for this lack of interaction, especially the failure of researchers and teachers to interact. The reasons for this lack of communication do not stem from any anti-intellectualism on the part of teachers. They stem, rather, from the failure of research to supply relevant input in the past, combined with the insistence on the part of theoreticians that *their* insights were the only legitimate determinant of teacher behavior and materials construction. In other words, we have, in the past, gone straight from theory to practice, and it simply has not worked.

Some well-known examples of this approach include the direct application of the principles of behaviorist psychology in the classroom, known as the audio-lingual method. Theoreticians insisted that dialogue and pattern drill were "the way" to teach language, and recommended techniques that felt wrong to many teachers and students. A more recent "application of theory" was what may be called the "applied transformational grammar" movement, which featured materials directly based on current work in theoretical syntax and phonology. Applied TG did not significantly advance language teaching, for reasons that will become clear as we proceed. Its only tangible effect, perhaps, was that it needlessly made many teachers feel unprepared because they had not been trained in the latest version of transformational theory. (Lest the reader get the wrong impression, my personal view is that transformational–generative grammar, and the progress it stimulated in formal linguistics, should be recognized as an extremely important contribution, and easily outdid previous theories of linguistic structure. My point here is that it does not necessarily follow that second language methods and materials should be based directly on TG.)

These two theories, then, failed. The first, behaviorist theory, failed to apply successfully to language teaching because it was, simply, not a theory of language acquisition. The second, TG, failed because it was a theory of the *product*, the adult's competence, and not a theory of how the adult got that competence. It is not a theory of the *process* of language acquisition.

The "new" theory, which I will present in Chapter II, is a theory of second language acquisition, and attempts to deal with the process of language acquisition, not its product. Despite these virtues, it should only be considered one of several possible sources of information in determining methods and materials for second language teaching.

Compounding the failure of theoreticians to supply relevant theory has been the feeling among practitioners that failure to make the theory "work" has been their fault. They incorrectly concluded that it was their ignorance of theory that caused these theory-based methods to fail. As a result of this, teachers in recent years have appealed mostly to area III, their own ideas and intuitions, in determining what they do in the classroom. What teachers actually do is no longer based on theoretical or applied research. Materials, and many books on methodology, are based primarily on what seems to work in the classroom, and only rarely on a theory (recall earlier books based on audiolingualism or TG), and are usually not field-tested.

C. What the Three Approaches Have to Say About Method

The purpose of this book is to summarize one current theory and state the implications of the theory to method. I will briefly summarize here what some of these implications are, anticipating Chapter III. What current theory implies, quite simply, is that language acquisition, first or second, occurs only when comprehension of real messages occurs, and when the acquirer is not "on the defensive", to use Stevick's apt phrase. Language acquisition does not require extensive use of conscious grammatical rules, and does not require tedious drill. It does not occur overnight, however. Real language acquisition develops slowly, and speaking skills emerge significantly later than listening skills, even when conditions are perfect. The best methods are therefore those that supply "comprehensible input" in low anxiety situations, containing messages that students really want to hear. These methods do not force early production in the second language, but allow students to produce when they are "ready", recognizing that improvement comes from supplying communicative and comprehensible input, and not from forcing and correcting production.

In several places in this book I will attempt to make the point that research in applied linguistics is very consistent with the theoretical research in second language acquisition and its implications. The "best methods" according to comparative research studies (comparing methods A and B, as described earlier) appear to be "input methods", those methods that focus on supplying comprehensible input in pressure-free situations.

We can get an idea of what the "ideas and intuitions" area feels is the "best method" by a survey of pedagogically-oriented papers in current journals and the titles of presentations at teacher workshops. The titles have changed markedly over the years! A decade ago teacher-oriented articles and presentations focussed on grammatical description, reflecting the concern with *product*, and procedures for drilling.[1]* Current titles more clearly reflect promoting real communication in the classroom, helping students *understand* spoken and written input and participate in conversations.[2]

In workshops and mini-conferences, we no longer see presentations on fine points of grammar, or on types of substitution drill. "Ideas that work" are ideas about role-playing, using the newspaper as a teaching aid, socio-drama, etc. Moreover, newer methodology has, as a primary goal, the lowering of student anxiety (see Chapter III).

D. Goals of This Book

The primary goal of this book is to present current theory and its implications. There is another goal, however, and that is to reintroduce

* Superscript numbers refer to Notes at end of chapters.

teachers to theory and hopefully to gain their confidence again. The time has come to look to theory again, realizing that the most current theory may still not be the final word on second language acquisition. I am not asking practitioners or materials developers to follow all of the implications of theory blindly. My hope is only that our results will be considered as another source of ideas and input to methods and materials, in partnership with conclusions reached by practitioners themselves from their own experience as language teachers and language acquirers.

Notes

[1] Consider, for example, the table of contents of *Language Learning*, vol. 9, 1959, which included:
  "Grammatical theory and practice in an English grammar class"
  "Teaching the French verb"
  "Noun-classes and the practical teacher"
  "Morpheme alternants in Spanish verb forms"
  " 'Technemes' and the rhythm of class activity"
Volume 12, 1962, contained:
  "Annotated bibliography of generative grammar"
[2] The 1979 volume of the *TESOL Quarterly*, for example, contains articles such as:
  "Using radio commercials as supplementary materials in ESL listening classes"
  "Communicative writing"
  "Joke-telling as a tool in ESL."
reflecting the current emphasis on communication in the classroom.
  (Notes 1 and 2 certainly do not represent a wide sample of activity in the field, but they are representative. In recent years, the journal *Language Learning* has focussed on theoretical and applied research, rather than pedagogy. For this reason, I used the *TESOL Quarterly*, which began publication in 1967, for current titles.)

Chapter II

Second Language Acquisition Theory

This chapter summarizes current second language acquisition theory. To do this, it first describes some very important hypotheses. The first three, the acquisition–learning distinction, the natural order hypothesis, and the Monitor hypothesis, are reviewed somewhat briefly, as they have been dealt with a great deal in several other books and professional papers. Enough detail will be provided, however, to give the uninitiated reader a good idea of the hypotheses and the sort of evidence that exists to support them. The fourth hypothesis, the input hypothesis, may be the single most important concept in second language acquisition theory today. It is important because it attempts to answer the crucial theoretical question of how we acquire language. It is also important because it may hold the answer to many of our everyday problems in second language instruction at all levels. Following the discussion of the input hypothesis, we turn to the concept of the affective filter, a hypothesis as to how affective variables relate to the process of second language acquisition.

The second portion of this chapter reviews a variety of factors that have been thought to be related to second language acquisition success, including instruction, different measures of exposure to the second language, and the age of the acquirer. These factors, it will be claimed, are not really causative factors. While they seem to relate to success or failure to acquire second languages, the true causative variables in second language acquisition derive from the input hypothesis and the affective filter—the amount of *comprehensible input* the acquirer receives and understands, and the strength of the affective filter, or the degree to which the acquirer is "open" to the input.

A. Five Hypotheses About Second Language Acquisition

1. THE ACQUISITION–LEARNING DISTINCTION

The acquisition–learning distinction is perhaps the most fundamental of all the hypotheses to be presented here. It states that adults have two distinct and independent ways of developing competence in a second language.

The first way is language *acquisition*, a process similar, if not identical, to the way children develop ability in their first language. Language acquisition is a subconscious process; language acquirers are not usually aware of the fact that they are acquiring language, but are only aware of the fact that they are using the language for communication. The result of language acquisition, acquired competence, is also subconscious. We are generally not consciously aware of the rules of the languages we have acquired. Instead, we have a "feel" for correctness. Grammatical sentences "sound" right, or "feel" right, and errors feel wrong, even if we do not consciously know what rule was violated.

Other ways of describing acquisition include implicit learning, informal learning, and natural learning. In non-technical language, acquisition is "picking-up" a language.

The second way to develop competence in a second language is by language *learning*. We will use the term "learning" henceforth to refer to conscious knowledge of a second language, knowing the rules, being aware of them, and being able to talk about them. In non-technical terms, learning is "knowing about" a language, known to most people as "grammar", or "rules". Some synonyms include formal knowledge of a language, or explicit learning.[1]*

Some second language theorists have assumed that children acquire, while adults can only learn. The acquisition–learning hypothesis claims, however, that adults also acquire, that the ability to "pick-up" languages does not disappear at puberty. This does not mean that adults will always be able to achieve native-like levels in a second language. It does mean that adults can access the same natural "language acquisition device" that children use. As we shall see later, acquisition is a very powerful process in the adult.

---

* Superscript numbers refer to Notes at end of Chapters.

Error correction has little or no effect on subconscious acquisition, but is thought to be useful for conscious learning. Error correction supposedly helps the learner to induce or "figure out" the right form of a rule. If, for example, a student of English as a second language says "I goes to school every day", and the teacher corrects him or her by repeating the utterance correctly, the learner is supposed to realize that the /s/ ending goes with the third person and not the first person, and alter his or her conscious mental representation of the rule. This appears reasonable, but it is not clear whether error correction has this impact on learning in actual practice (Fanselow, 1977; Long, 1977).

Evidence from child language acquisition confirms that error correction does not influence acquisition to any great extent. Brown and his colleagues have shown that parents actually correct only a small portion of the child's language (occasional pronunciation problems, certain verbs, and dirty words!). They conclude from their research that parents attend far more to the truth value of what the child is saying rather than to the form. For example, Brown, Cazden, and Bellugi (1973) report that a sentence such as:

Her curl my hair

"was approved, because the mother was, in fact, curling Eve's hair" (p. 330). On the other hand,

Walt Disney comes on on Tuesday

was corrected, despite its syntactic correctness, since Walt Disney actually came on television on Wednesday. Brown *et al*. conclude that it seems to be "truth value rather than syntactic well-formedness that chiefly governs explicit verbal reinforcement by parents—which renders mildly paradoxical the fact that the usual product of such a training schedule is an adult whose speech is highly grammatical but not notably truthful" (p. 330).

The acquisition–learning distinction may not be unique to second language acquisition. We certainly "learn" small parts of our first language in school (e.g. for most people, the who/whom distinction), and similar distinctions have been made in other domains (see, for example, Reber, 1976; Hall, 1959; and the review in d'Anglejan, 1978).

2. THE NATURAL ORDER HYPOTHESIS

One of the most exciting discoveries in language acquisition research in recent years has been the finding that the acquisition of grammatical structures proceeds in a predictable order. Acquirers of a given language tend to acquire certain grammatical structures early, and others later. The agreement among individual acquirers is not always 100%, but there are clear, statistically significant, similarities.

English is perhaps the most studied language as far as the natural order hypothesis is concerned, and of all structures of English, morphology is the most studied. Brown (1973) reported that children acquiring English as a first language tended to acquire certain grammatical morphemes, or functions words, earlier than others. For example, the progressive marker *ing* (as in "He is play*ing* baseball".) and the plural marker /s/ ("two dog*s*") were among the first morphemes acquired, while the third person singular marker /s/ (as in "He live*s* in New York") and the possessive /s/ ("John'*s* hat") were typically acquired much later, coming anywhere from six months to one year later. de Villiers and de Villiers (1973) confirmed Brown's longitudinal results cross-sectionally, showing that items that Brown found to be acquired earliest in time were also the ones that children tended to get right more often. In other words, for those morphemes studied, the difficulty order was similar to the acquisition order.

Shortly after Brown's results were published, Dulay and Burt (1974, 1975) reported that children acquiring English as a second language also show a "natural order" for grammatical morphemes, regardless of their first language. The child second language order of acquisition was different from the first language order, but different groups of second language acquirers showed striking similarities. Dulay and Burt's results have been confirmed by a number of investigators (Kessler and Idar, 1977; Fabris, 1978; Makino, 1980). Dulay and Burt used a subset of the 14 morphemes Brown originally investigated. Fathman (1975) confirmed the reality of the natural order in child second language acquisition with her test of oral production, the SLOPE test, which probed 20 different structures.

Following Dulay and Burt's work, Bailey, Madden, and Krashen (1974) reported a natural order for adult subjects, an order quite similar to that seen in child second language acquisition. As we shall see later, this natural order appears only under certain conditions (or rather, it disappears only under certain conditions!). Some of the studies confirming the natural order in adults for grammatical morphemes include Andersen (1976), who used composition, Krashen, Houck, Giunchi, Bode, Birnbaum, and Strei, 1977, using free speech, and Christison (1979), also using free speech. Adult research using the SLOPE test also confirms the natural order and widens the data base. Krashen, Sferlazza, Feldman, and Fathman (1976) found an order similar to Fathman's (1975) child second language order, and Kayfetz-Fuller (1978) also reported a natural order using the SLOPE test.

As noted above, the order of acquisition for second language is not the same as the order of acquisition for first language, but there are some similarities. Table 2.1, from Krashen (1977), presents an average

TABLE 2.1. *"Average" order of acquisition of grammatical morphemes for English as a second language (children and adults)*

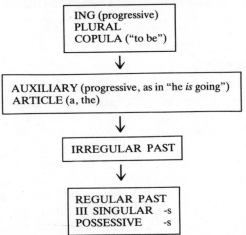

Notes:
   1. This order is derived from an analysis of empirical studies of second language acquisition (Krashen, 1977). Most studies show significant correlations with the average order.
   2. No claims are made about ordering relations for morphemes in the same box.
   3. Many of the relationships posited here also hold for child first language acquisition, but some do not: In general, the *bound* morphemes have the same relative order for first and second language acquisition (ING, PLURAL, IR, PAST, REG. PAST, III SINGULAR, and POSSESSIVE) while AUXILIARY and COPULA tend to be acquired relatively later in first language acquisition than in second language acquisition.

order for second language, and shows how the first language order differs. This average order is the result of a comparison of many empirical studies of grammatical morpheme acquisition.

While English is the best studied language, it is not the only one studied. Research in order of acquisition for other languages is beginning to emerge. As yet unpublished papers by Bruce (1979), dealing with Russian as a foreign language, and van Naerssen (1981), for Spanish as a foreign language, confirm the validity of the natural order hypothesis for other languages.

We will deal with the pedagogical implications of the natural order hypothesis later. I should point out here, however, that the implication of the natural order hypothesis is not that our syllabi should be based on the order found in the studies discussed here, that is, I do not recommend teaching *ing* early and the third person singular /s/ late. We will, in fact, find reason to reject grammatical sequencing in all cases where our goal is language acquisition. We will deal with this later, however, after we have finished laying the theoretical groundwork.

(a) Transitional forms

Studies supporting the natural order hypothesis show only the order in which mature, or well-formed structures emerge. Other studies reveal the path acquirers take *en route* to mastery. (For a review, see Dulay, Burt, and Krashen, in press. Ravem, 1974; Milon, 1974; Gillis and Weber, 1976; Cancino, Rosansky, and Schumann, 1974; Wode, 1978 and Nelson, 1980 are some second language studies in this area.) There is surprising uniformity here as well—acquirers make very similar errors, termed developmental errors, while they are acquiring. For example, in acquiring English negation, many first and second language acquirers pass through a stage in which they place the negative marker outside the sentence, as in:

	No Mom sharpen it.	(from Klima and Bellugi's (1966) study of child L1 acquisition)
and	Not like it now.	(from Ravem's (1974) study of child L2 acquisition)

A typical later stage is to place the negative marker between the subject and the verb, as in:

> I no like this one. (Cancino *et al.* (1975) study of child L2 acquisition)
>
> and This no have calendar. (from Schumann's (1978a) study of adult L2 acquisition)

before reaching the correct form.

Predictable stages in the acquisition of *wh-* questions in English include an early stage in which the *wh-* word appears before the rest of the sentence, which is otherwise left in its normal uninverted form, as in:

> How he can be a doctor? (Klima and Bellugi, 1966, child L1 acquisition)
>
> and What she is doing? (Ravem, 1974, child L2 acquisition)

Only later do acquirers begin to invert the subject and verb of the sentence. (A detailed review can be found in Dulay *et al.*, in press.)

Transitional forms have been described for other languages and for other structures. The stages for a given target language appear to be strikingly similar despite the first language of the acquirer (although particular first languages may influence the duration of certain stages; see Schumann, 1979). This uniformity is thought to reflect the operation of the natural language acquisition process that is part of all of us. (For a discussion of some of the current issues and controversies concerning the natural order hypothesis, see Krashen, 1981.)

3. THE MONITOR HYPOTHESIS

While the acquisition–learning distinction claims that two separate processes coexist in the adult, it does not state how they are used in second language performance. The Monitor hypothesis posits that acquisition and learning are used in very specific ways. Normally, acquisition "initiates" our utterances in a second language and is responsible for our fluency. Learning has only one function, and that is as a Monitor, or editor. Learning comes into play only to make changes in the form of our utterance, after it has been "produced" by the acquired system. This can happen before we speak or write, or after (self-correction). Figure 2.1 models this process.

Fig. 2.1. Acquisition and learning in second language production.

Conscious learning is available only as a "Monitor", which can alter the output of the acquired system before or after the utterance is actually spoken or written. It is the acquired system which initiates normal, fluent speech utterances.

The Monitor hypothesis implies that formal rules, or conscious learning, play only a limited role in second language performance. These limitations have become even clearer as research has proceeded in the last few years. This research, reviewed in Chapter IV, strongly suggests that second language performers can use conscious rules only when three conditions are met. These conditions are *necessary* and not *sufficient*, that is, a performer may not fully utilize his conscious grammar even when all three conditions are met. I list these conditions here, with a brief description. We will discuss them in greater detail in Chapter IV:

(i) *Time*. In order to think about and use conscious rules effectively, a second language performer needs to have sufficient time. For most people, normal conversation does not allow enough time to think about and use rules. The over-use of rules in conversation can lead to trouble, i.e. a hesitant style of talking and inattention to what the conversational partner is saying.

(ii) *Focus on form*. To use the Monitor effectively, time is not enough. The performer must also be focussed on form, or thinking about correctness (Dulay and Burt, 1978). Even when we have time, we may be so involved in *what* we are saying that we do not attend to *how* we are saying it.

(iii) *Know the rule*. This may be a very formidable requirement. Linguistics has taught us that the structure of language is extremely complex, and they claim to have described only a fragment of the best known languages. We can be sure that our students are exposed only to a small part of the total grammar of the language, and we know that even the best students do not learn every rule they are exposed to.

The evidence for the production schema shown in Fig. 2.1 comes originally from the natural order studies. (Confirming evidence has been also produced from other sources, see, for example, Bialystok and Frohlich, 1977, 1978a, 1978b.) These studies are consistent with this generalization: we see the natural order for grammatical morphemes, that is, the child's (second language) difficulty order (similar to the order of acquisition; Krashen, 1977), when we test subjects in situations that appear to be "Monitor-free", where they are focussed on communication and not form. When we give our adult subjects tests that meet the three conditions, i.e. a pencil and paper "grammar"-type test, we see "unnatural" orders, orders unlike the child L2 order of acquisition or difficulty order. The interpretation of this result is that the natural order reflects the operation of the acquired system alone, without the intrusion of the conscious grammar, since adult second language acquisition is posited to be similar to child (second) language acquisition. When we put people in situations where the three conditions are met, when they have time, are focussed on form, and know the rule, the error pattern changes, reflecting the contribution of the conscious grammar.

It appears to be the case that unnatural orders are the result of a rise in rank of certain morphemes, the late-acquired, more "learnable" items. In English as a second language, when performers are put in situations where they can and do Monitor, we see a rise in rank of the third person singular morpheme and the regular past, both late-acquired, low on the list in Table 2.1, and both relatively straightforward, both syntactically and semantically. (See studies by Larsen-Freeman, 1975, described in Chapter IV, Table 4.1; and Brown, described in Note 4, Chapter IV.)[2]

Use of the conscious Monitor thus has the effect of allowing performers to supply items that are not yet acquired. As we shall see in Chapter IV, however, only certain items can be supplied by most Monitor users; the Monitor does a better job with some parts of grammar than with others. Specifically, it seems to do better with rules that can be characterized as "simple" in two different ways. First, rules that do not require elaborate movements or permutations; rules that are syntactically simple. Easy rules in this sense include bound morphology, such as the third person singular in English, or the $de + le = du$ contraction in French. Difficult rules in this sense include the English *wh-* question rule, which requires moving the questioned word to the front of the sentence, a subject–auxiliary inversion, and in some cases the insertion of *do* in the right place. Rules can also be easy and difficult due to their semantic properties. The English article system is easy to describe formally—one simply inserts *the* or *a* or sometimes nothing before the noun. But its semantics are very difficult to describe (see, for example, Hawkins, 1978).

To summarize thus far, Monitor use results in the rise in rank of items that are "late-acquired" in the natural order, items that the performer has learned but has not acquired.[3] Only certain items can rise in rank, however. When Monitor use is heavy, this rise in rank is enough to disturb the natural order. (As discussed in Chapter IV, it is possible to see small changes in certain late-acquired morphemes that are not enough to disturb the natural order; this may be termed *light* Monitor use. See especially Note 5, Chapter IV.)

As we shall see in Chapter IV, it is not easy to encourage noticeable Monitor use. Experimentation has shown that anything less than a real grammar test will not bring out the conscious grammar in any force. Keyfetz (1978) found natural orders for both oral and written versions of the SLOPE test, showing that simply using the written modality is not enough to cause an unnatural order. Houck, Robertson and Krashen (1978a) had adult subjects (university level international students) correct their own written output, and still found a natural order for the corrected version. Krashen, Butler, Birnbaum, and Robertson (1978) found that even when ESL students write compositions with plenty of time and under instructions to be very "careful", the effect of Monitor use was surprisingly light. The best hypothesis now is that for most people, even university students, it takes a real discrete-point grammar-type test to meet all three conditions for Monitor use and encourage significant use of the conscious grammar.

(a) Individual variation in Monitor use

Some of the individual variation we see in adult second language acquisition and performance can be accounted for in terms of differential use of the conscious Monitor. Studies of case histories suggest that there may be three basic types of performer (Krashen, 1978; Stafford and Covitt, 1978; Kounin and Krashen, 1978).

(i) *Monitor Over-users*. These are people who attempt to Monitor all the time, performers who are constantly checking their output with their conscious knowledge of the second language. As a result, such performers may speak hesitantly, often self-correct in the middle of utterances, and are so concerned with correctness that they cannot speak with any real fluency.

There may be two different causes for over-use of the grammar. Over-use may first of all derive from the performer's history of exposure to the second language. Many people, victims of grammar-only type of instruction, have simply not had the chance to acquire much of the second language, and may have no choice but to be dependent on learning. Another type may be related to personality. These over-users have had a chance to acquire, and may actually have acquired a great deal of the second language. They simply do not trust this acquired competence and only feel secure when they refer to their Monitor "just to be sure".

(ii) *Monitor under-users*. These are performers who have not learned, or if they have learned, prefer not to use their conscious knowledge, even when conditions allow it. Under-users are typically uninfluenced by error correction, can self-correct only by using a "feel" for correctness (e.g. "it sounds right"), and rely completely on the acquired system.

Stafford and Covitt (1978) note that some under-users pay "lip service" to the value of conscious grammar. Their subject "I" felt that people need conscious rules to speak "correctly", and that "grammar is the key to every language". "I" himself, however, hardly used conscious rules at all, in speech or writing.

(iii) *The optimal Monitor user*. Our pedagogical goal is to produce optimal users, performers who use the Monitor when it is appropriate and when it does not interfere with communication. Many optimal users will not use grammar in ordinary conversation, where it might interfere. (Some very skilled performers, such as some professional linguists and language teachers, might be able to get away with using considerable amounts of conscious knowledge in conversation, e.g. Rivers, 1979, but this is very unusual. We might consider these people "super Monitor users", after Yorio, 1978.) In writing, and in planned speech, however, when there is time, optimal users will typically make whatever corrections they can to raise the accuracy of their output (see, for example, Krashen and Pon, 1975).

Optimal Monitor users can therefore use their learned competence as a supplement to their acquired competence. Some optimal users who have not completely acquired their second language, who make small and occasional errors in speech, can use their conscious grammar so successfully that they can often produce the illusion of being native in their writing. (This does not imply that conscious learning can entirely make up for incomplete acquisition. Some unacquired rules will be learnable and others not. The optimal user is able to fill *part* of the gap with conscious learning, but not all of it.)

4. THE INPUT HYPOTHESIS

We will take much more time with this hypothesis than we did with the others for two reasons. First, much of this material is relatively new, while the other hypotheses have been described and discussed already in several published books and articles. The second reason is its importance, both theoretical and practical. The input hypothesis attempts to answer what is perhaps the most important question in our field, and gives an answer that has a potential impact on all areas of language teaching.

The important question is: How do we acquire language? If the Monitor hypothesis is correct, that acquisition is central and learning more peripheral, then the goal of our pedagogy should be to encourage acquisition. The question of how we acquire then becomes crucial.

This section is organized as follows: I will first present the input hypothesis before giving any supporting evidence. Following this is a description of the evidence from research in first and second language acquisition. We will then briefly cover evidence from applied linquistics research, which is discussed in more detail in Chapter V.

(a) Statement of the hypothesis

Let us first restate the question of how we acquire: given the correctness of the natural order hypothesis, how do we move from one stage to another? If an acquirer is at "stage 4", how can he progress to "stage 5"? More generally, how do we move from stage i, where i represents current competence, to $i + 1$, the next level? The input hypothesis makes the following claim: a necessary (but not sufficient) condition to move from stage i to stage $i + 1$ is that the acquirer understand input that contains $i + 1$, where "understand" means that the acquirer is focussed on the meaning and not the form of the message.

We acquire, in other words, only when we understand language that contains structure that is "a little beyond" where we are now. How is this possible? How can we understand language that contains structures that we have not yet acquired? The answer to this apparent paradox is that we use more than our linguistic competence to help us understand. We also use context, our knowledge of the world, our extra-linguistic information to help us understand language directed at us.

The input hypothesis runs counter to our usual pedagogical approach in second and foreign language teaching. As Hatch (1978a) has pointed out, our assumption has been that we first learn structures, then practice using them in communication, and this is how fluency develops. The input hypothesis says the opposite. It says we acquire by "going for meaning" first, and as a result, we acquire structure! (For discussion of first language acquisition, see MacNamara, 1972.)

We may thus state parts (1) and (2) of the input hypothesis as follows:

(1) The input hypothesis relates to acquisition, not learning.
(2) We acquire by understanding language that contains structure a bit beyond our current level of competence ($i + 1$). This is done with the help of context or extra-linguistic information.

A third part of the input hypothesis says that input must contain $i + 1$ to be useful for language acquisition, but it need not contain only $i + 1$. It says that if the acquirer understands the input, and there is enough of it, $i + 1$ will automatically be provided. In other words, if communication is successful, $i + 1$ is provided. As we will discuss later, this implies that the best input should not even attempt to deliberately aim at $i + 1$. We are all familiar with syllabi that try to deliberately cover $i + 1$. There is a "structure of the day", and usually both teacher and student feel that the aim of the lesson is to teach or practice a specific grammatical item or structure. Once this structure is "mastered", the syllabus proceeds to the next one. This part of the input hypothesis implies that such a deliberate attempt to provide $i + 1$ is not necessary. As we shall see later, there are reasons to suspect that it may even be harmful.

Thus, part (3) of the input hypothesis is:

(3) When communication is successful, when the input is understood and there is enough of it, $i + 1$ will be provided automatically.

The final part of the input hypothesis states that speaking fluency cannot be taught directly. Rather, it "emerges" over time, on its own.[4] The best way, and perhaps the only way, to teach speaking, according to this view, is simply to provide comprehensible input. Early speech will come when the acquirer feels "ready"; this state of readiness arrives at somewhat different times for different people, however. Early speech, moreover, is typically not grammatically accurate. Accuracy develops over time as the acquirer hears and understands more input. Part (4) of the input hypothesis is thus:

(4) Production ability emerges. It is not taught directly.

(b) Evidence supporting the hypothesis

(i) *First language acquisition in children.* The input hypothesis is very consistent with what is known about "caretaker speech", the modifications that parents and others make when talking to young children. The most interesting and perhaps the most important characteristic of caretaker speech for us is that it is not a deliberate attempt to teach language. Rather, as Clark and Clark (1977) point out, caretaker speech is modified in order to aid comprehension. Caretakers talk "simpler" in an effort to make themselves understood by the child.

A second characteristic of interest to us here is the finding that caretaker speech, while it is syntactically simpler than adult–adult speech, is "roughly-tuned" to the child's current level of linguistic competence, not "finely-tuned". In other words, caretaker speech is not precisely adjusted to the level of each child, but *tends* to get more complex as the child progresses. Very good evidence for rough-tuning comes from the research of Cross (1977) and Newport, Gleitman, and

Gleitman (1977), who report that correlations between input complexity and measures of the child's linguistic maturity, while positive and often significant, are not usually very large. An interpretation of this finding is that caretakers are not taking aim exactly at $i + 1$. The input they provide for children includes $i + 1$, but also includes many structures that have already been acquired, plus some that have not ($i + 2$, $i + 3$, etc.) and that the child may not be ready for yet. In other words, caretakers do not provide a grammatically based syllabus! (For a more complete review of rough-tuning, see Krashen, 1980, 1981.)

A third characteristic of caretaker speech that concerns us is known as the "here and now" principle. It is well established that caretakers talk mostly about what the child can perceive, what is in the immediate environment. Discourse with children is far more likely to deal with what is in the room and happening now ("See the ball?") than what is not in the room and not current ("What will we do upstairs tomorrow?"). As Newport *et al.* (1977) points out, this is a topical constraint—the "here and now" principle reflects the common interests of the caretaker and child.

While there is no direct evidence showing that caretaker speech is indeed more effective than unmodified input, the input hypothesis predicts that caretaker speech will be very useful for the child. First, it is, or aims to be, comprehensible. The "here and now" feature provides extra-linguistic support (context) that helps the child understand the utterances containing $i + 1$. As MacNamara (1972) pointed out, the child does not acquire grammar first and then use it in understanding. The child understands first, and this helps him acquire language.

As discussed earlier, roughly-tuned caretaker speech covers the child's $i + 1$, but does not focus on $i + 1$ exclusively. Part (3) of the input hypothesis claims that this is optimal. Rough-tuning has the following advantages in child first language acquisition:

1. It ensures that $i + 1$ is covered, with no guesswork as to just what $i + 1$ is for each child. On the other hand, deliberate aim at $i + 1$ might miss!
2. Roughly-tuned input will provide $i + 1$ for more than one child at a time, as long as they understand what is said. Finely-tuned input, even if accurate (i.e. even if it "hits" $i + 1$), will only

benefit the child whose $i + 1$ is exactly the same as what is emphasized in the input.
3. Roughly-tuned input provides built-in review. We need not be concerned with whether a child has "mastered" a structure, whether the child was paying attention to the input that day, or whether we provided enough. With natural, roughly-tuned input, $i + 1$ will occur and reoccur.

In other words, if part (3) is correct, if it is the case that with enough natural communication and understanding that $i + 1$ is always provided, the caretaker need not worry about consciously programming structure.

This must be a good thing! Adding the responsibility of grammatical sequencing to parenthood would make parent–child communication much less spontaneous and far more difficult.

(ii) *Evidence from second language acquisition: simple codes.* The input hypothesis also holds for second language acquisition. First, as presented earlier, the second language acquirer, child or adult, is also an "acquirer", just like the child acquiring first language. Also, according to hypothesis (2), there is a natural order of acquisition for second language as well as first language, so we can talk about the second language acquirers' $i + 1$ as well. Third, second language acquirers can also receive the kind of modified input that children get.

This modified input is of three sorts. Foreigner-talk results from the modifications native speakers make with less than fully competent speakers of their language (see, for example, Hatch, Shapira, and Gough, 1978 for some good examples). Teacher-talk is foreigner-talk in the classroom, the language of classroom management and explanation, when it is in the second language. A third simple code is interlanguage talk, the speech of other second language acquirers.

While there are some differences between these simple codes and caretaker speech (Long, 1980; Freed, 1980), there are important similarities. As is the case with caretaker speech, modifications made in foreigner-talk and teacher-talk[5] are not made for the purpose of language teaching, but are made for the purpose of communication, to help the second language acquirer understand what is being said. Second, the available research indicates that foreigner-talk and teacher-talk are roughly-tuned to the level of the acquirer, and not finely-tuned (Freed, 1980; Gaies, 1977; for a review, see Krashen, 1980); more advanced second language performers tend to get more complex input, but the correlation between proficiency and input complexity is less than perfect.

Foreigner-talk and teacher-talk may not always be in the "here and now",[6] but helpful native speakers and teachers find other ways to make input comprehensible. In addition to linguistic alterations, they take advantage of the acquirer's knowledge of the world, which is, of course, greater than that of the child acquiring a first language. Teachers, in addition, use pedagogical aids, such as pictures and realia (see discussion in Chapter III).

The input hypothesis predicts that these simplified codes will be very useful for the second language acquirer, just as caretaker speech is posited to be useful for the child. (For some preliminary case history data supporting this hypothesis, see Krashen, 1980, 1981.) The input hypothesis also predicts that natural, communicative, roughly-tuned, comprehensible input has some real advantages over finely-tuned input that aims directly at $i + 1$, in other words, classroom exercises that aim to teach the structure of the day.

The case against the grammatical syllabus is presented in fuller detail in Chapter III, but here is a brief summary. The arguments are very similar to those presented against giving the child finely-tuned input:

(1) All students may not be at the same stage. The "structure of the day" may not be $i + 1$ for many of the students. With natural communicative input, on the other hand, some $i + 1$ or other will be provided for everyone.

(2) With a grammatical syllabus, each structure is presented only once. If a student misses it, is absent, is not paying attention, or if there simply has not been enough practice (input), the student may have to wait until next year, when all structures are reviewed! On the other hand, roughly-tuned comprehensible input allows for natural review.

(3) A grammatical syllabus assumes we know the order of acquisition. No such assumption is necessary when we rely on comprehensible input, on roughly-tuned natural communication.

(4) Finally, a grammatical syllabus, and the resulting grammatical focus, places serious constraints on what can be discussed. Too often, it is difficult, if not impossible, to discuss or read anything of real interest if our underlying motive is to practice a particular structure. In other words, a grammatical focus will usually prevent real communication using the second language.

If these arguments are correct, they mean that we should not attempt to teach along the natural order, or any other order, when our goal is acquisition. (This is not necessarily true when the goal is conscious learning; see Chapter IV.)

(iii) *Evidence from second language acquisition: the silent period and L1 influence.* The input hypothesis is also consistent with other findings and hypotheses in second language acquisition. One of these can be termed the "silent period", a phenomenon that is most noticeable in child second language acquisition.

It has often been noted that children acquiring a second language in a natural, informal linguistic environment, may say very little for several months following their first exposure to the second language. What output there is consists usually of memorized language, whole sentences learned as if they were one word. Hatch (1972), for example, reported that Paul, a five-year-old Chinese speaker acquiring English as a second language, did not really use "creative" language for his first few months in the United States. His only output was memorized sentences, such as

> Get out of here.
> It's time to eat and drink.

He had clearly learned these as whole utterances without a real understanding of their components (e.g. he probably would not understand the word "out" or "time" if it were used in another sentence). Such memorized sentences were probably very useful for Paul, both in the classroom and playground.[7] When "real" languages did start to emerge, it looked very much like first language development, with short, simple sentences such as

> This kite.
> Ball no.

The explanation of the silent period in terms of the input hypothesis is straight-forward—the child is building up competence in the second language via listening, by understanding the language around him. In accordance with the input hypothesis, speaking ability emerges on its own after enough competence has been developed by listening and understanding. We should note that case histories dealing with children acquiring second languages (see also Hakuta, 1974; Ervin-Tripp, 1974), agree that several months may elapse until they start talking, and that the speech that emerges is not error-free. This finding has important pedagogical considerations, as we shall see in Chapter III.

Adults, and children in formal language classes, are usually not allowed a silent period. They are often asked to produce very early in a second language, before they have acquired enough syntactic competence to express their ideas. According to a hypothesis first proposed by Newmark (1966), performers who are asked to produce before they are "ready" will fall back on first language rules, that is, they will use syntactic rules of their first language while speaking the second language.

Stated more formally, an acquirer will substitute some L1 rule for $i + 1$, a rule of the second language, if the acquirer needs $i + 1$ to express himself but has not yet acquired it. The L1 rule used may be quite similar to the L2 $i + 1$, but may also differ in certain ways. When the L1 and L2 rules are different, the resulting error is referred to often as "interference". But according to Newmark, it is not interference at all; it is not the result of the L1 interfering with second language performance, but the result of ignorance—the lack of acquisition of an L2 rule that is needed in performance.

(iv) *Advantages and disadvantages of L1 rule use.* The substitution of some L1 rule for some $i + 1$ has both advantages and disadvantages. The advantages are short term, however, while the disadvantages appear to be quite serious.

One obvious advantage is that the use of an L1 rule allows the performer to "outperform his competence", to meet a practical need in L2 communication before he has acquired the relevant $i + 1$ rule. When the L1 rule used is identical to a rule in the L2 ("positive transfer"), the performer seems to have got something for free. Even if the L1 rule is not the same as the L2 rule, one could argue that the performer still comes out ahead, as, quite often, he can still communicate his point despite the incorrect form.

Another advantage is that the early production allowed by the use of L1 rules also helps to invite input—it allows the performer to participate more in conversation, and this could mean more comprehensible input and thus more second language acquisition.

There are real disadvantages to falling back on the L1, however. First, the L1 rule may not be the same as an L2 rule, as noted above, and errors can result. The conscious Monitor can note and repair these errors in some cases, but not all, since, as we have seen, the constraints on Monitor use are severe. Thus, use of L1 rules requires constant vigilance on the part of the Monitor, and is an awkward way to produce formally-correct sentences in a second language. (Note that Monitor correction of such errors will not, according to the theory, produce acquisition, or permanent change. It will not eradicate the L1 rule, even if done effectively over long periods of time. Real acquisition comes only from comprehensible input.)[8]

There may be another serious disadvantage to the use of L1 rules in second language performance. Even if the L1 rule is similar to an actual L2 rule or transitional form, it is not clear that these rules will help the acquirer progress—they may not take the place of "true" L2 rules in the developmental sequence. In Krashen (1982) I discuss the hypothesis that acquisition requires a comparison between i and $i + 1$ (Clark and Andersen, 1980; Lamendella, 1979). It may be the case that the "distance" between i and $i + 1$ cannot be too great—i and $i + 1$ can only differ in small ways. Transitional forms, I hypothesize, may be useful in that they can temporarily serve as i, helping to decrease the amount of distance between i and $i + 1$.

If, for example, the target rule in English is the negative ($i + 1$, presented to the system by input), the intermediate form no + v (provided by the creative construction system internally) may be closer to the mature negative form. The acquirer may thus use no + v as i, rather than a more primitive form of the negative (e.g. no + S).

If transitional forms can temporarily serve as i, the next question is whether L1 rules, even when they happen to be similar to L2 rules or transitional forms, can perform this function. The answer may be "no". For example, Spanish speakers often have a long period in their acquisition of English in which they produce no + v for the English negative, a structure that is similar to a transitional form in English as a first and second language (Schumann, 1979). It may be the case that earlier no + v performance is the use of the L1 rule, while later no + v performance is the "true" intermediate form. It may be the case that only the latter can help the system "move forward".[9]

To summarize, use of L1 rules is hypothesized to be the result of falling back on first language knowledge when a second language rule is needed in production but is not available. It may temporarily enhance production, but may not be real progress in the second language. The real cure for "interference", according to Newmark, is not drill at the points of contrast between the two languages (Newmark and Reibel, 1973, p. 239). Drill will, at best, produce learning, and, as we have seen, this is only a short term cure. The real cure "is simply the cure for ignorance" (Newmark, 1966, p. 81): real language acquisition. This can happen only when the acquirer obtains comprehensible input.[10,11,12]

(v) *Applied linguistics research.* The input hypothesis is also consistent with the results of what can be called "method comparison" experiments. Several scholars and groups of scholars have attempted to determine directly which teaching methods are best by simple comparison. Groups of students studying second and foreign languages using two different methods are compared, both in long-term and short-term studies. We will have a detailed look at this research in Chapter V, but I will state my own conclusions in advance. My reading of studies comparing the more commonly used methods (audio-lingual as compared to grammar-translation or cognitive-code) is as follows:

(1) "Deductive" methods (rule first, then practice, e.g. grammar-translation and cognitive-code) are slightly more efficient than audio-lingual teaching for adults. The differences are often statistically significant, but are not huge. Students clearly make some progress using any of these approaches.

(2) For adolescents, there is no measurable difference.

I interpret this failure to find large differences in this way: none of the methods compared in these studies provides much in the way of comprehensible input! The input hypothesis predicts, moreover, that an approach that provides substantial quantities of comprehensible input will do much better than any of the older approaches.

There are several newer methods that do this, such as Asher's Total Physical Response Method (Asher, 1966, 1969) and Terrell's Natural Approach (Terrell, 1977). In these methods, class time is devoted to providing comprehensible input, where the focus is on the message and not the form, and students are not expected to produce in the second language until they themselves decide they are "ready". Reports confirming the superiority of such "input methods" have been appearing in the professional literature over the last ten years (e.g. Asher, 1972; Gary, 1975; Postovsky, 1974; more detail is provided in Chapter V). (The focus on comprehensible input is not the only reason for the success of the newer methods, however; see discussion below of affect, and Chapters III and V.)

Since the bulk of this book is intended to deal with implications of second language acquisition theory (Chapters III, IV, and V), this section should really be delayed until later. I cannot resist, however, briefly stating one implication here, since, in my opinion, the implications of the input hypothesis are truly exciting for all of us interested in language acquisition. Most important, the input hypothesis predicts that the classroom may be an excellent place for second language acquisition, at least up to the "intermediate" level. For beginners, the classroom can be much better than the outside world, since the outside usually provides the beginner with very little comprehensible input, especially for older acquirers (Wagner-Gough and Hatch, 1975). In the classroom, we can provide an hour a day of comprehensible input, which is probably much better than the outside can do for the beginner. We will elaborate on this a bit more after discussion of the Affective Filter.

5. THE AFFECTIVE FILTER HYPOTHESIS

The Affective Filter hypothesis states how affective factors relate to the second language acquisition process. The concept of an Affective

Filter was proposed by Dulay and Burt (1977), and is consistent with the theoretical work done in the area of affective variables and second language acquisition, as well as the hypotheses previously covered in this chapter.

Research over the last decade has confirmed that a variety of affective variables relate to success in second language acquisition (reviewed in Krashen, 1981). Most of those studied can be placed into one of these three categories:

(1) *Motivation*. Performers with high motivation generally do better in second language acquisition (usually, but not always, "integrative"[13]).

(2) *Self-confidence*. Performers with self-confidence and a good self-image tend to do better in second language acquisition.

(3) *Anxiety*. Low anxiety appears to be conducive to second language acquisition, whether measured as personal or classroom anxiety.

In several places I have hypothesized that these attitudinal factors relate directly to acquisition and not learning, since they tend to show stronger relationships to second language achievement when communicative-type tests are used, tests that tap the acquired rather than the learned system, and when the students taking the test have used the language in "acquisition-rich" situations, situations where comprehensible input was plentiful.

The Affective Filter hypothesis captures the relationship between affective variables and the process of second language acquisition by positing that acquirers vary with respect to the strength or level of their Affective Filters. Those whose attitudes are not optimal for second language acquisition will not only tend to seek less input, but they will also have a high or strong Affective Filter—even if they understand the message, the input will not reach that part of the brain responsible for language acquisition, or the language acquisition device. Those with attitudes more conducive to second language acquisition will not only seek and obtain more input, they will also have a lower or weaker filter. They will be more open to the input, and it will strike "deeper" (Stevick, 1976).

The Affective Filter hypothesis, represented in Fig. 2.2, claims that the effect of affect is "outside" the language acquisition device proper. It still maintains that *input* is the primary causative variable in second language acquisition, affective variables acting to impede or facilitate the delivery of input to the language acquisition device.

The filter hypothesis explains why it is possible for an acquirer to obtain a great deal of comprehensible input, and yet stop short (and sometimes well short) of the native speaker level (or "fossilize"; Selinker, 1972). When this occurs, it is due to the affective filter.

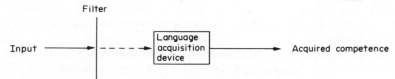

Fig. 2.2. Operation of the "affective filter".

The "affective filter", posited by Dulay and Burt (1977), acts to prevent input from being used for language acquisition. Acquirers with optimal attitudes (see text) are hypothesized to have "low" affective filters. Classrooms that encourage low filters are those that promote low anxiety among students, that keep students "off the defensive" (Stevick, 1976).

This picture does not diminish, in any way, the importance of affective variables in pedagogy. The Affective Filter hypothesis implies that our pedagogical goals should not only include supplying comprehensible input, but also creating a situation that encourages a low filter. As discussed in Chapter V, several methods focus on just this (e.g. Counseling–Learning and Suggestopedia).

The input hypothesis and the concept of the Affective Filter define the language teacher in a new way. The effective language teacher is someone who can provide input and help make it comprehensible in a low anxiety situation. Of course, many teachers have felt this way about their task for years, at least until they were told otherwise by the experts![14]

B. The Causative Variable in Second Language Acquisition

1. THE CAUSATIVE VARIABLES

Our review of second language acquisition theory thus far can be summarized as follows:

1. Acquisition is more important than learning.

2. In order to acquire, two conditions are necessary. The first is comprehensible (or even better, comprehen*ded*) input containing $i + 1$, structures a bit beyond the acquirer's current level, and second, a low or weak affective filter to allow the input "in".

This is equivalent to saying that comprehensible input and the strength of the filter are the true causes of second language acquisition. Other variables may relate to second language success, that is, we may see positive correlations between other variables and measures of achievement in second language, but in all cases in which language *acquisition* is attained, analysis will reveal that the relationship can better be explained in terms of comprehensible input plus filter level.

In this section, we will perform such an analysis, looking at several factors that have been shown to relate to success in second language acquisition. We will see that not only can they be re-analyzed, but that the comprehensible input + filter explanation helps to solve some apparent problems and contradictions in the research literature.

We will begin with the effect of language teaching on second language acquisition, then examine variables relating to exposure (length of residence in the country where the language is used and reported use of the second language), and then turn to age. Finally, we will consider Schumann's acculturation hypothesis, to see whether it too can be re-analyzed in this way.

2. LANGUAGE TEACHING: DOES IT HELP?

If acquisition is more central, and learning of less use to second language performance, and if comprehensible input and the filter are the essential causative variables for second language acquisition, the classroom should help only to the extent it supplies comprehensible input in an environment conducive to a low filter. This may indeed be, as mentioned earlier, its main function.

It seems reasonable to hypothesize that the classroom should be especially valuable for beginners, those who cannot easily utilize the informal environment for input. It will be of less value to those who can, who have other sources of comprehensible input, and who are linguistically advanced enough to take advantage of it.

The question then becomes not "Does language teaching help?" but

"When does language teaching help?". A possible answer is this: language teaching helps when it is the main source of low filter comprehensible input, that is, for beginners and for foreign language students who do not have a chance to get input outside the class. It will be of less help when rich sources of input are available. If the research literature supports these generalizations, it confirms the generalization that language teaching helps second language acquisition when it supplies comprehensible input, which is the true cause of second language acquisition.

(a) When language teaching helps

Brière (1978) investigated the factors that predicted successful acquisition of Spanish as a second language among 920 native Mexican children, ages four through twelve. Among the best predictors of Spanish proficiency was attendance in class in the village school (promotoria). This makes sense in terms of our hypothesis, since the promotoria was the major source of comprehensible input in Spanish, as opportunities to use Spanish outside the classroom were not plentiful. (The two other significant predictors were the father's ability to speak Spanish and the parents' need for Spanish.)

Some adult studies report fairly large positive correlations between the amount of classroom exposure to the second language and proficiency. In each case, however, it can be argued that the class was the primary source of comprehensible input. Krashen, Zelinski, Jones, and Usprich (1978) tested students in an extension (evening and weekend) program in English as a second language at Queens College in New York, and reported robust correlations between reported years of formal study and performance on a variety of ESL tests, i.e.:

Test	Correlation with years of formal study
Michigan (Lado)	$r = 0.50$
Composition	$r = 0.34$
Cloze	$r = 0.47$
SLOPE	$r = 0.42$ (reported in Krashen, 1976)

All correlations were very significant ($p < 0.01$ or better).

Despite the fact that these students were in the United States and technically in a second language and not a foreign language environment, it is likely that, in many cases, they did not have a rich input source available to them outside the class. First, some had not been in the country for a long time, their primary exposure to English having been in a foreign language situation. Second, since these were extension and not regular day-time university students, there was the strong possibility that many of them were not utilizing English very much in their daily lives, even though they were living in New York. This is confirmed below, when we note the lack of a strong relationship found for these same students between length of residence in the United States and proficiency, and when we examine the effect of instruction on regular university students who do have a rich source of input outside the classroom. (See Krashen, Seliger, and Hartnett, 1974 and Krashen and Seliger, 1976, for similar results.)

Chihara and Oller (1978) also report substantial correlations between length of formal study and second language proficiency, finding a correlation of $r = 0.45$ for performance on a cloze test and similar results for other measures. Their subjects were Japanese studying English as a foreign language in Japan, a clear foreign situation in which the classroom was the main, if not only, source of comprehensible input.

(b) When language teaching does not help

Not all the research literature concludes that language teaching is good for second language acquisition! (I must admit that I am astounded to see that so few studies have investigated such a crucial issue! What is presented in this section is practically the entire literature on this question.) There are generalizations that can be made about studies that seem to decide against second language teaching, however. In all cases, students have a rich source of comprehensible input outside the classroom, and are competent enough in the second language to be able to take advantage of it, i.e. understand.

Two studies deal with child second language acquisition and both with English as a second language. Fathman (1975) found no significant differences in English proficiency between children who had ESL instruction and children who did not. All children in her study, however, were enrolled in English-medium public schools in Washington, D.C. and all had been in the United States from one to three years. It can be hypothesized that they were getting comprehensible input from the school and playground, and the extra input from the ESL class did not make a difference (nor did grammar and drill!).

Hale and Budar (1970) studied immigrant adolescents in Hawaiian junior high schools. In their paper (titled "Are TESOL classes the only answer?"), they noted that the subjects formed a natural division. One group was composed of students who spoke less common languages. These students did not have the "benefit" of a formal ESL program and were isolated from speakers of their own language. The second group consisted of students who had the chance to associate with other students who spoke their own first language. These students did attend ESL classes. Hale and Budar report that the first group actually made better progress in acquiring English, a finding that seems to question the value of ESL classes. The first group, however, may have had more comprehensible input, possibly through having to associate more with English speakers and with other non-native speakers using English as a *lingua franca*. This study also fits our generalization and confirms that the issue is not plus or minus ESL or language teaching but plus or minus low filter comprehensible input.

Two adult studies also appear to decide against the classroom. Upshur (1968) studied three groups of ten foreign students studying law at a special summer session at the University of Michigan. All students took seminars and classes that used English as the medium of instruction. In addition, they took formal ESL classes, each group taking a different amount, depending on placement scores. Upshur's analysis of their progress in English over the summer revealed no significant effects attributable to the amount of instruction they received: those with more ESL did not necessarily acquire more than those with less over the course of the summer. Mason (1971), in a study done at the University of Hawaii, simply allowed a small group of intermediate[15] level international students to postpone a required ESL class for a semester. Their progress in ESL was compared to students who actually took the course. Mason reported no significant differences between the two groups.

The two adult studies are consistent with the hypothesis. In both cases, students had a rich source of comprehensible input outside the classroom, and in both cases they were advanced enough to be able to utilize it.

I conclude from this that language teaching certainly *can* help. Its primary function is to supply comprehensible input for those who can not get it elsewhere, those constrained by their situation (i.e. foreign language students who do not have input sources outside the class) or by their competence (those unable to understand the language of the outside world). While it is less useful for those who have other sources of input, there still are things the competent classroom can contribute to the intermediate student. It can supply conscious learning for optimal Monitor use (see Chapter IV), and give tools to help the acquirer utilize the outside environment more fully for further acquisition (Chapter III). Table 2.2 summarizes studies discussed in this section.[16]

3. EXPOSURE VARIABLES

Several exposure variables have been investigated with respect to second language acquisition. Some studies show a clear relationship between the amount of exposure and proficiency and some do not. We shall see again that the hypothesis that comprehensible input plus low filter are the true causative variables predicts quite well when exposure variables relate to second language acquisition and when they do not. Thus, exposure variables are also indirect and not in themselves causative.

Several studies have examined *length of residence* (LOR) in the second language environment. For those studies of child second language acquisition, it can be plausibly argued that LOR may reflect simply the amount of comprehensible input the child obtains. (This is of course not always the case in child second language acquisition; all too often children living in a country do not get comprehensible input, either in or out of school.) We thus see, in these studies, a clear relationship between LOR and second language proficiency.

Fathman (1975) was discussed above. In addition to her finding on the non-effects of formal instruction on ESL achievement, Fathman also reported that LOR did predict proficiency for her sample of children (ages 6–14, enrolled in public school in Washington, D.C.).

TABLE 2.2. *Formal instruction and second language acquisition*

Study	Subjects	Level	Other sources of comprehensible input available?
Studies that claim instruction helps:			
Briere (1978)	Native Mexican children	Beginning	No; promotoria is main source of Spanish
Krashen *et al.* (1978)	"Extension" univ. students	Beginning to intermediate	Only in some cases; some students new in U.S., others do not use English in daily life
Chihara and Oller (1978)	Adult English students (EFL) in Japan	Beginning to intermediate	No; foreign language situation with little use of English outside the class
Studies that claim instruction does not help:			
Fathman (1975)	Children	Intermediate[a]	Yes; classes (public school), playground
Hale and Budar (1970)	Adolescents	Beginning to intermediate	Yes; classes in English, playground, possible inter-language talk (see text)
Upshur (1968)	Adult ESL in university (summer session)	Intermediate	Yes; classes and seminars given in English informal environment available
Mason (1971)	Adult ESL university	Intermediate	Yes; course work in English, also informal environment

[a] All subjects had been in the U.S. at least one year.

Those who had been in the United States for three years did better on the SLOPE test than those who had been in the United States for two years, and this group, in turn, outperformed those who had been in the United States for only one year.

Walberg, Hase, and Rasher (1978) studied Japanese-speaking children who had been in the United States a range of zero to 12 years, with most reported a LOR of three to four years. Self-report and report of teachers were used as estimates of the children's proficiency in English. Walberg *et al.* did find a significant relationship between LOR and proficiency in English as a second language, but note that even higher correlations were found with a "diminishing returns" model: "For children of all ages in the sample, acquisition proceeds at a fast rate initially, but the amounts of gain diminish with time" (p. 436). Specifically, "it may be estimated that equal . . . units are gained in the first two months, the next five months, the following one year, the next two years, and the next eight years" (p. 436).

Ekstrand (1976), however, found no relationship between LOR and child second language proficiency in his study of immigrant children in Sweden. The median LOR in his study was only 10.5 months, and it may be the case that LOR effects are not seen unless the children have been in the country for some minimum length of time (one year?). This condition is satisfied in the Fathman and Walberg *et al.* studies, and may be due to the fact that approximately one year is necessary to offset the advantage the older children have in rate of acquisition in early stages (Krashen, Long, and Scarcella, 1979; see also discussion below on *age*).

Walberg *et al.*'s diminishing returns hypothesis predicts that there is also a maximum LOR, beyond which we see no relationship between LOR and second language acquisition. Data from some other studies confirm this. Seliger, Krashen and Ladefoged (1974), Oyama (1976, 1978), and Patkowski (1980) all report no relationship between LOR and proficiency in English as a second language using a variety of measures for groups of subjects who had arrived in the United States at different ages, some arriving as children and some as adults. In all cases, however, very long LORs were involved, the minimum being five years with most being much longer.

Two other studies that bear on the issue of LOR and child second language acquisition will be covered in a subsequent section (Ramsey and Wright, 1974; Minoura, 1979).

Adult studies of the relationship between LOR and second language proficiency show, in my view, that LOR "counts" when there is evidence that it reflects high interaction and therefore comprehensible input. Because of the variability in filter level in adults, however, we might expect lower correlations for adults in general, as compared to children (see discussion of *age* below).

International university students fully involved in the academic environment should give us significant correlations between LOR and proficiency in the second language, provided a large enough range of LOR is examined, since students should have access to large amounts of comprehensible input, both in and out of class. Two studies utilized international students. Murakami (1980) studied 30 Japanese-speaking students at Southern Illinois University and found a significant correlation between performance on a dictation test of ESL and LOR ($r = 0.68$), and a positive but not significant correlation using a cloze test ($r = 0.29$). These results are nearly identical to those of Oller, Perkins, and Murakami (1980), who examined a group of 182 students, also at SIU (which did not include the 30 students Murakami studied alone). They also report a significant correlation between LOR and dictation ($r = 0.46$) but no significant correlation for cloze (correlation not reported).

LOR and proficiency was also probed in our study of extension students at Queens College (cited above; Krashen *et al.*, 1978). Correlations were occasionally significant (due to the large sample size) but were quite modest.

Correlation	Measure
0.18	Michigan test (Lado)
0.22	Composition
0.24	Cloze
0.014	SLOPE test (Krashen, 1976)

These results are predictable. We would expect extension students to have variable, and often very low, contact with English as compared to full-time students. Some may have lived in the United States many years without much comprehensible input. (Similar results are reported in Krashen, Seliger, and Hartnett, 1974, and Krashen and Seliger, 1976.)

Two studies examine "time abroad" to foreign language students, but differ somewhat in environment and also in results. Carroll (1967) reported that foreign language majors in American universities who were able to spend their junior years abroad in the country where the language was spoken performed better on the FSI test of listening comprehension than those who had only spent a summer abroad. The summer travelers, in turn, outperformed those who had never been abroad. These clear results probably reflect the fact that such students, most likely, sought out interaction, and thus comprehensible input in the second language while they were abroad.

In Chihara and Oller (1978), students of English as a foreign language in Japan were studied. No relationship was found, however, between the amount of time spent abroad and tests of English ($r = 0.04$ for cloze, with other measures producing similar results; Chihara and Oller report higher correlations between time abroad and self-report of English proficiency; $r = 0.24$ for speaking and $r = 0.23$ for listening comprehension). In contrast to Carroll's American foreign language majors study, in which acquirers were in daily contact with the target language, time abroad in this case need not have a direct relationship with amount of comprehensible input. Table 2.3 summarizes LOR studies.

A second exposure variable that has been studied is *reported use of the second language*. Several studies (but surprisingly few) have asked whether those who say they use the second language more actually acquire more. We would expect a significant relationship between "use" and acquisition, since use nearly always entails comprehensible input. Of the three studies I know of that explore this variable, two do in fact show a clear relationship with second language proficiency. (Failure to find a clear relationship in every case may be due to the unreliability of self-report; see Oller and Perkins, 1978.)

All studies examining reported use involve adult subjects. Johnson and Krug (1980) studied 72 international students at Southern Illinois University and found a modest but significant 0.34 correlation between proficiency in English (as measured by accuracy of grammatical morphemes in obligatory occasions in an interview situation) and subjects'

TABLE 2.3. *Length of residence (LOR) and second language acquisition (SLA)*

Study	Subjects	Duration of LOR	Linguistic environment; does LOR = CI?
Studies claiming LOR relates to SLA:			
Fathman (1975)	Children	1–3 years	Public school/playground; yes
Walberg et al. (1978)	Children	0–12 years[b]	Public school/playground; yes
Murakami (1980)	Adults	Not reported	Full-time university; yes
Oller et al. (1980)	Adults	Not reported	Full-time university; yes
Carroll (1967)	Adults	1 yr/summer	"Junior year abroad"; yes
Studies showing weak or no relationship between LOR and SLA:			
Ekstrand (1976)	Children	Medium = 10.5 months	Public school/playground; yes[c]
Krashen et al. (1978)	Adults	Mean = 4 years	Variable, including some with very little; not necessarily
Chihara and Oller (1978)	Adults	Not reported	"Travel abroad"; not necessarily

[a] CI = comprehensible input.
[b] Average LOR = 3–4 years.
[c] No relationship between LOR and SLA presumably due here to relatively short LOR.

report of the amount of leisure time they spent speaking and listening to English. Oller, Perkins, and Murakami (1980), however, examining a similar sample, found no relationship between a report of "time spent with English speakers" and second language proficiency, as measured by dictation and a cloze-type grammar test.

The Heidelberg project, as cited in Schumann (1978b), examined factors predicting proficiency in German as a second language for guest-workers (Italian and Spanish speakers) in Germany. They reported a correlation of 0.64 between German syntactic proficiency and "leisure contact" with Germans and one of 0.53 between German proficiency and "work contact". Both leisure and work contact can plausibly be interpreted as indicating comprehensible input.

4. AGE

It has been popularly assumed that age itself is a predictor of second language proficiency, that younger acquirers are better at second language acquisition than older acquirers. It can be argued, however, that age is not in itself a predictor of second language rate or attainment, and that here too everything reduces down to the quantity of comprehensible input and the level of the affective filter.

Krashen, Long, and Scarcella (1979) reviewed the available empirical research on the effect of age and second language acquisition and concluded that all published studies were consistent with these three generalizations:

1. Adults proceed through the early stages of second language development faster than children do (where time and exposure are held constant).
2. Older children acquire faster than younger children, time and exposure held constant.
3. Acquirers who begin natural exposure to second languages during childhood generally achieve higher second language proficiency than those beginning as adults.

Thus, it is not simply the case that "younger is better"; children are superior to adults only in the long run.

The explanations for these observed differences that seem most plausible to me involve input and the level or strength of the affective filter. First, let us consider the older acquirer's *rate* superiority (generalizations (1) and (2) above). Scarcella and Higa (forthcoming) found that younger acquirers actually received "simpler" input in a block building task, a result that confirms observations made by Wagner-Gough and Hatch (1975), and that seems to predict greater speed for younger, and not older acquirers. Scarcella and Higa noted that the older acquirers (adolescents) were better able to regulate both the quantity and quality of their input. They were better at encouraging speech and at getting the native speaker to modify it for greater comprehensibility. They could, for example, ask for help, change the topic, and direct the conversation better. They had, in other words, more "conversational competence". Thus, despite the simpler input directed at the younger children, it is likely that older acquirers actually get more comprehen*ded* input, and this may be a key factor in their faster initial progress.

There may be other reasons for the older acquirers' superiority in rate of acquisition. Adults have means of producing language earlier, of "beating the Silent Period", means that have nothing to do with natural language acquisition but that may nevertheless help them participate in conversation and hence obtain comprehensible input.

I have hypothesized in earlier papers (see, for example, Krashen, 1981) that significant Monitor use is only possible after the acquirer has undergone formal operations, a stage in cognitive development that generally occurs at about puberty (Inhelder and Piaget, 1958). The availability of the conscious grammar, the Monitor, allows adults to produce formally acceptable utterances using first language rules repaired by the Monitor, as discussed earlier in this chapter. While the use of this mode does not require comprehensible input, it helps the acquirer to talk early, to participate in conversations, and thereby obtain input, at least some of which will be comprehensible.

Both explanations for the older acquirers' rate superiority reduce to the greater ability of the adult and older child to obtain comprehensible input. Thus, comprehensible input again is hypothesized to be the causative variable, and not age *per se*.

The child's superiority in ultimate attainment has been hypothesized to be due to the strengthening of the affective filter at about puberty, an event that may also be related to formal operations (Krashen, 1981). As argued elsewhere, this hypothesis has several advantages. First, it claims that child–adult differences in attainment are not due to any change in the "language acquisition device" (LAD) but are due to the filter, a factor that is, in a sense, external to the LAD. Second, it is consistent with the claim that adults are still "acquirers", that they retain the natural language acquisition capacity children have. It also allows for the possibility that some adults can achieve extremely high levels of competence in a second language and may even be taken for native; it predicts that such "Good Language Learners" will be, above all, good acquirers, with the ability to obtain a great deal of comprehensible input with a low affective filter. In many cases, the filter prevents the adult only from going the last few inches.[17]

5. ACCULTURATION

A similar argument can be made concerning Schumann's Acculturation Hypothesis. Schumann (1978b) has hypothesized that acculturation is the "major casual variable in second language acquisition" (p. 29). Schumann maintains that "Second language acquisition is just one aspect of acculturation, and the degree to which the learner acculturates to the target language group will control the degree to which he acquires the target language" (p. 34).

While the Acculturation Hypothesis seems to account for second language acquisition data in extended sojourn situations, it is easily expressible in terms of comprehensible input and low filter level. Acculturation can be viewed as a means of gaining comprehensible input and lowering the filter. Moreover, the comprehensible input hypothesis accounts for second language acquisition in situations that acculturation does not attempt to deal with.

Schumann defines two types of acculturation:

"In type one acculturation, the learner is socially integrated with the TL group and, as a result, develops sufficient contacts with TL speakers to enable him to acquire the TL. In addition, he is psychologically open to the TL such that input to which he is exposed becomes intake. Type two acculturation has all the characteristics of type one, but in this case the learner regards the TL speakers as a reference group whose life styles and values he consciously or unconsciously desires to adopt. Both types of acculturation are sufficient to cause acquisition of the TL, but the distinction is made to stress that social and psychological contact with the TL group is the essential component in acculturation (as it relates to SLA) that that adoption of the life style and values of the TL group (characteristics traditionally associated with the notion of acculturation) is not necessary for successful acquisition of the TL" (p. 29).

Type one acculturation is thus "weaker" than type two in that it does not involve adoption of the new life style. Since Schumann hypothesizes that type one is all that is necessary for successful second language acquisition, we restrict our discussion to type one acculturation.

Type one acculturation is easily restatable in terms of the framework presented in this chapter: social integration with resulting contacts lead to comprehensible input, while the open psychological state Schumann refers to is equivalent to a low filter. The evidence Schumann presents in support of the Acculturation Hypothesis can be similarly interpreted.

The Heidelberg project, mentioned earlier, studied variables correlating with successful acquisition of German by foreign workers. Reported amounts of leisure contact with speakers of German correlated with syntactic performance ($r = 0.64$) as did amount of work contact ($r = 0.55$). Apparently, either form of interaction was effective in encouraging second language acquisition. (Schumann notes that "among the best speakers, those who had little leisure contact with Germans all had considerable work contact" (p. 39); thus, some guest-workers who acquired German did so without much leisure contact.) This confirms that it is interaction, and the resulting comprehensible input, that "causes" second language acquisition, a view consistent with both the comprehensible input plus low filter view as well as the Acculturation Hypothesis.

Schumann, in reporting the Heidelberg research, also notes that "learners whose work required communication with co-workers did better in German than workers who provided services (hairdressers, kitchen help, etc.)" Also, "learners who worked in an environment that was noisy or which constrained movement were at a disadvantage". These results also suggest that those who were able to interact more in the target language acquired more German, all of which means more input meeting the requirements of the input hypothesis.

Schumann draws a parallel between natural ("free" or informal) second language acquisition and the pidginization–decreolization continuum, suggesting that early second language acquisition is similar to pidginization (secondary hybridization) and that late second language acquisition is similar to the mesolect and acrolect stages of decreolization.[18] As evidence, he describes the case of Alberto, a Spanish-speaking adult living in the United States who appeared to be at a considerable psychological and social distance[19] from English speakers, and whose speech showed marked signs of pidginization, i.e. lack of several grammatical morphemes, little use of inversion in questions, and use of more primitive transitional forms in negation (Schumann, 1978a provides details). Alberto thus fits the Acculturation Hypothesis, since he showed little second language acquisition and little acculturation, defined as the degree of social and psychological distance. Albert is also quite consistent with the theoretical framework presented here and the hypothesis that comprehensible input and filter level are primary determinants of second language acquisition. Alberto, it can be claimed, received little comprehensible input in English (he worked nights, did not own a TV set, did not attend ESL classes, and made little effort to get to know English speakers, according to Schumann, 1978a), and probably had a strong affective filter as well.[20]

Stauble's subjects, reported in Stauble (1978) are also considered to be evidence for the Acculturation Hypothesis. All three were Spanish speakers who had been in the United States for many years, and who had apparently "fossilized" at different levels in their development of negation. Stauble attempted to relate their progress in second language acquisition, as reflected by the transitional forms they used for negation, and acculturation, measured by an informal questionnaire probing social and psychological distance from speakers of English. The subject Xavier showed the least progress in English negation, but also showed the least social distance. Stauble's questionnaire revealed that his psychological distance, however, was greater than that of the others, which is consistent with the Acculturation Hypothesis. Paz, the most advanced speaker, had the greatest social distance, but, along with Maria, the other subject, had relatively low psychological distance. Stauble's interpretation of these findings is that psychological distance may be a more important determinant of acculturation, and hence language acquisition, than social distance.

Stauble's data can also be analyzed in terms of our theoretical framework. Since all three subjects had been in the United States for many years, all three had had considerable comprehensible input (recall our earlier generalization that LOR, when over a long period of time, does not predict SLA, a hypothesis consistent with Walberg *et al.*'s diminishing returns hypothesis), enough to allow a "zero filter" acquirer to reach native-speaker levels. We can then simply hypothesize that it was Paz's lower filter, reflected by the lower psychological distance score, that allowed this acquirer to make more progress.[21]

Finally, it can be claimed that the comprehensible input plus filter position is more general. The acculturation hypothesis predicts second language acquisition only in immigration and extended sojourn situations. (Indeed, it is unfair to ask it to account for other situations, since Schumann has made it very clear in his writings that the acculturation hypothesis is designed to account for second language acquisition *only* in this situation.) The theory of SLA presented in this chapter can not only account for extended sojourn and immigrant SLA but also predicts success in the classroom, as detailed in Chapters III, IV, and V, and is claimed to be applicable to *all* language acquisition.

The Acculturation Hypothesis has considerable merit. It may be the case that acculturation is the most effective way of lowering the affective filter and getting input for immigrants and long-term visitors. Figure 2.3 attempts to capture the parallel between second language acquisition and the pidginization–decreolization continuum, and the effect of acculturation on both. "Free" second language acquisition and the continuum are similar in that acculturation may be the "motivating force" behind both.[22] Creole speakers gradually acquire closer versions of the standard as they are acculturated into the target culture. This acculturation brings them into contact with speakers of the standard, and makes them more "open" to the input (lowers the filter). Also, acculturation may "motivate" second language acquisition. As the individual acquirer acculturates into a culture, he obtains more input via more interaction, and is more "open" to it. The differ-

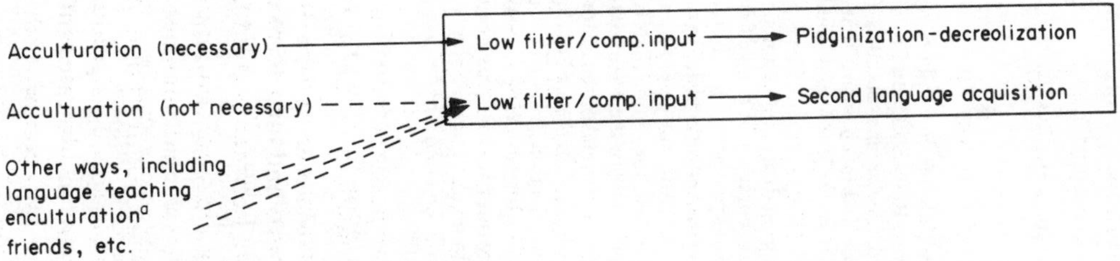

Acculturation (necessary) ──────→ Low filter/comp. input ──────→ Pidginization-decreolization

Acculturation (not necessary) ── ── ── → Low filter/comp. input ──────→ Second language acquisition

Other ways, including
language teaching
enculturation[a]
friends, etc.

Fig. 2.3. Acculturation, pidginization–decreolization, and second language acquisition.

Second language acquisition and the pidginization-decreolization continuum are similar in that both progress via comprehensible input supplied in a low filter situation (area inside the box).

────── Obligatory process
── ── ── Optional process

[a] *Enculturation* = "the process by which an individual assimilates to his own culture or to some segment of it", i.e. the case of European élite professionals who acquire English in their own countries. (For discussion, see Schumann (1978b), pp. 47–48.)

ence is that acculturation is the necessary motivating force for movement along the decreolization continuum, while it is only one way to bring the filter down and obtain comprehensible input. Input can be obtained with acculturation, and there are many techniques for bringing down the filter that have nothing to do with acculturation.

Notes

[1] The acquisition–learning distinction is not new with me. Several other scholars have found it useful to posit similar kinds of differences. Bialystock and Frohlich (1972) distinguish "implicit" and "explicit" learning, and Lawler and Selinker (1971) discuss mechanisms that guide "automatic" performance and mechanisms that guide "puzzle and problem solving performance" (p. 35). Also, Corder (1967) and Widdowson (1977) suggest similar ideas.

[2] Those of us who have studied languages with a great deal of inflectional morphology in school, using methods that focus on grammatical accuracy, often have first-hand experience with this phenomenon. Consider what happens just before a grammar test in a language such as German; students carefully review the inflectional system (der–das–die; den–das–die; plus the list of prepositions that take different cases) on the way to the exam. As soon as they sit down in class to take the test, they immediately scribble what they can remember of the inflectional system on the side of the page, so that when they need the correct marker, they can find it and use it. At the end of the exam, before handing in the paper, they erase their notes. The morphology on the side of the page is, most likely, late-acquired, and unavailable in rapid conversation for most people. The notes on the side, then, act like a conscious Monitor, raising the accuracy of the output in situations where the student has time, is focussed on form, and can access the rule; grammar tests fill these conditions nicely. Students thus do much better in terms of grammatical accuracy on such tests than they would in free conversation, the late-acquired, or not-yet-acquired, items that are learnable rising in rank.

[3] An interesting parallel hypothesis is that we will see greater numbers of *transitional forms* in Monitor-free conditions. The literature is consistent with this hypothesis, since the transitional forms noted for adult acquirers have all been found in subjects who appear to be non-users, or under-users of the conscious Monitor. For example, Schumann's Alberto (Schumann, 1978); Nelson's McGill university janitors (Nelson, 1980), and Hanania and Gradman's Fatmah (Hanania and Gradman, 1977). This is predictable, since transitional forms are hypothesized to reflect the operation of the acquired system.

[4] To be more precise, speaking skills that depend on *acquired* competence emerge over time as a result of comprehensible input. There appear to be, however, at least two ways of beating the system, at least over the short run. We can produce using memorized language, or routines and patterns (Krashen and Scarcella, 1978), and we can also produce by using the first language surface structure plus conscious grammar (L1 plus Monitor Mode). As we shall see later, both of these methods of performing without acquired competence have drawbacks and limitations.

[5] Interlanguage talk, the speech of second language acquirers to each other, may or may not be useful for acquisition. This is an important question that, to my knowledge, has not been directly dealt with in the professional literature. Arguments in favor of its utility for language acquisition are these: it satisfies the input hypothesis in that it is meant

for communication and might contain input at some acquirers' $i + 1$. On the other hand, there is the question of whether the ungrammaticality of much interlanguage talk outweighs these factors. Also, much interlanguage talk input might be too simple and may not contain $i + 1$ for the more advanced acquirer. See Krashen (1980, 1981) for a discussion of some of the empirical evidence that might shed light on this issue.

[6] In a recent study, M. Long (1980) reported that foreigner talk discourse did not contain significantly more verbs marked for present tense than native speaker–native speaker discourse. It is thus not more in the "now" of the "here and now", to paraphrase Long.

[7] A look at some of the memorized sentences and phrases children pick up during the silent period confirms their utility in a variety of social situations. Quite often, however, the children do not always acquire the knowledge of exactly when and how to use them. A particularly vivid example is the child, who had been in the United States approximately two months, who greeted an acquaintance of mine with "I kick you ass."

[8] Conscious Monitoring need not always result in the full repair of an L1 influenced error. If the repair job appears to be too complex for the Monitor to deal with, the performer may simply abort the entire sentence and try to express the idea in a simpler way. This may be the cause of the avoidance phenomena, first reported by Schachter (1974). In Schachter's study, it was shown that Chinese and Japanese speakers produced fewer relative clauses in English as a second language than did Farsi and Arabic speakers, but were more accurate. Schachter relates this result to L1–L2 differences: Chinese and Japanese relative clauses are constructed to the left of the head noun, while Farsi and Arabic, like English, have relative clauses to the right of the head noun.

One possible interpretation is that the Chinese and Japanese speakers in Schachter's study consciously knew the correct English relative clause rule but had not acquired it. Also, in their production of English, they utilized their L1 rule. Their Monitor was thus presented with the task of moving relative clauses around a head noun, a very complex operation. In many cases, subjects simply decided that it was not worth the effort! When they did produce relative clauses, however, they were accurate. These were the cases when they went to the trouble of applying a difficult rule.

Avoidance is thus predicted in cases where a rule has been consciously learned but not acquired, and when the L1 and L2 rules are quite different, where repair by the Monitor requires difficult mental gymnastics.

Avoidance is also predicted in cases where the performer consciously knows the rule imperfectly, not well enough to make the necessary change but well enough to see a mismatch between the L1 rule he has used and the correct target language rule. Since he cannot repair but knows there is an error, he can exercise his option to avoid the structure. Kleinman's avoidance data (Kleinman, 1977) fits this description. His Arabic-speaking subjects showed evidence of avoiding the passive in English, and his Spanish- and Portuguese-speaking subjects avoided infinitive complements and direct object pronouns in sentences with infinitive complements (e.g. "I told her to leave"). In both cases, according to Kleinman, contrastive analysis predicts difficulties. These subjects, unlike Schachter's, were not unusually accurate with these constructions when they produced them. In this case, it is possible that the subject's knowledge of the rule was not complete enough to effect a perfect repair, so avoidance was the result.

In both cases described above, conscious rules serve a filtering function, telling the performer where his L1 rule differs from the L2 rule. In one case, repair is possible but difficult, and in the other the conscious rule does not permit repair.

[9] Based on Hyltenstam's data on the acquisition of negation by adult acquirers of Swedish (Hyltenstam, 1977), Hammarberg (1979) argues that acquirers may begin at

different developmental stages depending on their first language. The normal course of development in the acquisition of negation in Swedish consists of the following transitional stages:

(1a) Acquirers place the negative marker before all other parts of the VP, before the auxiliary and the main verb.
(1b) Acquirers place the negative marker after the auxiliary but before the main verb.
(2)   Post-verbal negation.

In subsequent stages, acquirers move closer to the Swedish rule of post-verbal negation in main clauses and pre-verbal negation in subordinate clauses.

According to Hammarberg, speakers of languages that have pre-verbal negation (Serbo-Croatian) typically start this developmental sequence at the beginning, at stage 1a. English speakers, however, appear to begin at 1b. We do not see English speakers, in Hyltenstam's data, who produce "neg + aux" structures. Since 1b "is an English-like solution" (p. 10), one can hypothesize that English speakers skipped the (1a) transitional stage.

There are several possibilities here. First, Hammarberg's suggestion may be true. If so, if acquirers can skip a transitional stage t_j when their language has a rule identical to t_{j+1}, this implies that t_j was not essential—it did not have to serve as i. This does *not* rule out the possibility that t_j would have been useful.

A second possibility is that t_j was present, but escaped the observer's notice. Indeed, it may have been present as t_j but never uttered. Adult performers who have consciously learned the target language rule, or who have even learned parts of it, may be able to use the conscious Monitor to detect transitional errors and either avoid them in performance or repair them (see discussion in footnote 7 on avoidance). They may, however, have more of a tendency to accept such transitional forms when they coincide with an L1 rule, even if they are errors (Schachter *et al.*, 1976). This could explain why transitional forms that are unlike L1 rules are less frequently seen in performance. It should be noted, however, that the Serbo-Croatian speakers in Hyltenstam's study did show clear signs of stage 1b, which does not correspond to any rule in Serbo-Croatian.

There are thus at least two possibilities—the English speakers did indeed skip a stage, which implies that the skipped stage may not have been crucial to further development, or the stage was "there" but undetected, due to its short duration and/or its having not been used in the performer's output. Consistent with Schumann's findings (Schumann, 1979), the transitional stage that coincides with the L1 rule was quite evident, both in the case of Serbo-Croatian speakers (stage 1a) and English speakers (stage 1b). As suggested in the text, this stage may have, in each case, been two stages in one, first the L1 rule, and then the "real" transitional stage, with only the latter helping real progress to continue.

[10] Several scholars have pointed out that this view of transfer is too strong in that it predicts the occurrence of "transfer" errors that in fact do not occur. This problem can be resolved by positing several constraints on transfer, or conditions that must be met before a performer can substitute a first language rule for some $i + 1$.

Zobl (1980a, b, c) notes that the L1 rule itself must be a productive one. This accounts for the fact that French speakers acquiring English as a second language do not make errors of the kind:

John comes he?

after the French:

Jean vient-il?

The French rule, according to Zobl, is no longer productive in French. Citing Terry (1970), Zobl notes that it is mainly limited to present tense contexts, an indication that the rule is becoming unproductive.

Kellerman (1978) provides another condition on transfer: the performer must perceive the transferred rule to be potentially non-language specific. Kellerman's original experiments in lexical transfer showed that foreign language students were less willing to transfer features of words they considered to be less "core". For example, a Dutch-speaking student of English would be more likely to presume that he could transfer the Dutch verb 'brechen' (break) in an English sentence:

He broke his leg.

than in:

The waves broke on the shore.

A similar constraint exists in syntax. Dutch students of English, Kellerman reports, were not willing to accept a literal translation into English of the Dutch equivalent of:

This book reads well.

apparently because the intransitive use of *read* was perceived to be language-specific and infrequent (see also Jordans and Kellerman, 1978).

Another constraint comes from the work of Wode (1978), and accounts for the finding that L1 influenced errors do not seem to occur at all stages of the acquirer's development. Wode states that for an interlinguistic error to occur, the L1 rule and the L2 rule it substitutes for must meet a "crucial similarity measure" (p. 116). In other words, if an L1 rule is to be utilized, it must be preceded by some i of the L2 that differs from it only in minimal ways. Wode's example, from child second language acquisition of English by German speakers, illustrates this point nicely. Wode notes that errors such as:

John go not to school.

occur in which German-like post-verbal negation is used. These errors are not found in beginning acquirers, but occur, according to Wode, only after the acquirer has reached the "aux-negation" stage and already produces sentences such as:

John can not go.

The acquirer then overgeneralizes the negative rule from post-auxiliary to post-verbal, and uses the first language rule.

[11] There is another way in which use of the L1 may indirectly help second language acquisition. The existence of cognates will help to make input comprehensible, even if form and meaning are not identical across languages. This factor will increase the rate of acquisition but not alter the order.

[12] The hypothesis that L1 rules cannot contribute to real progress implies that fossilized use of a L1 rule is the "end of the line" for acquisition. Does this mean that a single L1 error, a single prolonged substitution of some $i + 1$ halts all acquisition? It only implies this if we accept a strictly linear view of the natural order hypothesis, that there is only one stream of progress that acquirers follow in strict sequence. Clearly, this is not the

case. If it were, acquirers would always show us just one transitional error at a time! Of course, individuals show us many error types at once. This indicates that several streams of development are taking place at the same time. These streams appear to be correlated; a performer at a given stage in one stream will usually be at a predictable stage in another stream. Schumann (1980) provides good evidence for this, noting that his subjects who were at the *no + v* stage in negation produced few relative clauses or relative clauses without relative pronouns. For L1 acquisition, Shipley, Smith and Gleitman (1969) report that verb phrase related items are correlated fairly highly for order of acquisition, and noun phrase related items are correlated, but agreement across the groups is not high (see also Krashen, Madden and Bailey, 1975; and Andersen, 1978, for similar suggestions). Of course, it is quite possible that transitional forms or rules from one stream may help out those in any other by serving as *i*. If say ten parallel streams of development occur at any given time in an acquirer, it may be the case that a given stream will interact with some, but not all, of the others in this way.

[13] "Integrative" motivation refers to the desire to "be like" speakers of the target language. In foreign language situations (e.g. studying French in Anglophone Canada), students with more integrative motivations are usually superior, especially over the long run (Gardner and Lambert, 1972). In situations where there is some urgency in second language acquisition and/or where there is less desire to "integrate", the presence of integrative motivation may not relate to second language achievement. Rather, "instrumental" motivation, the desire to use the language for practical means, may predict success better (Lukmani, 1972; Gardner and Lambert, 1972; Oller, Baca, and Vigil, 1977).

[14] Stevick (1980) provides a poignant example, a story related to him by one of his students:

"Four years ago I was looking for any kind of job I could find. I happened to get one teaching ESL to a class of six women from various parts of the world who spoke no English. I had never heard of ESL before. The salary was poor and I didn't know if I wanted to pursue a teaching career, therefore my approach was very casual and low pressure. My method usually consisted of thinking up a topic to talk about, introducing it, and encouraging each student to express her feelings.

In spite of my casual approach, the teaching job was extremely pleasant. I had a deep empathy for anyone who was facing a language barrier because I had just returned from a trip around the world alone as a monolingual.

They all started speaking English fairly well after the first two weeks of class. I remember a woman from Columbia telling me that she hadn't spoken English before because she was afraid of making mistakes. After being in class for a while, she spoke English and made mistakes and didn't care. I didn't attach much significance to the progress that the women made. I had no idea how long it took people to learn a language.

Gradually I became quite career-oriented, and made a conscious decision to try to be a top-notch ESL teacher. I had guilt feelings about the casual way in which I had taught those first six women, and my teaching evolved into the traditional authoritarian style with the textbook dominant. Over the years, it has gotten to where I feel frustrated if a student takes class time to relate a personal anecdote.

I can look back on these four years and see a gradual decline in the performance of my students. Until recently, I have been assuming that I needed to be more attentive to their mistakes in order to speed their progress. My present style of teaching bypasses the students' feelings and basic needs, and concentrates on method. I never see successes like those first six ladies." (From Stevick, 1980, pp. 4–5).

[15] "Intermediate" here means knowing enough English to be able to take at least a partial academic load, but not being able to "pass out" of the required university English as a second language requirement. The normal situation for the intermediate at the university is to be enrolled in at least one ESL class in addition to one or more subject matter courses.

[16] The research cited here deals exclusively with the effect of instruction on the acquisition of syntax and morphology. Until recently, little work had been done that examined the effect of instruction on the acquisition of pronunciation. Purcell and Suter (1980) report that acquisition of pronunciation of English as a second language was predicted by the following factors: (1) The acquirer's first language (speakers of Arabic and Farsi were superior to speakers of Japanese and Thai); (2) The amount of interaction with English speakers; (3) Performance on a test of phonetic ability; and (4) The degree of concern the speaker had about his accent. Factor (2) appears to be related to comprehensible input, while (3) and (4) may be related to learning. (1) Reflects the consequences of falling back on the first language. The amount of formal classroom training in ESL, however, did not relate to pronunciation ability, even when courses were specifically aimed at teaching pronunciation.

[17] Some studies seem to show that age of arrival (AOA) predicts second language attainment for children—that is, that the child who arrives at age six, for example, will attain higher levels of proficiency than the child who arrives at age ten. While AOA *does* predict ultimate attainment for children as a group as compared to adults as a group, closer examination reveals that AOA *per se* is not a factor for children considered alone. In cases where AOA seems to be a factor, it can be argued that LOR, and ultimately CI, is really causative. Cummins (1980) has performed such a reanalysis of Ramsey and Wright's data on 1,200 immigrant children in Canada (Ramsey and Wright, 1974), and reaches this conclusion, noting that when AOA is controlled in Ramsey and Wright's data, children with longer LOR's perform better in a variety of tasks. Cummins also found that when LOR is controlled, however, children with younger AOA's are not necessarily better—in many cases, the opposite is true. Minoura (1979) can also be reinterpreted. She studied 44 Japanese children who had been in the United States for a range of one to eight years. While LOR predicted attainment ($r = 0.79$), so did AOA ($r = -0.75$) (a sentence imitation test was used). All the children in the sample had arrived in the United States at about the same time, however, so LOR and AOA were highly correlated ($r = -0.95$). It thus may be argued that LOR, and thus comprehensible input, was the true causative factor. (According to my calculations, the correlation between AOA and SLA reduces to $r = 0.005$ when the effect of LOR is removed!) The Heidelberg project, discussed in the text, also reports a relationship between AOA and SLA, this time among adults taken as a group. This also seems to be a confound, since older subjects seemed to spend less time speaking German ($r = -0.32$ between AOA and reported leisure time use of German). Partial correlation partialling out the effects of interaction with German speakers reduces the reported correlation of -0.57 between AOA and SLA to $r = -0.49$. This could (and should) go even lower with a more reliable measure of the amount of comprehensible input subjects actually got.

[18] Pidginization "occurs when speakers of different languages come into limited contact and an auxiliary vehicle of communication develops to facilitate interaction among them." (Schumann, 1978b, p. 40). Secondary hybridization is a form of pidginization that occurs if a "standard form" of a target language is available. It persists only if speakers remain at social and psychological distance from speakers of the norm. (From Whinnom, 1971, cited by Schumann, 1978b).

Decreolization occurs when speakers of a creole (a pidgin that has becomer a native language of a group) "gain varying degrees of contact with the group that speaks the base language of the creole" (Schumann, p. 41). It is the process of moving toward the "standard form" of the language. Creolists refer to several stages of decreolization, ranging from the creole itself, to the basolect, which is close to the creole, the mesolect, the acrolect, and finally, the standard form.

[19] Psychological distance is determined by factors such as motivation, language and culture shock, and other affective variables. Social distance results from social factors, such as the relative dominance of the social group of the acquirer and speakers of the target language, the cohesiveness of the groups, similarity in culture, etc. In Schumann's view, factors causing psychological and social distance "put the learner in a situation where he is largely cut off from target language input and/or does not attend to it when it is available" (Schumann, 1977, pp. 266–267).

[20] Also of interest is the fact that Alberto's grammatical morpheme difficulty order (one cross-section) correlates significantly with the "natural order" proposed earlier ($r = 0.73$, $p < 0.05$; analysis in Krashen, 1977). The data was collected from his spontaneous speech.

[21] This is not the only interpretation of this result, as Earl Stevick has pointed out to me. Something else may have caused Paz' superior second language acquisition, and the low psychological distance score may be a result of this and not a cause.

[22] Or the "remote cause". See discussion in Schumann (1978b), p. 48.

Chapter III

Providing Input for Acquisition

In this chapter, we take the difficult step from theory to practice. Before we do this, let me remind the reader of the main point of Chapter I: I consider theory to be only one of several possible determinants of method and materials. These implications need to be confirmed by further research (even though several implications do have empirical confirmation) and by the experiences of teachers and students. The "ideal" state is a relationship whereby theoretical and applied researchers and practitioners learn (and acquire) from each other.

We will cover one aspect of application in this chapter: how we can encourage subconscious acquisition. This is an important question, since the major implication of second language acquisition theory is that acquisition is central. It therefore follows that our major pedagogical efforts need to be devoted to encouraging language acquisition.

This portion begins with a brief discussion of some of the implications of the input hypothesis with respect to the role and potential of the second language classroom, as well as its limitations, as compared with the informal environment. Following this, we discuss the contribution that actual output can make. As explained in Chapter II, it is hypothesized that we acquire via input, what we read and hear, and not via output, actual talking and writing. Output does have an indirect role to play in encouraging acquisition, however.

The major portion of this chapter is concerned with characterizing what "good input" is, listing the features that input should have if it is to encourage acquisition. In subsequent chapters, we will discuss how conscious language learning fits into the pedagogical schema, and in the final chapter we will examine some common language teaching methods and some aspects of the informal environment, to see to what extent they provide the input discussed in this section and the type of learning discussed in Chapter IV.

The goal of this exercise is to provide a framework that helps us see what materials and methods actually do for the second language student. This will hopefully help uncover gaps and provide us with ways to supplement and improve existing materials and techniques.

A. The Potential of the Second Language Classroom

We often hear that you have to "live in the country" in order to achieve any real proficiency in a second language, and that the informal real world environment is always superior to the classroom, or formal environment. As we saw in Chapter II, there are several studies that appear to support this assertion. Other studies, however, suggested that the classroom does help after all. I attempted to resolve this apparent conflict by hypothesizing that what was really at issue was *comprehensible input*. The classroom is of benefit when it is the major source of comprehensible input. When acquirers have rich sources of input outside the class, and when they are proficient enough to take advantage of it (i.e. understand at least some of it), the classroom does not make an important contribution.

Thus, the real advantage of the informal environment is that it supplies comprehensible input. If, however, we fill our second language classrooms with input that is optimal for acquisition, it is quite possible that we can actually do better than the informal environment, at least up to the intermediate level. As we mentioned in Chapter II, the informal environment is not always willing to supply comprehensible input to the older second language student. As Hatch and her colleagues have pointed out, input to the adult is more complicated grammatically, contains a wider range of vocabulary, deals with more complex topics, and is generally harder to understand. This is simply a reflection of the fact that the adult world is more complex than the world of the child, and our expectations for adult comprehension are much higher.

In the case of the adult beginner, the classroom can do much better than the informal environment. In the second language classroom, we have the potential of supplying a full 40–50 minutes per day of comprehensible input, input that will encourage language acquisition. The true beginner in the informal environment, especially if he or she is not adept at skills of conversational management and negotiation of meaning (see discussion later in this chapter; also Scarcella and Higa, forthcoming), may require days or even weeks before he or she can "pick out" that much comprehensible input from the barrage of language heard. The beginning student will simply not understand most of the language around him. It will be noise, unusable for acquisition.

The value of second language classes, then, lies not only in the grammar instruction, but in the simpler "teacher talk", the comprehensible input. It can be an efficient place to achieve at least the intermediate levels rapidly, as long as the focus of the class is on providing input for acquisition.

B. Limitations of the Classroom

Despite my enthusiasm for the second language classroom, there are several ways in which the outside world clearly excels (or some "modification" of the outside world, a fascinating alternative that we shall discuss later), especially for the intermediate level second language student. First, it is very clear that the outside world can supply *more* input. Living in the country where the language is spoken can result in an all-day second language lesson! As we mentioned earlier, however, for the informal environment to be of any use, the input language has to be comprehensible. The informal environment will therefore be of more and more use as the acquirer progresses and can understand more and more.

Second, as many scholars have pointed out, the range of discourse that the student can be exposed to in a second language classroom is quite limited, no matter how "natural" we make it. There is simply no way the classroom can match the variety of the outside world, although we can certainly expand beyond our current limitations.

The classroom will probably never be able to completely overcome its limitations, nor does it have to. Its goal is not to substitute for the outside world, but to bring students to the point where they can begin to use the outside world for further acquisition, to where they can begin to understand the language used on the outside. It does this in two ways: by supplying input so that students progress in language acquisition, so that they understand "real" language to at least some extent, and by making the student conversationally competent, that is, by giving the student tools to manage conversations despite a less than perfect competence in the second language. We return to both of these important points in the discussion that follows.

C. The Role of Output

A second point that needs to be dealt with before describing the characteristics of optimal input for acquisition is the role of output, most commonly, the role of speech, in language acquisition.[1] *

The Input Hypothesis makes a claim that may seem quite remarkable to some people—we acquire spoken fluency *not* by practicing talking but by understanding input, by listening and reading. It is, in fact, theoretically possible to acquire language without ever talking. This has been demonstrated for first language acquisition by Lenneberg (1962), who described the case of a boy with congenital dysarthria, a disorder of the peripheral speech organs, who was never able to speak. When Lenneberg tested the boy, he found that the child was able to understand spoken English perfectly. In other words, he had acquired "competence" without ever producing. The child was tested at age eight, and there is no way to tell directly whether his lack of output had slowed down his language acquisition. It is quite possible that if he had been able to speak, he would have acquired language somewhat faster, due to the *indirect* contribution speaking can make to acquisition.

Output has a contribution to make to language acquisition, but it is not a direct one: Simply, the more you talk, the more people will talk to you! Actual speaking on the part of the language acquirer will thus affect the *quantity* of input people direct at you.

It will also affect the *quality* of the input directed at the acquirer. Conversational partners often try to help you understand by modifying their speech ("foreigner talk"). They judge how much to modify by seeing whether you understand what is said, and also *by listening to you talk*. A second language speaker who makes lots of mistakes, has a poor accent, and is hesitant, will most likely receive, in general, more modified input than a speaker who appears competent and fluent.

Engaging in conversation is probably much more effective than

* Superscript numbers refer to Notes at end of Chapters.

"eavesdropping" for language acquisition. In conversation, the second language acquirer has some degree of control of the topic, can signal to the partner that there is a comprehension problem, etc. In other words, he can manage and regulate the input, and make it more comprehensible. There is no such control in eavesdropping! But in order to participate in conversation, there must be at least some talk, some output, from each partner. Hence, the indirect contribution of speech.

1. "CONVERSATION" AND LANGUAGE ACQUISITION

Some scholars have suggested that "participation in conversation" is responsible for language acquisition. In the light of the above discussion, we can see that this is true, in a sense. "Conversation", however, is not in itself the causative variable in second language acquisition. It is one way, and a very good way, to obtain input. It is theoretically quite possible to acquire without participating in conversation, however.[2]

Figure 3.1 illustrates the indirect, but often considerable, contribution output can make to language acquisition.

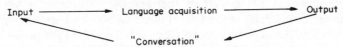

Fig. 3.1. How output contributes to language acquisition indirectly.

Comprehensible *input* is responsible for progress in language acquisition.
Output is possible as a result of acquired competence.
When performers *speak*, they encourage *input* (people speak to them). This is *conversation*.

2. OUTPUT AND LEARNING

As suggested in Chapter II, output can play a fairly direct role in helping language *learning*, although even here it is not necessary. Output aids learning because it provides a domain for error correction. When a second language user speaks or writes, he or she may make an error. When this error is corrected, this supposedly helps the learner change his or her conscious mental representation of the rule or alter the environment of rule application. (See discussion of Hypothesis (1), Chapter II.)

We may thus compare an "output approach" to the input approach promoted here. Could we teach language primarily by encouraging production, with little or no input, and correcting all errors? Such a technique, in addition to being maddening, relies entirely on the students' ability to learn grammar.

This is not to say that error correction is totally useless and that learning is of no value. Learning has a role to play, and error correction may be of use in certain situations. We will return later to the question of "putting learning in its place".

By now the reader has seen enough promises of "more on this topic later", and it is time to turn to the major portion of this chapter, a description of the characteristics of optimal input for second language acquisition, where, hopefully, the promises this introduction has made will be kept.

D. Characteristics of Optimal Input for Acquisition

I will attempt in this section to present a set of requirements that should be met by any activity or set of materials aimed at subconscious language acquisition. The (testable) prediction that this set of characteristics makes is that an activity that fits the characteristics fully will encourage acquisition at the fastest possible rate. An activity that fits none of them could result in zero acquisition, or very little acquisition. (The latter, "very little", is more likely. The "language acquisition device" may be so powerful, even in the adult, that some minimal acquisition may occur as a result of *any* exposure to language.)

The characteristics described below are not "weighted". There is no attempt to claim that one is more important than another, although such claims should possibly be made. I will leave this to future refinements. Also, there is no attempt here to "support" these conclusions by empirical evidence. They derive from second language acquisition theory, the hypotheses presented in Chapter II. It is these hypotheses that are supported by empirical evidence. In other words, we are looking here only at implications of theory. This does not mean that the characteristics cannot be treated as predictions and further tested; indeed, they should be confirmed by both applied linguistics research as well as teacher and student intuition, as I discussed in Chapter I.

We discuss each characteristic separately, showing what predictions each characteristic makes with respect to different aspects of method, materials, and informal input. Following these descriptions, I will attempt to point out some new possibilities, and underscore the importance of some neglected traditional sources of input (Chapter V).

1. OPTIMAL INPUT IS COMPREHENSIBLE

This is clearly the most important input characteristic. It amounts to the claim that when the acquirer does not understand the message, there will be no acquisition. In other words, incomprehensible input, or "noise", will not help.

Positing *comprehensibility* as a fundamental and necessary (but not sufficient) requirement makes several predictions that appear to be correct. It explains why it is practically impossible for someone to acquire a second or foreign language merely by listening to the radio, unless the acquirer speaks a very closely related language. A monolingual English speaker, for example, hearing Polish on the radio, would acquire nothing because the input would be only "noise".[3]

This requirement also explains the apparent failure of educational TV programs to teach foreign languages. The input is simply not comprehensible. My own children watched programs such as Ville Allegre faithfully for years, and acquired about as much as I did: They could count from one to ten in Spanish and recognize a few words such as *casa* and *mesa*! The comprehensibility requirement predicts that TV would, in general, be somewhat more successful than radio as a language teacher, but that even TV would be inadequate in beginning stages. Ervin-Tripp (1973) has noted that hearing children of deaf parents do not acquire language from TV or radio, an observation consistent with this requirement.[4]

This characteristic also explains why children sometimes fail to pick up family languages. My own case is, I think, quite typical. My parents spoke Yiddish around the house for years, occasionally to each other (to tell secrets), and constantly to my grandparents. Nevertheless, my sister and I failed to acquire Yiddish, with the exception of a few phrases and routines. On the other hand, in many families children do grow up speaking the family language as well as the language of the community. What appears to be crucial is whether the family language is directed at the child, in other words, whether an attempt is made to make the language *comprehensible*. What we heard via eavesdropping was not comprehensible. It dealt with topics that were not easily identified and that were also often beyond our range of experience. Language directed at us in Yiddish would have been simplified, and more relevant to us, and hence more comprehensible.

Another prediction that the comprehensibility requirement makes is that "just talking", or "free conversation", is not language teaching. In other words, simply being a native speaker of a language does not in of itself qualify one as a teacher of that language. Conscious and extensive knowledge of grammar does not make one a language teacher either. Rather, the defining characteristic of a good teacher is someone who can make input comprehensible to a non-native speaker, regardless of his or her level of competence in the target language. This leads naturally to another topic, how teachers make input comprehensible.

(a) How to aid comprehension

If we are correct in positing comprehensibility as a crucial requirement for optimal input for acquisition, the question of how to aid comprehension is a very central one for second language pedagogy. Indeed, the comprehension requirement suggests that *perhaps the main function of the second language teacher is to help make input comprehensible*, to do for the adult what the "outside world" cannot or will not do.

There are basically two ways in which the teacher can aid comprehension, linguistic and non-linguistic. Studies have shown that there are many things speakers do linguistically to make their speech more comprehensible to less competent speakers. Hatch (1979) has summarized the linguistic aspects of simplified input which appear to promote comprehension. Among these characteristics are:

(1) slower rate and clearer articulation, which helps acquirers to identify word boundaries more easily, and allows more processing time;
(2) more use of high frequency vocabulary, less slang, fewer idioms;
(3) syntactic simplification, shorter sentences.

Such characteristics and others appear to be more or less common to different types of simple codes, such as caretaker speech, foreigner-talk, and teacher-talk (see also Krashen, 1980), and clearly help make input language more comprehensible. There is considerable empirical evidence that these codes are significantly "simpler" than native speaker–native speaker language, and, as mentioned in Chapter II, there is evidence of some correlation between the linguistic level of the acquirer and the complexity of the input language: more advanced acquirers tend to get more complex input.

Does this mean that teachers should consciously try to simplify their speech when they talk to students? Should they think about slowing down, using more common vocabulary, using shorter sentences, less complex syntax with less embedding, etc.? Consciously referring to these "rules" might be helpful on occasion, but it appears to be the case that we make these adjustments automatically when we focus on trying to make ourselves understood. Roger Brown, commenting on studies of caretaker speech in first language acquisition, comes to a similar conclusion. He gives the following advice to parents wanting to know how to "teach" their children language in the least amount of time:

> Believe that your child can understand more than he or she can say, and seek, above all, to communicate. . . . There is no set of rules of how to talk to a child that can even approach what you unconsciously know. If you concentrate on communicating, everything else will follow. (Brown, 1977, p. 26.)

As I have argued in several places (Krashen, 1980, 1981), the same situation may hold for the language teacher. If we focus on comprehension and communication, we will meet the syntactic requirements for optimal input.

While we free teachers of the responsibility to consciously control the grammar of their output speech, other responsibilities become more important. One is to make sure that the input is indeed comprehensible. I have nothing startling to add to the literature on comprehension checking, other than to underscore and emphasize its importance. Comprehension checking can range from simply asking "Do you understand?" occasionally, to monitoring comprehension via students' verbal and non-verbal responses.

Another main task of the teacher is to provide non-linguistic means of encouraging comprehension. In my view, providing extra-linguistic support in the form of realia and pictures for beginning classes is not a frill, but a very important part of the tools the teacher has to encourage language acquisition. The use of objects and pictures in early second language instruction corresponds to the caretaker's use of the "here and now" in encouraging first language acquisition, in that they all help the acquirer understand messages containing structures that are "a little beyond" them.

Good teachers also take advantage of the student's knowledge of the world in helping comprehension by discussing topics that are familiar to the student. Certainly, discussing or reading about a topic that is totally unknown will make the message harder to understand. There is a danger, however, in making the input too "familiar". If the message is completely known, it will be of no interest, and the student will probably not attend. We want the student to focus on the message, and there must be some message, something that the student really wants to hear or read about. This requirement is perhaps the hardest one to meet, and we shall have more to say about it below, in our discussion of characteristic II.[5]

As pointed out just a moment ago, comprehension is a *necessary* condition for language acquisition, but it is not *sufficient*. It is quite possible to understand input language, and yet not acquire. This can happen in several different ways: First, it is quite possible that the input simply does not contain $i + 1$, that it does not include structures that are "a bit beyond" the student. Second, in many cases we do not utilize syntax in understanding—we can often get the message with a combination of vocabulary, or lexical information, plus extra-linguistic information. Finally, the "affective filter" may be "up", which can result in the acquirer understanding input, even input with $i + 1$, but not utilizing it for further acquisition.

2. OPTIMAL INPUT IS INTERESTING AND/OR RELEVANT

Optimal input focusses the acquirer on the message and not on form. To go a step further, the best input is so interesting and relevant that the acquirer may even "forget" that the message is encoded in a foreign language.

Creating materials and providing input that meet this characteristic may appear to be an easy and obvious task, but my view is that, in reality, this requirement is not easy to meet, nor has the profession considered it obvious. It is very *difficult* to present and discuss topics of interest to a class of people whose goals, interests, and backgrounds differ from the teacher's and from each other's. I also claim that relevance and interest have not been widely perceived as requirements for input, since so many materials fail to meet this requirement!

It is fairly easy to think up examples of input that, while comprehensible, are universally perceived to be uninteresting and irrelevant. Among the most obvious examples are pattern drill, and most dialogue type exercises. Experimental evidence suggests that students pay little or no attention to meaning after the first few repetitions in pattern drill (Lee, McCune, and Patton, 1970), and the same result is most likely true for dialogues that are memorized by rote. Grammatical exercises also fail as input for acquisition on similar grounds. Granted, the goals of these exercises are not "acquisition", and we will have occasion to examine whether these input-types fill other needs in the second language program. Nevertheless, they fail this requirement dismally.

Somewhat less obvious is the failure of "meaningful drill" to qualify as optimal input for acquisition. "Meaningful drill" is distinguished from "mechanical drill", in that the former requires that real meaning be involved (Paulston, 1972). Since meaningful drill is designed to provide practice on particular grammatical structures, however, it is very difficult to also build in the exchange of truly relevant or interesting information, as in:

What time does he get up in the morning?
What time do they get up in the morning?

At best, such information is of only mild interest to members of a language class. I believe that it is an impossible task for teachers to embed truly interesting or relevant information into the form of a meaningful drill on a daily basis!

Some other fairly widespread input types that fall very short of the mark of true relevance are the reading assignments that most foreign language students work through in introductory courses. Generally, these selections bear very little resemblance to the kind of reading the students would do in their first language on their own time.

Before the reader feels I am being overly critical and unfair, I must say that it seems to me that the interest-relevance requirement is nearly impossible to satisfy in the standard American foreign language course given in the high school or college, especially when such a course is taken as a requirement. It is far easier to satisfy in ESL situations, where there is a perceived need for the language. For example, in classes composed primarily of immigrants, input will typically contain a great deal of information that is useful to the student for survival "on the outside". University ESL courses for foreign students often include study skills, English for academic purposes, introduction to university life, and even useful academic skills.[6] ESL teachers often serve officially or unofficially as friends and counselors, and therefore provide a great deal of truly relevant input.[7,8]

3. OPTIMAL INPUT IS NOT GRAMMATICALLY SEQUENCED

In acquisition-oriented materials, we should not be consciously concerned about including $i + 1$ in the input. Part (3) of the Input Hypothesis claims that when input is comprehensible, when meaning is successfully negotiated, $i + 1$ will be present automatically, in most cases.[9]

This requirement could be stated in a weaker form. 3 could be rephrased as follows: there is no *need* to deliberately include $i + 1$, since it will occur naturally. The strong form may be called for instead: it may be better not to even attempt to include $i + 1$! The arguments against a deliberate attempt to grammatically sequence were given briefly in Chapter II, and will be expanded on here.

1. If we sequence, and each lesson, or group of lessons, focusses on one structure, this assumes that everyone in the class has the same $i + 1$, that everyone is at the same developmental stage in the second language. Because there are individual differences in the rate of acquisition (due to the strength of the affective filter and the amount of comprehensible input obtained), and differences among students as to out of class contact with the language, it is extremely unlikely that all the students in any class are at the same stage. Unsequenced but natural input, it is hypothesized, will contain a rich variety of structure—if it is comprehensible, there will be $i + 1$ for everyone as

long as there is *enough* input (we return to the *quantity* question below).

2. When we attempt to present a "finely-tuned" sequence, we generally present each structure or rule once. (There is the "review" lesson and there are attempts at recycling, but review does not usually work through the entire sequence of activities—its goal is generally to "remind" and provide some additional practice for a rule that is supposedly already "internalized".[10]) What happens to the student who misses the rule the first time around? Traditional review, meant as a reminder, will often not help. In traditional foreign language learning, as done in the United States, the student may even have to wait until next year, when the rule is presented again! Unsequenced communicative input contains built-in review. We don't have to worry if we miss the progressive tense today, it will be part of the input again . . . and again! Comprehensible input thus guarantees us natural review and recycling, assuming, as mentioned above, that there is enough of it.

Some readers may feel that I am setting up and attacking a straw man. It can be argued that some grammatically-based courses, despite a lockstep structural orientation, do provide input at $i + 1$ as well. While there may be a "structure of the day", not every utterance contains the target structure. For example, if the lesson's focus is the progressive tense marker, other tenses will be used as well in both classroom input and in the readings.

This may appear to be the case, but there is, nevertheless, a real problem with this approach. With a grammatical focus, communication will *always* suffer, there will always be less genuinely interesting input. The teacher's mind, and the materials writer's mind, is focussed on "contextualizing" a particular structure, and not on communicating ideas.

As my colleague Steven Sternfeld has pointed out to me, what is proposed here is fundamentally different from "contextualization". Contextualization involves inventing a *realistic* context for the presentation of a grammatical rule or vocabulary item. The goal in the mind of the teacher is the learning or acquisition of the rule or word. What is proposed here is that the goal, in the mind of both the teacher and the student, is the idea, the message.

This objection can be summarized as follows:

3. The very orientation of the grammatically-based syllabus reduces the quality of comprehensible input and distorts the communicative focus. Teachers will be concerned with *how* they are speaking, reading selections will be aimed at including *x* number of examples of structure *y* along with a certain vocabulary sample, a sure guarantee of boring and wooden language.

4. Still another problem is that the grammatical sequence attempts to guess the order of acquisition. Several years ago, I suggested (Krashen *et al.*, 1975) that an application of the Natural Order Hypothesis was the construction of "natural syllabi" following the natural order. My position has changed. As Fathman (1979) has pointed out, the practical implication of the Natural Order Hypothesis may lie in what it has taught us about the underlying process of language acquisition. It seems to me now that we should not attempt to teach according to an order similar to that given in Table 2, Chapter II (or according to any other grammatical sequence!).

Comprehensible input, it is claimed, will automatically follow a natural order insofar as $i + 1$ will be provided (along with many other structures).

We now summarize the advantages of natural input (the well-balanced diet of wholesome food) over the lockstep grammatical syllabus (single or even multiple vitamin therapy).[11]

(a) The case against the grammatical syllabus

Grammatical syllabus (deliberate attempt to supply $i + 1$)	Communicative input ($i + 1$ included naturally, given enough input)
1. All students may not be at the same stage. The structure of the day may not be the $i + 1$ for many of the students.	1. $i + 1$ will be provided for all students eventually
2. Each structure presented only once. (See text for discussion of "review".)	2. Natural and extensive review.
3. Grammatical focus may prevent real and natural communication.	3. Conscious focus of both student and teacher is communication of ideas.
4. Assumes we know order of acquisition.	4. Does not assume we know order of acquisition.

4. OPTIMAL INPUT MUST BE IN SUFFICIENT QUANTITY

It is difficult to say just how much comprehensible/low filter input is necessary to achieve a given level of proficiency in second language acquisition, due to a lack of data. We know enough now, however, to be able to state with some confidence that the profession has seriously underestimated the amount of comprehensible input necessary to achieve even moderate, or "intermediate" levels of proficiency in second language acquisition.

Theoretical arguments for quantity derive from the immediately preceding discussion. I hypothesized that natural communicative input could supply $i + 1$ for all students if two conditions were met;

(1) The input was not artificially constrained (limited range of discourse types)
(2) It was supplied in sufficient quantity.

Clearly, five minutes of talk, or a single paragraph of reading, has little chance of including a given student's $i + 1$. Rather than take a more careful aim at that student's needs, rather than "overindividualizing" instruction, it is far easier, I am suggesting, to increase the amount of comprehensible input. Again, if there is enough, $i + 1$ will be provided, and will be provided over and over!

As mentioned above, we do not have enough data to state, with confidence, how much input is necessary to reach a given stage. The literature does provide us with enough to state some initial hypothesis, however. Below, we briefly examine what the literature implies about reaching the initial "readiness to speak" stage, and more advanced levels.

(a) Quantity requirements for initial readiness to speak

How much input is needed to end the "silent period"? How much input is necessary so that second language acquirers can produce utterances using acquired competence?

Asher's work on Total Physical Response teaching, a method that requires students to obey commands given in the second language, often with a "total physical response" (e.g. standing up), gives us some idea as to how much input is necessary for initial speaking readiness.

As we will see in Chapter V, the chief virtue of Total Physical Response may be its ability to supply concentrated comprehensible input. Asher has noted in several papers (reviewed in Chapter V) that TPR students are generally ready to start production in the target language after about ten hours of Total Physical Response input.[12]

Informal language acquisition research presents what at first may seem to be a different picture. The "silent period" seen in informal child second language acquisition may last as long as six months! During this time, the child may produce very little in the second language, other than routines and a few patterns. The greater length of the "natural" silent period, as compared to Asher's observation that ten hours may suffice may be due to the fact that a great deal of the input that the child in the natural environment receives may be incomprehensible. As stated earlier in this chapter, the main advantage of "formal instruction" may be its potential for providing comprehensible input in early stages, bringing the acquirer to the point where he or she can begin to take advantage of the natural environment. The long silent period in informal child second language acquisition may be further evidence that the informal environment is inefficient in early stages.[13]

(b) Quantity requirements for higher levels of proficiency

We know even less about the amount of low filter/comprehensible input necessary for progress to higher levels of competence. We can get some idea from the United States Foreign Service Institute chart, an estimate of the amount of class time necessary to achieve a FSI 2+ rating in different foreign languages (2+ is defined as "halfway between minimal professional proficiency and working professional proficiency", Diller, 1978, p. 100) for adult English speakers. According to the Foreign Service Institute estimates (reproduced in Diller, 1978), European languages such as German, French, and Italian require approximately 720 hours of classtime for the "average" student to attain the 2+ level, while more "exotic" languages (such as Arabic, Korean, and Chinese) require 1950 hours of classtime.[14]

These figures may, however, represent an upper bound. They are based on "classroom hours", which, if traditional methods are employed, may not entail optimal input. In other words, we can do better!

"How much input?" remains an empirical question, one that can probably be adequately answered by research. To be more precise, we would like to know: "How much low filter/comprehensible input is necessary for students to acquire enough competence in the second language, so that they can use the informal environment to continue improving?" Despite our current paucity of data, what seems clear to me now is that we are not using enough of the available instruction time for supplying comprehensible input, and that we will be able to stimulate more rapid (and more comfortable) second language acquisition if we put greater focus on input.

Before concluding this section, I should point out that what I am suggesting is not at all new: along with Newmark (1971), I am suggesting that the "extensive" side of the extensive–intensive reading debate is correct, that students profit more from reading for meaning, and reading great quantities of material, than from what Newmark calls "cryptoanalytic decoding" of difficult paragraphs, and that students gain more from participating in conversations, many conversations, than from focussed listening comprehension exercises.

We turn now to two other features programs should contain if they are to encourage language acquisition.

E. Other Features that Encourage Acquisition

1. THE STUDENT SHOULD NOT BE PUT ON THE DEFENSIVE

The phrase "on the defensive" comes from Stevick's well known book *Memory, Meaning, and Method*. What it means to me is that methods and materials should not be a test of the student's abilities or prior experiences, should not merely reveal weaknesses, but should help the student acquire more.

More generally, we are talking about keeping the affective filter "low", making sure the student is open to the input. It may be the case that if we use procedures that are "true" to the input hypothesis, and that satisfy all the other characteristics of optimal input, the kind of input that results, and the classroom procedures that evolve, will satisfy this requirement as well and help keep the filter low. I will attempt, in this section, to outline a few general procedures and practices that do this.

First, and I apologize for harping on this issue so much, if we concentrate on supplying comprehensible input where the focus is on the message and not on the form, this will in of itself contribute to a low filter. If the topic being discussed is at all interesting, and if it is comprehensible, much of the "pressure" normally associated with a language class will be "off", anxiety will be lowered, and acquisition will result. As mentioned earlier, I think a desirable goal is that the student "forget", in a sense, that the message is actually encoded in another language.

Second, we will be able to keep the filter low by not insisting on too-early production, before the student is "ready". Language teachers (and students) associate progress in second language acquisition with speaking fluency ("Do you *speak* French?"), and the logical consequence of this is that we want our students to talk from the beginning. My personal view is that forcing early production, before the student has built up enough competence through comprehensible input, is perhaps the single most anxiety-provoking thing about language classes! While some students may want to talk as soon as possible, others may feel less secure until they have built up more competence. In other words, the length of the silent period is variable (see Note 12); Asher's ten-hour estimate may be "average", but it is not carved in stone. A safe procedure is simply not to force production and let the student decide when to start talking.

Closely related to speaking readiness for production is the question of error and error correction. Second language acquisition research tells us clearly that errors are inevitable, and that they will be plentiful in early stages. To give the reader an estimate, in an experiment we conducted at Queens College, we found approximately one error for every five words in compositions written by ESL students in a placement examination for our extension course (Krashen *et al.*, 1978). The better students averaged about one error for every ten words, and the least proficient about one error for every two words! A sure method of raising the filter is attempting to correct errors, especially in beginning stages and especially in spoken language! Error correction is, unfortunately, the profession's typical reaction to error, and in my view it has been a serious mistake. There are several reasons why it is a mistake. We focus here on what is probably the most serious flaw in error correction, its effect on the affective filter.

Error correction has the immediate effect of putting the student on the defensive. It encourages a strategy in which the student will try to avoid mistakes, avoid difficult constructions, focus less on meaning and more on form. It may disrupt the entire communicative focus on an exchange. This was brought home to me in a demonstration I often employ to illustrate how the Input Hypothesis applies to classroom teaching. In the demonstration, which I have borrowed from Steven Sternfeld, I tell the audience that I am going to give them two lessons in a foreign language (I usually use German). For the first lesson, I simply start talking, saying things like "I am now going to give you a German lesson, but first of all let me tell you something about the German language, etc. etc." This is done entirely in German, and is nearly completely incomprehensible to those in the audience who have never been exposed to German. The second lesson is something like this:

> This is my shoe. (*Point to shoe*)
> This is my hand. (*Point to hand*)
> This is my head. (*Point to head*)
> This is a head. (*Draw picture on board*)
> Here are two eyes. (*Draw eyes, hold up two fingers*)
> Here is a mouth. (*Draw in a mouth*)
> Here is a cigarette. (*Draw in a cigarette*)
> Do you have a cigarette for me? (*Walk up to class member, make cigarette smoking motion, point to self.*)

The point of lesson number two is that while it may not be very interesting, it is quite comprehensible, thanks to the simple language, the extra-linguistic support, etc. There is also an attempt to bring down the filter by drawing a funny head and asking for a cigarette. In the discussion following this brief lesson, I explain these things and make the claim that if such input is provided over a period of time, speech will emerge on its own. What is of interest to us here is the reaction of the audience: it is one of relief. Several people have come up to me after the lecture, and said something like: "When you said you were going to give us a language lesson, I got very nervous. I was afraid you would call on me and I would have to say something, and I would make a mistake." What this tells me is that language lessons inspire fear even among professional language teachers, and one of the reasons for this is our insistence on early speaking and our attitudes towards errors. Why make students suffer from procedures that are unpleasant even to us?

There is more to say on the topic of error correction; it has some advantages, and other disadvantages, and we will look at these later on when we discuss conscious learning in the classroom. What needs to be said here is only that error correction is not the basic mechanism for improving second language performance; rather, we acquire via comprehensible input, according to the theory. Since overuse of correction has such negative effects for acquisition, and since error correction is not of direct benefit to language acquisition (see Chapter II, discussion of hypothesis one), a safe procedure is simply to eliminate error correction entirely in communicative-type activities, a procedure used with great success in Terrell's Natural Approach. Improvement will come without error correction, and may even come more rapidly, since the input will "get in", the filter will be lower, and students will be off the defensive.

2. PROVIDE TOOLS TO HELP STUDENTS OBTAIN MORE INPUT

Our responsibility goes beyond the language classroom.[15] Indeed, as I have stated earlier, our task is to provide the students with the tools they need to continue improving without us. We need to provide enough input so that they can gain the linguistic competence necessary to begin to take advantage of the informal environment, the outside world. In other words, they need to know enough of the second language so they can understand significant portions of non-classroom language. Building their linguistic competence to this point, however, is not enough.

Even if we do succeed in bringing our students to this stage, they will have problems in using the language on the outside. They will still not understand a great deal of the input they hear, even if it is modified. They will find themselves at a loss for words, and will make mistakes at all levels. If we focus only on providing the input for purely "linguistic" competence, we will have students who avoid contact with native speakers for fear they will not understand much of what is said to them, and who will have real problems when they are engaged in conversation, including painful silences while they search for words, confusion and embarrassment due to misunderstanding, etc.

This is, I think, the typical situation in the foreign language teaching scene in the United States. After two years of instruction, the student who is even willing to participate in a conversation with a speaker of the language he or she has studied is rare! The solution to this problem is to give our students the tools they need to overcome these difficulties, to make them *conversationally competent*. By giving them the means of managing conversations, we can help them to continue improving by allowing them to participate in conversation despite their inadequacies. We can prepare them for the certainty that they will not be able to find the right word, that they will not understand everything, and we can help insure that they will *continue to obtain comprehensible input*.

What are the tools students need to manage conversation and thus continue to gain input outside the classroom? In other words, how can we help our students to converse despite less than perfect competence?

Scarcella (forthcoming) has stated that there are at least two ways conversational competence can help the acquirer gain more comprehensible input: devices that help control the *quantity* of input, and devices that help control the *quality*. The former will help the acquirer get more input, the latter will help to make that input comprehensible.

Components of conversational competence included under the quantity category include ways of starting conversations (greetings) and ways of keeping conversations going (e.g. politeness formulae). Scarcella's subject Miguel, a 21 year old speaker of English as a second language, despite only modest "linguistic" competence, was quite adept at these tools of conversational competence, as the following brief excerpt shows:

Miguel: Hi! How are ya?
NS: Okay.
Miguel: What's new?
NS: Not much. Had a test today.
Miguel: Oh that's too bad. What test?

Miguel, by using a few well-chosen routines, is able to initiate and maintain conversations. Second language performers such as Miguel are not the rule, however, as research has shown that second language acquirers often have surprising and serious gaps when it comes to conversational competence (see over).

There are various techniques that are used to make input more comprehensible, to control the quality of the input. Perhaps the most obvious is simply asking the native speaker for help, "getting the native speaker to explain parts of the conversation . . . by using discourse devices" (Scarcella, p. 5). These devices range from focussing on a single problem word by repeating it, as in

> NS: Salvador Dali also put out a cookbook because he is a
>   great expert on cuisine.
> Miguel   *(looking confused)*: Cookbook?
> NS   *(picking up a cookbook)*: Recipes from Maxime's, places
>   like that.
>
> (Scarcella, p. 5)

to utterances such as "What?", or "I don't understand."

Scarcella also notes that the quality of input can be improved by the use of "back channel cues", cues that provide the native speaker with evidence that the conversational partner is indeed following the conversation. These include verbal cues such as "Uhuh", "Yeah", and non-verbal cues such as head nodding at appropriate time and eye gaze behavior.

Finally, there are conversational strategies that avoid incomprehensible input, including ways of changing the subject to something easier to understand or more familiar to the acquirer. Scarcella's subject Miguel is quite good at this, as the following demonstrates:

> NS: . . . I like classical music too—Beethoven, Schubert—
>   you know that kinda stuff.
> Miguel: You play the piano?
> Joe: Yeah.
> Miguel: Me too.

F. "Teaching" Conversational Competence

Knowledge of the components of conversational competence is one thing. Developing conversational competence in students is another. The question that needs to be asked here is whether conversational competence is learned or acquired.

There are good arguments, I think, against the hypothesis that all of conversational competence is learnable (see also discussion in Scarcella, forthcoming). First, it is simply too complex. As Scarcella points out:

> "Most discourse rules and strategies are very complex, characterized by vocabulary, pronunciation, and prosodic features, features of non-verbal communication, and, perhaps to a lesser degree, syntactic features. Moreover, all of these features may vary according to the social context. For instance, some greetings are appropriate in some situations, but not in others. They are sometimes shouted, and sometimes spoken quite stiffly. In any given situation, an appropriate greeting depends on a variety of factors. These include: the person being greeted, the time of day, the location and the interaction, other people present, and the sort of interaction which is expected (pleasant, scornful, etc.)" (p. 10).

Second, even if the student manages to learn some rules of conversational competence, they will not always be available when they are needed: in Monitor-free situations.

Most likely, the non-universal aspects of conversational competence have to be acquired. An initial hypothesis is that they are acquired the same way grammar is, via comprehensible input, and that the requirements presented in this chapter need to be satisfied for the acquisition of conversational competence as well, a very difficult task given the time and discourse constraints of the classroom.

It is possible, however, that a small sub-set of conversational management tools can be directly taught, either as rules or as memorized routines, as long as they are easy to learn (see section on learning, to follow). These include routines for starting a conversation, some pause filters, and expressions that ask for help (Scarcella, p. 11). Also, a host of in-class and out-of-class activities have been introduced in recent years to encourage conversational competence.

My main point in this section is that conversational competence gives students the tools they need to manage conversation, and is thus an essential part of instruction, since it helps to insure that language acquisition will take place outside of class, and after the instructional program ends. Our responsibility does not end with the completion of the semester: indeed, in my view, the purpose of language instruction is to provide students with what they need so that they can progress without us.

Notes

[1] As detailed in Chapter II, speech production can come from any of three different sources. First, we can use our acquired competence, as illustrated in the Monitor model for production in Chapter II. According to the input hypothesis, this sort of production takes some time to develop. Another way is via memorized patterns and routines (see Krashen and Scarcella, 1978). A third way is by extensive use of first language structures, as explained in Chapter II. The latter two methods of speech production are ways of "performing without competence" (borrowing R. Clark's terminology). A second language performer can "learn to speak" very quickly using these methods, and they are explicitly encouraged by some techniques. They are severely limited modes, however. (See discussion in Chapter II, Krashen and Scarcella, 1978, and Krashen, 1981.)

[2] This raises the interesting question of whether participation in conversation is even *practically* necessary for truly successful second language acquisition. It probably is. In addition to being an effective means of obtaining comprehensible input, conversation offers some other real advantages that will become clearer as we proceed in this chapter. Scarcella (forthcoming) points out that there are many aspects of "communicative competence" that are probably not acquirable by observation and input alone (see discussion later in this chapter). Also, Scarcella points out that real conversation entails "a high degree of personal involvement", what Stevick (1976) terms "depth" and a lowered affective filter.

[3] In a review of the science fiction literature, Hatch (1976) points out several examples in which authors assume that it is possible to acquire human languages by listening to radio broadcasts. Even these authors seem to understand, however, that acquiring language by listening to incomprehensible input is an ability possessed only by certain aliens with different, and apparently superior "language acquisition devices".

[4] There are anecdotal cases of people who have picked up second languages via television. Larsen-Freeman (1979), for example, cited a case of a German speaker who acquired Dutch via TV. This is not at all strange, as much input in Dutch would be comprehensible to a speaker of such a closely related language. Note that I am not claiming that it is *impossible* to acquire language from TV. I am only saying that comprehensible input is necessary for acquisition and that television provides little comprehensible input for a beginner. Intermediate level students may profit quite a bit from television and even radio.

[5] Another way teachers help students understand messages containing structures that are "beyond" them is by emphasizing vocabulary. Both Evelyn Hatch and I have stated the argument for increased vocabulary work in recent years (Hatch, 1978a; Krashen, 1981), and our argumentation is, I think, similar. While knowledge of vocabulary may not be sufficient for understanding all messages, there is little doubt that an increased vocabulary helps the acquirer understand more of what is heard or read (see e.g. Ulijn and Kempen, 1976; Macha, 1979, on the role of vocabulary in reading comprehension). Thus, more vocabulary should mean more comprehension of input, and more acquisition of grammar. This "new view" is quite different from earlier positions. Language teachers had been told to restrict introduction of new vocabulary in order to focus on syntax. Now we are saying that vocabulary learning will actually contribute to the acquisition of syntax.

The practical implications of this position are not clear to me, however. Should we teach vocabulary in isolation in an effort to boost the amount of input that is comprehensible? Unfortunately, there is little research that speaks directly to the question of how vocabulary is best acquired, and, most important, retained. There is some agreement among teachers that vocabulary should be taught in context, rather than by rote memorization of lists (see Celce-Murcia and Rosenzweig, 1979, for several techniques), but it may even be the case that vocabulary should not be directly taught at all! It may be the case that if we supply enough comprehensible input, vocabulary acquisition will in fact take care of itself.

Let me restate this suggestion in the form of an informal experiment: Given ten minutes of study time (waiting for a bus, etc.), which activity would be more useful for the language acquirer interested in long-term retention of vocabulary?

(1) Rote learning of a list, using flash cards or some equivalent technique.
(2) Reviewing a story that has "new words" carefully included (Contextualization).
(3) Reading for pleasure, trying only to understand the message and looking up new words only when they seem to be essential to the meaning or when the acquirer is curious as to their meaning.

Method (3) relies on comprehensible input to supply new vocabulary in enough frequency, and to help the acquirer determine the meaning. In method (3) there is no conscious focus on vocabulary, only on meaning. The prediction (hope?) is that really important words will reoccur naturally and their meanings will be made increasingly obvious by the context. It does not exclude the possibility that the acquirer may be helped by occasional glances at the dictionary or occasional definitions by a teacher.

[6] The American Language Institute at USC, for example, offers a course in typing along with its offerings in English as a Second Language for foreign students.

[7] There may be further opportunities for providing optimal input for second language acquirers at the university level, which we will discuss in Chapter V.

[8] For some Monitor users and linguists, explicit grammatical information is, oddly enough, interesting and relevant, since such acquirers *believe* it will help their performance. In this case, the medium is the message. If a course on the structure of the target language is taught in the target language, and if the students are "analytic" types, the course will be a success! (See comments in Krashen, 1980, and in Chapter V.)

[9] There are exceptions, examples of comprehensible input in which $i + 1$ may not be present. These include situations in which the discourse is limited, as in many classrooms, where the possibilities for discourse variation are limited, and in many instrumental uses of language in which familiarity with a few routines and patterns may suffice for successful communication (e.g. dealing with gas station attendants, clerks, etc.).

[10] "Internalization", in my interpretation, seems to mean the acquisition of a rule that was first learned, where learning is assumed to have *caused* the subsequent acquisition. According to the theory of second language acquisition presented in Chapter II, this does not occur. I have discussed this in several technical papers (Krashen, 1977) and will review this point in a later section.

[11] Another analogy that comes to mind is "shotgun" versus single bullet. The former has a better chance of hitting the target.

[12] Varvel (1979) describes a silent period in formal instruction (Silent Way methodology) that lasted considerably longer, indicating that there may be a fair amount of individual variation in the duration of the silent period for adults in language classes:

"There was a woman from Taiwan who after several weeks was still conspicuously silent in class. She never talked, and when called upon would only answer in a whisper, saying only what was required. It was clear, however, that she was one of the most attentive students in the class, had a clear understanding of what was being done, and seemingly enjoyed the class. She also had a positive attitude towards what and how she was learning. At no time was she coerced into active participation.

"Then one day in the ninth week of school she sat in the front row and actively participated throughout the whole hour. From that point on, she continued to participate actively in a more limited way and at times helped others and was helped by others . . ." (p. 491)

While there may have been other reasons for this student's silence, this example suggests that the silent period should be respected, and that some students develop speaking readiness later than others.

[13] Given the same amount of comprehensible input, the child's silent period in second language acquisition may turn out to be longer than the average adult silent period for other reasons. What I am suggesting here is that the silent period in child second language acquisition would not be as long if more of the input the child hears is comprehensible.

[14] Note that if we assume that an acquirer in the natural environment receives about two hours per day of comprehensible input, 720 hours translates into about one year "abroad". This assumes that classtime = comprehensible input, which may not be true with the traditional methods the FSI chart is based on. It is, however, in accord with the informally accepted idea that a year abroad will result in a fair degree of fluency in the case of European languages.

[15] The material contained in this section is simply my summary of what I have learned from discussions with Steven Sternfeld, Robin Scarcella, and Batyia Elbaum. I thank them not only for the information and intellectual stimulation, but also for their patience.

Chapter IV

The Role of Grammar, or Putting Grammar in its Place

As should be apparent by now, the position taken in this book is that second language teaching should focus on encouraging acquisition, on providing input that stimulates the subconscious language acquisition potential all normal human beings have. This does not mean to say, however, that there is no room at all for conscious learning. Conscious learning does have a role, but it is no longer the lead actor in the play. The purpose of this section is to discuss what that role is, how we can put conscious learning, or "grammar" in its proper place in the second language program.

A. Learning Does Not Become Acquisition

Chapter II attempted to make clear what learning does and what it does not do in the theoretical model of second language performance. According to the Monitor model for performance, conscious learning acts as an editor, as a Monitor, "correcting" the errors, or rather what the performer perceives to be errors, in the output of the acquired system. This can happen before the sentence is spoken or written, or after. Conscious knowledge of rules is therefore not responsible for our fluency, it does not initiate utterances.

A very important point that also needs to be stated is that learning does not "turn into" acquisition. The idea that we first learn a new rule, and eventually, through practice, acquire it, is widespread and may seem to some people to be intuitively obvious. This model of the acquisition process was first presented to me when I was a student of TESL, and seemed to be very sensible at the time. It was, I thought, exactly the way I learned languages myself. I accepted as penetrating insight Carroll's characterization of how language learning proceeds from the point of view of the then new "cognitive-code" school of thought:

> "Once the student has a proper degree of cognitive control over the structures of a language, facility will develop automatically with the use of the language in meaningful situations" (Carroll, 1966, p. 102).

As mentioned in Note 10 of the previous section, this process of converting learned rules into acquired rules was called "internalization".

Despite our feelings that internalization does occur, the theory predicts that it does not, except in a trivial way. Language acquisition, according to the theory presented in Chapter II, happens in one way, when the acquirer understands input containing a structure that the acquirer is "due" to acquire, a structure at his or her "$i + 1$".

There is no necessity for previous conscious knowledge of a rule. (The trivial sense in which a conscious rule might "help" language acquisition is if the performer used a rule as a Monitor, and consistently applied it to his own output. Since we understand our own output, part of that performer's comprehensible input would include utterances with that structure. When the day came when that performer was "ready" to acquire this already learned rule, his own performance of it would qualify as comprehensible input at "$i + 1$". In other words, self-stimulation!)

In addition to the fact that the theory does not directly predict that learning needs to precede acquisition, there are very good reasons for maintaining this position that emerge from observing second language performers.

First, we often see acquisition in cases where learning never occurred. There are many performers who can use complex structures in a second language who do not know the rule consciously and never did. There have been several case histories in the second language acquisition literature that illustrate this phenomenon, one which I think is quite common.

Evelyn Hatch's students, Cindy Stafford and Ginger Covitt, interviewed one such second language performer, "V", an ESL student at UCLA, who exhibited considerable competence in English, but who admitted that he had conscious control of very few, if any, rules. The following exchanges come from an interview with "V", which takes place while one of the authors is reviewing his composition errors (from Stafford and Covitt, 1978; also quoted in Krashen, 1978):

> *Interviewer*: (When you write a composition) . . . do you think of grammar rules? Do you think "Should I have used the present tense here or would the present continuous be better or . . ."
>
> *V*: "I don't refer to the books and all that, you know. I just refer it to this, uh, my judgment and . . . sensing if I'm writing it right or wrong. Because I really don't know . . . what where exactly how . . . the grammatical rules work out.

Later in the interview, one investigator asks:

> Do you think grammar rules are useful?
> *V*: Useful? Yeah. When you want to write they are very very useful.
> *Int*: But you don't use them when you write.
> *V*: Yeah, I know. I don't use them . . . I don't know how to use them.

Another good example of an "under-user" of the conscious grammar is Hung, studied by Cohen and Robbins (1976), who stated:

> "I never taught any grammar. I guess I just never learned the rules that well. I know that every time I speak it's pretty correct, so I never think about grammars. I just write down whatever I feel like it. Everytime I write something I just stop thinking. I don't know which (rule) to apply" (p. 59).

Not only is what Hung says revealing, but so is *how* he says it. There are, for sure, errors in this passage, but there is also control of fairly complex syntax and a real ability for self-expression. (Not all under-users succeed, of course; see, for example, Schumann's description of Alberto in Schumann (1978a).) If conscious rules have to come first, how can we explain cases such as V, Hung, and others? (For other case histories, see Krashen, 1978; Stafford and Covitt, 1978; Kounin and Krashen, 1978.) Unless all cases such as these can be shown to be instances of the use of the first language or routines and patterns the existence of such cases shows that previous conscious learning is not necessary for language acquisition.

Second, we also see learning that never seems to become acquisition. Many fine ESL performers, while they have acquired a great deal of English, also know many conscious rules. They nevertheless make what they consider to be "careless" errors on rules that are linguistically quite straightforward. This occurs when the performer has learned a rule, but has not acquired it. This happens typically with late-acquired items, such as the third person singular ending on regular verbs in English ("He go*es* to work every day."). What is particularly interesting is that these performers may have known the rule and have practiced it for many years. Even after thousands of correct repetitions, and with a thorough understanding of the rule, such performers still make "careless" mistakes on certain items. What has prevented learning from "becoming" acquisition in these cases is the fact that the learned rule is still beyond the acquirer's $i + 1$.

A case history that illustrates this situation very well is that of "P" (Krashen and Pon, 1975). P was an excellent Monitor user (an optimal user, as described in Chapter II), an adult with a BA in Linguistics with honors, whose written English appeared nearly native-like. In casual conversation, however, P made occasional "careless" errors on "easy" rules that she had known consciously for twenty years. Thus, even well-learned, well-practiced rules may not turn into acquisition.

An explanation of P's problem is that the items she missed in casual conversation were those that are late-acquired, and her acquisition, while very advanced, had simply not gone the final few steps in syntax and morphology. She had learned the rules well, however, and was able to supply them under conditions where she could Monitor.

A third reason for doubting that acquisition requires previous learning is the fact that even the best learners master only a small subset of the rules of a language. As discussed earlier (Hypothesis 3, Chapter II), even professional linguists admit that their conscious knowledge of even the best studied languages is imperfect, and discoveries of new rules are reported with every issue of technical journals in linguistic theory. Linguists often succeed in describing, after years of analysis, what many second language performers have already acquired.

My explanation for these phenomena is that while learning may often precede acquisition, it need not, and in fact may not even help directly. Rather, we acquire along a fairly predictable natural order, and this occurs when we receive comprehensible input. Occasionally, we learn certain rules before we acquire them, and this gives us the illusion that the learning actually caused the acquisition.

Professional language teachers, with their fascination for the structure of language, and with the pleasure they derive from the mastery and use of conscious rules, are often not even aware that acquisition without prior conscious learning is possible. This was my unexamined assumption as well. The procedure described earlier seemed right and reasonable to me at one time: language learning, in the general sense, occurred when one first consciously grasped a rule, then practiced it again and again until it was "automatic". (This is actually deductive learning; there is another possibility, namely, "inductive" learning; see discussion below.) The great contribution of linguistics was to discover and describe rules, which "applied linguists" could transmit to language teachers, who, in turn, could tell students about them.

One experience that helped to change my thinking occurred when I was teaching English as a second language to an "advanced" adult education class at Queens College. As a member of a team, my responsibility was "structure". Since I was, at the time, the director of the English Language Institute at Queens, I felt obliged to present an impressive series of lessons that demonstrated my control of the subject. I therefore chose to concentrate on the verb system, and presented a complete survey of all tenses.

The first lesson of the session was focussed on the present progressive tense. My objective was to inform my students that the present progressive had three meanings: (1) a current, on-going action that would soon be completed, (2), an action that began some time ago in the past and may or may not be taking place at the moment, and would end sometime in the future, and (3) future tense. I illustrated this using the familiar time flow diagram

and by showing that sentences such as

John is playing the violin.

were three ways ambiguous:

(1) What is that noise from the other room? (John is playing the violin.)
(2) What's John doing this summer? (He is playing the violin for the local symphony.)
(3) What's John doing tomorrow? (He's playing the violin in the talent show.)

None of my advanced ESL students knew this rule consciously. In fact, very few people do. I have presented this example several times at lectures to practicing ESL teachers, and I often ask those who consciously "know" the rule that the progressive is three ways ambiguous to raise their hands. Very few do, and those that do claim they know it have usually just finished teaching it in class. ⟶

What was very interesting was that a significant number of students had a "Eureka" experience. After I explained the rule, they would remark: "That's right . . . it *is* three ways ambiguous . . . how about that!", or would make similar comments. My interpretation is that these students had already subconsciously acquired the progressive tense and its three meanings, and were confirming that their acquisition was correct. I had, in other words, succeeded in providing learning where acquisition was already present.

I would like to point out several things about this phenomenon. First, my students had apparently acquired the rule without having first learned it. (It could be argued that they knew it once but had forgotten it, and that this temporary learning had been essential, or at least useful, in acquiring the rule. This is possible, but unlikely, as all three functions are not usually taught. Another unlikely possibility is transfer from the first language. Most of the first languages of my students that semester did not have the progressive tense.) Second, those who learned what they had already acquired thought they were gaining a great deal from the class. This sort of knowledge is very satisfying to many people (including me). It is not, however, language teaching, even though it is of some value. (We return to this topic, which I refer to as "language appreciation", later in this chapter.)

Learning sometimes precedes acquisition in real time: A rule that is eventually acquired may have been, at one time, learned only. As I have maintained elsewhere (Krashen, 1977), this certainly does occur, but by no means establishes the necessity of prior learning for acquisition. Just because event A preceded event B does not demonstrate that A caused B. We see many cases of acquisition without learning, learning (even very good learning that is well practiced) that does not become acquisition, and acquired knowledge of rules preceding learning.

B. The Place of Grammar

"Grammar", a term I will use as a synonym for conscious learning, has two possible roles in the second language teaching program. First, it can be used with some profit as a Monitor. We will discuss this use in more detail in the section that follows. A second use for grammar is as subject-matter, or for "language appreciation" (sometimes called "linguistics"), and we will discuss this role later on. Neither role is essential, neither is the central part of the pedagogical program, but both have their functions.

Several isues will be discussed in relation to teaching grammar for Monitor use: *when* rules can be used, *which* rules should or can be learned, what the *effects* of Monitor use are, and what we can expect in terms of Monitor efficiency.

1. GRAMMAR FOR MONITOR USE: *WHEN* THE MONITOR IS USED

As stated in Chapter II (Hypothesis 3), one of our goals in pedagogy is to encourage optimal Monitor use. We would like our students to utilize conscious rules to raise their grammatical accuracy when it does not interfere with communication. Stated differently, the optimal Monitor user knows *when* to use conscious rules.

As mentioned earlier, one necessary condition for successful Monitor use is *time*. It takes real processing time to remember and apply conscious rules. We should not expect most students to successfully apply conscious rules to their output during oral conversation— there is, obviously, little time. People who do attempt to think about and utilize conscious rules during conversation run two risks. First, they tend to take too much time when it is their turn to speak, and have a hesitant style that is often difficult to listen to. Other overusers of the

Monitor, in trying to avoid this, plan their next utterance while their conversational partner is talking. Their output may be accurate, but they all too often do not pay enough attention to what the other person is saying!

Some people are better than others at Monitor use, and may actually be able to successfully use a fair number of conscious rules "on line". Most people run the risk of seriously endangering the success of the conversation when they try to Monitor during casual talking. (Success in Monitor use in free conversation also depends on other factors—one is the difficulty or complexity of the rule, which we discuss below. A second is the topic: I find it much easier to pay attention to the form of what I say in a second language when I am talking about something I am very familiar with and have discussed before, e.g. second language acquisition.)

The place for Monitor use is when the performer has time, as in writing and in prepared speech. As stated earlier, simply giving performers time does not insure that they will use the conscious Monitor; hence, condition 2 in Chapter II: The performer must be thinking about correctness or focussed on form. When given time, and when focussed on form, some people can use conscious grammar to great advantage. In the case of the second language performer who has acquired nearly all of the grammar of the second language, but who still has some gaps, the use of the conscious grammar can fill in many of the non-acquired items. This can, in writing at least, occasionally result in native-like accuracy.

I have often referred to "P", discussed above, as a performer who was able to do this. Despite her accent, and occasional morphological errors in free speech, P's writing (done in class) was nearly flawless. I have known many professionals who also use conscious grammar this way, colleagues in linguistics who speak with slight imperfections but whose writing is nearly error-free. Some very interesting cases involve specialists in grammar, in formal linguistics, scholars who certainly consciously know many of the rules they violate in free conversation. Two cases I personally know have, in fact, published papers on the theory of grammar that rely heavily on English, testifying to their deep and thorough grasp of English syntax. Yet, in unmonitored free speech, third person singulars drop off, the possessive marker is occasionally missing, etc. Both scholars publish all of their current work in English and do not consult anyone to review their papers for errors, nor is this necessary.

My own experience may be helpful to readers. I am, at the time of this writing, an "intermediate" level speaker of French as a second language. (This means, according to my definition, that I can converse comfortably with a monolingual speaker of French as long as (s)he makes some compensation. I cannot eavesdrop very well and have some trouble with radio and films. Also, my output is fairly fluent, but not error-free.) Many people at this level, including myself, make errors on rules that are easy to describe, but that are apparently fairly late-acquired. One rule like this I have noted is the simple contraction rule:

$$de + le = du.$$

I, and my classmates in intermediate conversational French at USC, occasionally miss this one in free conversation. On the occasions when I write French, however, I get it right every time. (My accuracy or difficulty order changes when I use my conscious knowledge of French grammar. Correctly applying the $de + le = du$ rule raises this item from a low position in the difficulty order to one near the top. This is exactly what I attempted to say in Chapter II, Hypothesis 3, in discussing distortions of the natural order in Monitored conditions. I differ from the average subject in that I do not require a discrete-point grammar test to focus me on form. Most readers of this book are probably like this as well.)

This kind of behavior is natural and normal. What is tragic, in my opinion, is that teachers expect perfect performance of such simple, yet late-acquired items in unmonitored performance. Even quite competent second language users, such as P, will "miss" such items in conversation. We often see, however, beginners, students who can barely converse in the target language, struggling to make correct subject–verb agreement in what are termed "communicative" exercises, fearful of the teacher's shattering corrections. The cause of this torture is, first of all, a confusion between linguistic simplicity and order of acquisition—it is not at all the case that the more linguistically simple an item is, the earlier it is acquired. Some very "simple" rules may be among the last to be acquired. Second, the cause is also a failure to distinguish between acquisition and learning, a failure to realize that conscious knowledge of an item bears no relationship to a performer's ability to use it in unmonitored speech. This ability comes from acquisition, and acquisition comes from comprehensible input, not from error correction. The result of such treatment is, at best, overuse of the Monitor. At worst, it results in the establishment of such a strong Affective Filter that acquisition is impossible.

2. WHAT CAN BE MONITORED

Condition three for Monitor use (Chapter II, Hypothesis 3) is relevant to discussing this point. In order for performers to Monitor successfully, they must know the rule they are applying. To expand on a point made in Chapter II, let me attempt to illustrate just how drastically this requirement limits Monitor use. Let this circle represent all the rules of a well-described language, such as English:

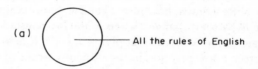

Let us now consider all the rules of English that the best linguists "know", or have succeeded in describing. How many rules did Jespersen (ever) know, how much of English have scholars such as Noam Chomsky described? While Chomsky often says that he and his colleagues have only described "fragments" of English, we will give the formal linguists the benefit of the doubt, and represent their accomplishments as a proper subset of the first circle:

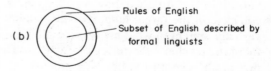

Now let us consider the rules that "applied linguists" know, where applied linguists here refers to the scholar whose task it is to study the work of the formal, theoretical linguist, and present it to the language teacher, and perhaps also to the language student. Let the additional smaller circle in the next figure represent what the applied linguist knows. This will have to be a proper subset of what the formal linguist knows, since the full-time job of the theoretician is to seek out new rules, while the applied linguist spends a great deal of time explaining this work:

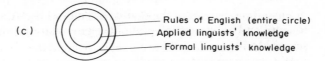

(c)
Rules of English (entire circle)
Applied linguists' knowledge
Formal linguists' knowledge

The next circle represents all the rules that the most knowledgeable language teachers know. This will be a proper subset of the circle introduced in the last figure. Teachers, after all, have a great deal to do besides study the work of applied linguistics:

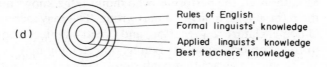

(d)
Rules of English
Formal linguists' knowledge
Applied linguists' knowledge
Best teachers' knowledge

Still another circle represents the number of grammar rules that the best teachers actually teach. This is, in turn, a proper subset of the set of circles they know, since teachers will undoubtedly present to their students only a part of their knowledge:

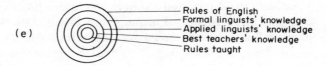

(e)
Rules of English
Formal linguists' knowledge
Applied linguists' knowledge
Best teachers' knowledge
Rules taught

We draw next still another circle, which represents all the rules that the best students actually succeed in learning. We should even put in one last circle, all the rules that students can carry around in their heads as mental baggage and actually use in performance:

(f)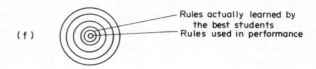

Rules actually learned by
the best students
Rules used in performance

By now, we are down to a very small circle, even giving every group discussed the benefit of the doubt. Even our best students will be able to learn and utilize a small part of the grammar of a language as a conscious Monitor.

We can draw an even smaller circle for some people. As we saw in the discussion of individual variation in Chapter II, some performers are either less willing or less able to utilize conscious rules. At the opposite extreme from the professional linguist or language teacher (see, for example, Yorio, 1978), we have the Monitor under-user, the performer who does all self-correction by "feel" and has no control of conscious grammar. Perhaps even more extreme is the incompetent Monitor user, the performer who thinks (s)he knows the rules but has them (or at least many of them) wrong. This may merely be a problem of nomenclature (e.g. Stafford and Covitt's subject who kept referring to "dead objects" instead of direct objects), but may be more serious. We should be aware that confusions may exist even for rules that appear to us to be very simple, and for rules that the performer may have already acquired and can utilize in an unmonitored situation. Such cases illustrate vividly the contrast between acquisition and learning.

(a) Incompetent Monitor use

Seliger (1979) reported a simple, yet interesting experiment which confirms the existence of incompetent Monitor users. The task was naming: Subjects were shown pictures and asked to say what the object pictured was in English (e.g. It's a pen). Seliger noted whether the subjects applied the "a/an" rule and whether they correctly used *an* when the following noun began with a vowel. The subjects were then asked, after completing the task, if they had noticed that sometimes *a* was called for and sometimes *an* was called for. If they said that they did notice, they were asked to give their reasons for the distinction. (In all cases, either *a* or *an* was required. There were no cases where the zero allomorph was appropriate.) Seliger's subjects included 29 monolingual English speaking children, ages 3 to 10.8, 11 "bilingual" children, ages 4 to 10, and 15 adult ESL students at Queens College in New York.

In my interpretation, this study contrasts acquisition and learning.[1]* The subjects' focus in the picture naming task was on supplying vocabulary. They were not told in advance that grammatical accuracy was an issue and certainly the a/an rule was not presented or discussed in advance. The task, then, encouraged use of the acquired system; it was relatively "unmonitored". This interpretation is consistent with the evidence reviewed in Chapter II, which concludes that for most subjects, one needs to deliberately focus subjects on form using a device such as a discrete-point grammar test in order to bring out extensive use of the conscious grammar. Of course, since the task was an "experiment", it is quite possible that some subjects may have been more careful than they normally would be. The results of the direct question about *a* and *an*, however, show that it is unlikely that subjects were accessing much conscious knowledge while identifying pictures.

Seliger reports "no relationship" between performance on picture identification and whether the subjects could state a rule! Many subjects did not "do what they say they do". If their responses to the post-task question represent conscious learning, this result confirms just how limited learning is for some people. Let us examine the results.

As we would expect from the discussion of age in Chapter II, none of the bilingual children produced correct conscious rules for a/an. This is consistent with the claim that pre-formal operations children have less extensive meta-awareness of grammar. The potential for extensive Monitor use is hypothesized to emerge with formal operations, at around puberty.

Among the adults, three of the four who "knew" the rule (could verbalize it after the test) "produced no instances on the picture test to show they understood how the rule was to be used" (p. 364). These subjects, in other words, had *learned* the a/an distinction but had not

* Superscript numbers refer to Notes at end of Chapters.

acquired it. They were unable, moreover, to apply this conscious knowledge to the picture identification task, since the necessary conditions for successful Monitor use were not met (condition three = know the rule, was met, but one = time, and two = focus on form, were not). This case is exactly analogous to the *de + le = du* case described above. These three students, I would predict, would perform well on this item under different conditions, i.e. if given a discrete-point grammar test that focussed them on form, containing items such as:

$$\text{That's} \begin{Bmatrix} a \\ an \end{Bmatrix} \text{pen}$$

Finally, and what is of most interest here, two children and one adult performed well on the picture identification test but produced incorrect rules (e.g. "You use *an* for something that's alive"). The child subjects are reminiscent of other cases in the literature and may simply reflect the inability of children to induce or learn correct conscious rules (e.g. a child in one study, acquiring French as a second language, decided that feminine gender was for "everything that was good and beautiful" (Kenyeres and Kenyeres, cited in Hatch, 1978b). The adult who performed perfectly on the test may be classified as an "incompetent" Monitor user. This subject had acquired the a/an rule, but had not learned it correctly. The fact that he did not apply his conscious rule to performance worked to his benefit! I would predict that such a subject would perform worse on a test that focussed him on form. (I do not wish to imply that some learners get all rules wrong while others get them all right. Clearly, many learners have learned some rules correctly and some incorrectly.)

What is remarkable here is that this subject had failed to learn what most teachers would consider to be an amazingly simple rule, yet he had apparently acquired it. This illustrates the independence of acquisition and learning, as well as just how limited learning can be for some performers.[2]

(b) Rule learnability

We see fairly wide individual variation in the ability to use the conscious Monitor. The range goes from the professional linguist, who may be able to consciously learn many rules of great complexity and even apply them while performing in a second language, to Monitor under-users and incompetent wrong-rule users. Despite this variation, we can begin to characterize the kinds of rules that are learnable for most adults, recognizing that even for super Monitor users (see e.g. Yorio, 1978), this set will be a small subset of the total number of rules in a language.

The professional literature supports what I think is the most reasonable hypothesis: "learnability" is related to linguistic simplicity, both formal and functional. The rules we can learn and carry around in our heads for use as a Monitor are not those that are earliest acquired, nor are they those that are important for communication. Rather, they are the simple rules, rules that are easiest to describe and remember.

I have pointed out elsewhere in other publications (first discussed in Krashen *et al.*, 1978) that simplicity can be defined in at least two ways, and both definitions are relevant here. First, a rule can be formally simple. Examples of relatively simple rules include our old friends the third person singular ending on regular verbs in English, and *de + le = du*. These rules require only the addition of a bound morpheme (an inflection), or contraction operations. Simple deletion is also probably not difficult for the conscious Monitor.

Other syntactic operations appear to be more difficult for the Monitor. Permutations, and movements of constituents from one part of a sentence to another are quite difficult to do "in your head" while in the middle of a conversation or even when writing for content. It is probably the case that rules requiring a great deal of movement and order change are either acquired or are never done well by most people. This applies to rules such as formation of wh- questions in English, which might involve the following separate operations: (1) placing the *wh-* word first; (2) performing subject–auxiliary inversion, unless there is a helping verb; (3) performing "do-support"; (4) inflecting "do" correctly for tense and number. This is a lot to remember, especially when the learner has other things on his mind, including remembering other parts of grammar (he might also be Monitoring pronunciation as well as syntax) and trying to keep up a conversation with a native speaker.

(The reader may argue that (s)he has no problem doing all these things at the same time, and with a little practice and good teaching everyone else can as well. If this is what is going through your mind, you are probably a Monitor super-user. This sort of interest and ability may be what brought you into language science in the first place; and got you interested in books such as this one. You are not typical. Other readers may argue that the way to make rules such as question formation automatic is to learn and drill the components one at a time until they become automatic. This is exactly the "learning becomes acquisition" argument reviewed at the beginning of this section. I maintain that in cases where this seems to work, one of two things is happening: (1) acquisition is occurring separately and catches up to the student's learning level; the learning that preceded the acquisition did not play any direct role, moreover, in helping acquisition develop. (2) The successful learner was a super Monitor user and very atypical.)

Simplicity also needs to be defined in terms of meaning. Rules that are formally simple will not be easily learnable if their meanings are subtle and hard to explain. Both the form and meaning of the third person singular ending and $de + le = du$ are straightforward. On the other hand, while the form of the definite and indefinite article in English is very simple, many of the uses of *a* and *the* are enormously complex. We certainly cannot expect ESL learners to understand, remember, and consciously apply descriptions such as that contained in Hawkins (1978), a full volume devoted to the article in English. We can also find examples in punctuation. Rules such as "capitalize the first letter of every sentence" are formally and functionally easy. Some of the uses of the comma and semi-colon, however, are difficult to describe and probably need to be acquired for effective use.

(c) Some evidence

There are no studies I know of that directly probe which structures are learnable by different student populations and which are not. Several papers, however, present evidence that is quite consistent with the claim that only "easy" rules are learnable by most people.

One sort of evidence is provided by studies and case histories that tell us what sorts of "careless" errors second language students make, errors that involve rules that the students had formally studied and that they could self-correct, given time and when focussed on form. In our terms, these are rules that have been learned but have not been acquired. They are, in all cases, what appear to be late-acquired and formally simple rules, involving mostly bound morphology. P, the optimal Monitor user we discussed earlier, made many errors on such easy items as the third person singular ending on regular verbs, the use of "much" and "many" with count and mass nouns, and the irregular past, among other errors. Two optimal Monitor users described in Cohen and Robbins (1976) also made what they themselves called "careless" errors on such items.

Both Ue-Lin and Eva, Chinese speaking ESL students at UCLA, had problems with the late-acquired third person singular /s/. Ue-Lin explained this omission "as a careless mistake since she reported knowing the rule" (Cohen and Robbins, 1976, p. 55). Similarly, "when Eva was shown sentences containing *s* deletion, she was actually able to identify the error and supply the *s* immediately. When asked to explain why she omitted the *s* she replied: 'Probably just careless.' " (p. 58). Eva had a similar explanation for omitting the regular past /ed/: When presented with one of her errors on this form, also known to be late-acquired (Hypothesis 3, Chapter II), she was able to supply the correct form. After correcting one sentence, "Eva remarked that she wrote down the sentence the way she would say it: 'For one thing, sometimes I would write something the way that I speak. We say a word more or less in a careless way. But if I take my time, sometimes go over it, that would be much easier . . .'." (p. 58). My interpretation is that given time, Eva was able to access her conscious knowledge of English, or Monitor, a procedure that can be effective for such late-acquired, simple rules.

Eva had had a fair amount of exposure to English and was considered to be advanced by Cohen and Robbins. She had lived in Australia for two and a half years and had studied English since grade 5 (at the time of Cohen and Robbins' study she was a junior in college). She also considered herself a "good language learner". Even Eva, however, had problems with what seem to language teachers to be simple rules. In explaining her error ("I have *talk* to Sylvia already") she attributed the error to being unclear about the rule. She remarked: "Yeah, I learned that. It's just something I'm not good at. I think the main problem is that I just learn the rule—one or two years, the whole time I was going to school . . . It was never drill enough to me" (Cohen and Robbins, p. 58). This confirms a point made earlier, and shows that while Monitor use may be limited to non-acquired, simple rules, even "good" learners may be able to use and recall only a small part of the rules we present, even those that seem transparent to us.[3]

A study by Duškova (1969) also confirms that the syntactic domain of the conscious Monitor, for many people, consists of relatively simple but late-acquired items. Duškova investigated written errors in 50 Czech university level students studying English (EFL). Duškova noted that ". . . many of the recurrent errors . . . reflect no real deficit in knowledge, since most learners know the pertinent rule and can readily apply it, but the mechanical operation does not yet work automatically" (p. 16). This generalization applies in particular, Duškova notes, to morphological errors. Examples include the omission of plurals on nouns (relatively early acquired among grammatical morphemes, I must admit). Duškova notes that for plurals ". . . the learner is aware of it when it is pointed out to him and is able to correct it himself" (p. 20). Another example is errors in subject–verb agreement. Again, for this error, "when the learner's attention is drawn to the fact that he has made a mistake, he is usually able to correct it" (p. 20). Other error types of this sort include confusion of past participle and infinitive, errors on irregular verbs, and adjective–noun agreement in number (e.g. this workers). In our terms, the errors reflect a failure to apply conscious rules, a failure to Monitor effectively. The students, Duškova tells us, "can certainly formulate the rule" for these error types.

The morpheme studies described in Chapter II also contribute to this point. As you may recall from Chapter II, changes or disturbances in the "natural order" were interpreted as intrusions of the conscious grammar. It is interesting to note just how the order was affected. In Larsen-Freeman's study (Larsen-Freeman, 1975), morpheme orders were presented for both monitored and unmonitored conditions (a discrete-point pencil and paper grammar test, and the Bilingual Syntax Measure, respectively). In the Monitor-free condition, Larsen-Freeman obtained the following order (Table 4.1) which is quite "natural".

TABLE 4.1

Morpheme order obtained in monitor-free condition (Larsen-Freeman, 1975)

ing
copula
article
auxiliary
short plural
regular past
third person singular
irregular past
long plural
possessive

Compare this to the unnatural order found in the Monitored condition (Table 4.2). (We use the writing task as an example; Larsen-Freeman's "reading" task gives similar results.)

TABLE 4.2

Morpheme order obtained in monitored condition (Larsen-Freeman, 1975; writing)

copula
auxiliary
third person singular
ing
regular past
irregular past
article
long plural
short plural
possessive

These orders differ largely due to the increase in relative rank of two morphemes, regular past and the third person singular marker, both late-acquired, or low in relative order of accuracy in the Monitor-free natural order. This interpretation is consistent with the claim that when performers focus on form they can increase accuracy in unacquired but learned parts of grammar.[4]

Still more evidence comes from our composition study (Krashen, Butler, Birnbaum, and Robertson, 1978). We asked ESL students at USC to write compositions under two conditions—"free" (instructions were to write as much as possible in five minutes) and "edited" (instructions were to pay careful attention to grammar and spelling and to "take your time"). Both conditions yielded natural orders for grammatical morphemes, which we interpreted as indicating little intervention of the conscious Monitor. This was due to the fact, we hypothesized, that our subjects focussed primarily on communication in both conditions, despite our instructions to the contrary in the second condition.

Closer analysis of our data does show some rise in the third person singular in the edited condition, however (we did not analyze regular past due to too few obligatory occasions). This rise was not enough to disturb the natural order, but enough to suggest some Monitor use. Again, we see the differences in the late-acquired, easy item. (To inject a more theoretical point, perhaps the correct interpretation of morpheme natural and unnatural orders is that unnatural orders, as in Larsen-Freeman (1975) reflect *heavy* Monitor use. Increases in certain items without changes in rank, as in our composition study, may reflect *light* Monitor use.) Table 4.3 shows this small improvement in the third person singular morpheme in the edited condition.[5,6]

TABLE 4.3

Accuracy differences in free and edited conditions for grammatical morphemes

Morpheme	Free I	Edited I	Free II	Edited II
ing	0.87	0.85	0.88	0.82
copula	0.79	0.95	0.86	0.85
plural	0.82	0.82	0.77	0.78
article	0.86	0.85	0.76	0.83
auxiliary	0.82	0.79	0.77	0.76
irregular past	0.69	0.81	0.82	0.77
third person singular	0.54	0.61	0.32	0.65

Free: "write as much as you can" in five minutes.
Edited: "pay careful attention to grammar and spelling and take your time".
I: same subjects ($n = 58$) performed both conditions.
II: different subjects for each condition.
Each morpheme was represented by at least 100 obligatory occasions.

(d) Consequences of teaching "hard" rules

Felix (1980) shows us what happens when students are asked to learn rules that are too difficult for them, rules that are not only difficult to learn but that are also not yet acquired. Not only were such students asked to learn difficult rules, they were also asked to use them in unmonitored situations. Felix observed and EFL class for ten and eleven year old students in Germany. Among his many interesting observations was this one: Teachers taught and demanded correct use of elliptic sentences (as in exchanges of the type: Is it a dog? Yes, *it is*). Despite the fact that this type of question–answer dialogue "was intensively drilled every day" (p. 8), Felix reports that correct elliptic sentences were only randomly supplied for a period of almost three months (i.e. Is it a dog? Yes, it isn't)!

This result is quite predictable: the rule was simply too hard to learn and was not yet acquired. Felix notes that according to the research literature elliptic sentences "do not appear until relatively late" (p. 9). Even with input containing sentences of this sort (assuming the input was comprehensible, interesting, etc.; see Chapter III), such structures were far beyond the $i + 1$ of these students.

Felix also reports that teachers valiantly tried to teach *do*-support and the English negation rules with little success. These are also quite difficult. Students, Felix found, would produce sentences like these in class:

> (1) It's no my cow.
> (2) Doesn't she eat apples.

Both of these sentences are interpretable as reliance on what has been acquired without the contribution of the conscious grammar. To fully appreciate the significance of these errors, we first need to briefly review what is known about the acquisition of negation in informal language acquisition (see also Chapter II). The following stages are found in child L1, child L2, and adult L2 acquisition (what follows is a simplification; see Dulay, Burt, and Krashen, in press, for details):

I. The negative marker goes outside the sentence, as in:

> no wipe finger
> wear mitten no (examples from Klima and Bellugi, 1966)

II. The negative marker is placed between the subject and verb, as in:

> He no bite you
> He not little, he big

III. Post auxiliary negation is acquired; the marker now appears after the auxiliary verb, as in:

> That was not me
> I didn't caught it

Felix's example (1) appears to be a stage II type transitional form. This "error" is a typical intermediate stage all acquirers (or nearly all) go through before fully acquiring the correct form. The appearance of such an error type is thus consistent with the hypothesis that these children, even though they are in a classroom, are undergoing normal language acquisition to at least some extent, and are relying on acquired language in classroom speech (note that German negation is always post verbal and post auxiliary).

Sentence (2), according to Felix, is *not* a yes/no question! Felix maintains that it is, instead, a negative declaration ("She doesn't eat apples"). Thus, as is the case with sentence (1), Felix interprets this error as a transitional form, this one being an example of stage I with *doesn't* acting as a monomorphemic negation marker. (It is quite common for *don't* to perform the same function in stage II in natural first and second language acquisition, e.g. sentences such as "I don't can explain" where "don't" acts as the negative marker; see, for example, Cancino, Rosansky and Schumann, 1974). The child's selection of *doesn't* (instead of *no*) is due to the particular kind of input presented in the classroom, the grammatical exercises in which *doesn't* appears in very high frequencies.

Such interpretations not only point to the reality and strength of subconscious acquisition, but they also confirm that conscious learning is quite limited, and that, except for certain conditions, acquisition is responsible for most second language performance.

C. The Effects of Learning: Accuracy of Self-correction

Previous sections of this chapter have discussed when performers Monitor and which rules are usable for Monitoring. We turn now to the question of how effective Monitoring is: How much can the second language performer improve accuracy by consulting the conscious grammar?

We can get some approximation of the efficiency of the conscious grammar by looking at how good performers are at self-correction of their own linguistic output. Noel Houck has pointed out to me that *self-correction* (as opposed to "other-correction", or correcting someone else's output, an activity that includes detecting errors on tests), is the most valid object of study in investigating Monitor strength, since this is what one's Monitor actually does in real performance.

Several studies have examined how effective self-correction is, but before surveying the data and drawing conclusions, we need to briefly look at some of the factors that cause accuracy of self-correction to vary.

1. FACTORS AFFECTING SELF-CORRECTION ACCURACY

First, as we can infer from the discussion in Chapter II, there is individual variation with respect to self-correction efficiency. To the extent that self-correction involves the conscious Monitor, if there is individual variation in degree of and ability for Monitor use, this will be reflected in self-correction efficiency. We might expect much better performance from a professional linguist who is an optimal Monitor user (e.g. "P", from Krashen and Pon, 1975), than from other performers, all other conditions (see below) held constant.

Second, we might expect variation depending on which aspects of output the performer attempts to correct. As we discussed above, the Monitor appears to work best for simple morphology, may be less efficient for complex syntax, and may have even more trouble with other parts of the grammar (there is, unfortunately, not even enough data to speculate about the learnability of much of the grammar; see Chapter III for a very brief discussion of the learnability of aspects of conversational competence).

Self-correction efficiency will also vary according to the conditions under which it is done. Houck, Robertson and Krashen (1978b) distinguished the following conditions. First, there is "free speech", or natural conversation. (In one sense, "free writing" belongs in this category, in another sense it does not, as some would argue that the written modality automatically entails a greater focus on form.) In "free speech", self-correction is up to the performer, and there is no special focus on form. Rather, the focus, in most cases, is on communication. We would expect natural difficulty orders when looking at errors in grammatical structures in this condition.

A second condition, moving in the direction of more focus on form, can be termed "careful" speaking or writing. This is roughly equivalent to the edited condition in Krashen *et al.* (1978), described earlier, and occurs when speakers or writers are attempting to speak or write "correctly". (We might subdivide this condition into two sub-conditions, one for careful speaking and one for careful writing, predicting more self-correction for writing.)

Conditions (1) and (2) cover most situations in real world informal communication. We can, however, specify other conditions typically used in language instruction that focus the performer still more on form. In condition (3), the student is informed that an error exists, but does not know where the error is or what rule has been broken. This is roughly equivalent to composition correction in which students are simply told that there are some errors in their paper and that they should be corrected.

A condition still more in the direction of focussing on form indicates to students where the error is, in addition to informing them that an error exists. This condition, condition (4), corresponds to composition correction in which the teacher underlines the errors. Still more focussed, according to Houck *et al.*, is condition (5) in which existence, location, and description of the violated rule are provided, as in feedback of this sort:

I saw two *pl.* b̲o̲y̲.

The more we move toward condition (5), the more effect of the conscious Monitor is predicted, and the greater the likelihood of "unnatural" orders for errors. According to research summarized in Chapter II and discussed again in this chapter, we see natural orders for conditions (1) (free speech, BSM, free composition) and (2) (edited writing), but might see some effect of the Monitor in condition (2) (i.e. rise in accuracy in third person singular in Krashen *et al.*, 1978). Larsen-Freeman's unnatural order was produced under conditions similar to condition (4) (but see Note 4, this chapter).

Table 4.4 summarizes the five conditions.

TABLE 4.4. *Self-correction conditions in second language performance*

Instructions:	(1) None	(2) Rewrite	(3) Correct the error	(4) Correct this error	(5) Correct this error use this rule
Includes error:					
Existence	No	No	Yes	Yes	Yes
Location	No	No	No	Yes	Yes
Rule broken	No	No	No	No	Yes

(1) Free speech or writing.
(2) Careful speech or writing.
From: Houck, Robertson and Krashen (1978b).

There are some studies available that give us an idea of the efficiency of self-correction for some of the conditions described here, that tell us what percentage of performers' errors are actually self-corrected. They thus tell us something about Monitor efficiency, since they report to what extent a performer's self-corrections improve output accuracy. In one sense, however, they may not truly show the effectiveness of the Monitor. They *underestimate* Monitor use, since they do not indicate covert self-correction, the correction that went on before the utterance was spoken or written, (Recall, in figure one, Chapter II, that there are two possible arrows leading from the Monitor to the output of the acquired system, one affecting output before and one affecting output after production.) On the other hand, studies that report the percentage of successful self-correction also *overestimate* the amount of actual conscious Monitor use, since self-correction can also be done using the acquired system alone, with one's "feel" for correctness. This is what performers do in their first language when correcting slips of the tongue.

Still another problem of interpretation of such studies is that we do not really know whether subjects had indeed had the chance to learn all the rules necessary for successful self-correction. Are we studying the efficiency of learning and/or the ability of performers to apply what they consciously know?

Self-correction studies do not provide us, therefore, with an exact picture, but the results are quite useful to the teacher interested in the overall efficiency of self-correction, and they probably give us an approximation of the efficiency of conscious learning and Monitoring.

THE DATA

Table 4.5 and Fig. 4.1 summarize the literature available to me on self-correction. With two exceptions, all deal with university level ESL students who, we expect, have been exposed to a fair amount of formal instruction in English grammar. The subject in one study is our old friend "P", a linguist. Fathman's subjects (Fathman, 1980) are described as 20 adults "learning English as a second language in the United States, primarily in an informal setting" and 20 adults "learning English in a formal setting, primarily in Mexico" (p. 3, manuscript).

TABLE 4.5. *Accuracy of self-correction in adult performance in English as a second language*

Study	Condition[1]	Error type analyzed	Results (% of errors self-corrected)
1. Schlue (1977)	Stream of speech (1)	All syntax, morphology	7.2% (99/1101)
2. Fathman (1980)	SLOPE test, oral interview, Picture description (1)	Morphology[2]	a. "Informal" adults (see text) = 20% (13/65) b. "Formal adults" = 32% (46/144)
3. Schlue (1977)	Listen to tape of own speech (2)	All syntax, morphology	31%
4. Houck *et al.* (1978a)	Inspect transcription of own speech[3] (2)	Nine morphemes	17.5% (36.5/236)
5. White (1977)	Inspect transcript of responses to BSM[4] (4)	a. Morphology b. Syntax c. "Omissions" d. Lexical	a. 52% (53/102) b. 27% (6/22) c. 53% (23/43) d. 9% (1/11) 47% (83/178)
6. Krashen and Pon (1975)	Inspect transcriptions[5] (4)	Morphology, syntax	95% (76/80)

[1] Number in parenthesis refers to conditions in Table 4.4.
[2] "Almost all the uncorrected errors were related to verbs, such as: omission of the copula and omission or incorrect use of inflections".
[3] Subjects transcribed tapes themselves.
[4] E transcribed tapes (". . . (S's) were presented with some of their errors").
[5] E = Subject transcribed tape.

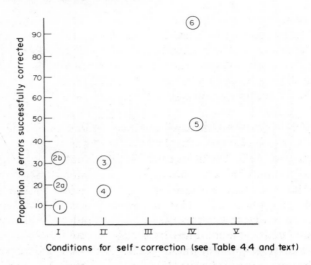

Fig. 4.1. Self-correction accuracy.

1: Schlue (1977).
2a, 2b: Fathman (1980).
3: Schlue (1977).
4: Houck *et al*. (1978a).
5: White (1977).
6: Krashen and Pon (1975).
         (see Table 4.5)

As for the domain of language analyzed, one study (Houck *et al.*, 1978a) focusses only on nine grammatical morphemes, while the others cover morphology and syntax in general.

It is hard to say whether any of the studies actually meet the description of condition (1), since in all cases the subjects knew they were being tested and that the focus of the investigation was the quality and accuracy of their speech. Thus, Fathman (1980), and Schlue (1977) may be overestimates of self-communication accuracy in "free speech" and might really belong in condition (2).

Figure 4.1 attempts to illustrate how conditions, and differences in subjects, affect self-correction accuracy, and gives us a picture of what we can expect, at least in the domain of syntax and morphology. It suggests, first of all, that training and type of student do make a difference: Fathman's "formal" students correct a higher percentage of their own errors than her informal students do, and our subject, "P", outperforms everyone. It is also consistent with the hypothesis that accuracy increases as we focus more on form. Further studies could easily be performed to fill in the holes in the figure; they would also hopefully control for proficiency level, since there may be a relationship between the sheer number of errors committed and self-correction accuracy. It would also be desirable to control for first language and some aspects of personality, due to the observed relationship between personality and avoidance behavior (Kleinman, 1977).

Possibly the most important result to emerge from these studies is the point that self-correction is never perfect, never reaches what some teachers would consider acceptable performance except in the case of one very good learner who was presented with her own errors! The fact is that many teachers assume self-correction should be 100%, that students should be able to apply all they have learned at all times.[7]

If second language performers do not focus heavily on form in self-correction, what do they do? Several studies, all classified as falling under condition (2), show that revisions are typically aimed at greater communicative effectiveness and not merely on form. Hassan (cited in Hatch, 1979) noted what changes ESL students made on second and third drafts of compositions. Hassan reported that the students "concentrated mainly on vocabulary choice, added minor details, and made fewer changes which resulted in overall grammar improvement" (Hatch, 1979, p. 136). Schlue (1977) came to similar conclusions, noting that "her subjects seemed to monitor their speech quite carefully, but not for grammatical correctness. Their speech awareness was for the most part focused on their success or failure in conveying their message. Thus, they were very concerned with such things as the appropriateness of their *lexical* choices . . . even in the self-analysis activity, it was often hard to make the subjects focus on form rather than on lexicon and pronunciation . . ." (p. 343). Houck, Robertson and Krashen (1978a) also noted that many of the corrections made by subjects were "obviously attempts at improved intelligibility, rather than grammatical form" (p. 337).

To summarize thus far: Our description of when we can Monitor, what can be Monitored, and the linguistic effect of Monitoring all reach similar conclusions. The use of conscious grammar is limited. Not everyone Monitors. Those who do only Monitor some of the time, and use the Monitor for only a sub-part of the grammar. As we have just seen, the effects of self-correction on accuracy is modest. Second language performers can typically self-correct only a small percentage of their errors, even when deliberately focussed on form (conditions 2 to 4), and even when we only consider the easiest aspects of the grammar.

D. Other Effects of Conscious Rules

Use of the conscious grammar, we have maintained, is limited to easily learned, late-acquired rules, simple morphological additions that do not make an overwhelming contribution to communicating the speaker or writer's message. For most people, only "local" rules can be learned and used (Burt and Kiparsky, 1972). Certainly, speakers of English understand sentences with missing third person singular markers and dropped regular past endings fairly well, thanks to the presence of other markers of tense and pragmatic knowledge.

There is, nevertheless, some real value in applying these rules when time permits, when rule use does not interfere with communication. Providing these local items, even though they may make a small contribution to communication, makes writing and speech more polished, it adds a cosmetic effect that may be very important for many second language students.

Indeed, in the advanced second language class, providing such polish may become the main goal, one that is quite justified for many students. "Advanced" second language acquirers, especially those who have been in the country where the target language is spoken for a few years, may have acquired a great deal, but not all, of the second language, enough to meet communicative needs, but still short of the native speaker standard. Their chief need may be conscious rules to use as a supplement to their acquired competence, to enable them to appear as educated in their second language as they are in their first.

I do not object to this sort of grammar teaching. What is unfair is to emphasize accuracy on communicatively unessential, late acquired items in beginning language classes, with students who are unable to understand the simplest message in the second language.

E. Presentation of Rules

A fair amount has been written about how grammar rules should be presented. One issue is whether rules should be given "directly" (deductive), or whether students should be asked to figure out the rules for themselves (inductive). Another issue is sequence—which rules should be presented first, and/or emphasized more. I will restrict my comments on these issues to the implications second language acquisition theory make for these questions.

1. THE DEDUCTIVE–INDUCTIVE ISSUE

This issue was one of some concern in the second language acquisition pedagogical literature for many years. For many scholars and teachers, deductive teaching seemed much more reasonable—why make students guess the rule? Present a clear explanation and have them practice until the rule is "internalized". Cognitive-code teaching, as well as grammar-translation, are examples of the "rule-first" deductive approach.

Proponents of inductive teaching argued that the best way to insure learning was for the student to work out the rule himself. Inductive teaching is very much like rule-writing in linguistics. The learner is given a corpus and has to discover the regularities.

Before proceeding to some of the research bearing on this issue, it is important to clarify one major point: both inductive and deductive learning are *learning*. Neither have anything directly to do with subconscious language acquisition. Inductive learning bears a superficial resemblance to acquisition, and has occasionally been confused with acquisition in the literature. As Table 4.6 indicates, both inductive

TABLE 4.6. *Acquisition and inductive learning: similarities and differences*

Acquisition	Inductive learning
Data first, rule follows	Data first, rule follows
Rule is subconscious	Rule is conscious
Focus on meaning	Focus on form
Slow process	May occur quickly
Requires large amounts of data	May occur after exposure to small amount of data

learning and acquisition share the features of data, or input, first, with the "rule" coming second. There are deep and fundamental differences, however. When the goal is inductive learning, the focus is on form, and the learner attempts to analyze formal aspects of the data presented. When the goal is acquisition, the acquirer attempts to understand the message contained in the input. Also, the "rule" developed by the two processes is different. An inductively-learned rule is a conscious mental representation of a linguistic generalization—an acquired rule is not conscious (we can, however, certainly learn later what we have acquired; see below), but is manifested by a "feel" for correctness. Also, inductive learning, since it is conscious problem-solving, may occur very quickly—an adept student may "see" the regularity after only a few examples. Acquisition, however, always takes time and requires a substantial quantity of input data. As discussed in Chapter II, it takes more than a single paragraph and a few exercises to acquire a rule.

Thus, from the point of view of second language acquisition theory, the deductive–inductive controversy is not a central one for second language pedagogy, since it focusses only on which learning style is best. The issue has some significance, however, and there have been several suggestions and experimental results relating to this controversy that are of interest.

It has been suggested (Hammerly, 1975) that certain structures "are most amenable to a deductive approach while others . . . can be learned very well by an inductive approach" (p. 17). Seliger (1975) presents data suggesting that retention over time is better with a deductive approach. Hartnett's data support the hypothesis that students who are successful in deductive foreign language classes employ different neurological mechanisms than learners successful in more inductive classes, deductive learners being more left-brained, analytic thinkers, and inductive learners being more right-brained, analogic thinkers (Hartnett, 1974; Krashen, Seliger and Hartnett, 1974).

If there are individual differences in preference of rule presentation, if some people prefer rules first and others prefer to figure things out for themselves, insistence on the "wrong" approach for the grammar portion of the language teaching program may raise anxieties and strengthen the affective filter.[8]

The theory of second language acquisition presented in Chapter II makes only indirect contributions to this question. The most important contribution is its insistence that both deductive and inductive approaches are learning-oriented. The "practice" used for rule practice (deductive) or rule-searching (inductive) will not be optimal input for acquisition, since the students' focus will be primarily on form rather than on the message.

2. SEQUENCING AND LEARNING

I argued, in Chapter III, that grammatical sequencing was undesirable when the goal is acquisition. It seems reasonable that we should present rules one at a time in some order when the goal is conscious learning, however ("rule isolation"; Krashen and Seliger, 1975). Several rationale for sequencing have been suggested. We (Krashen, Madden and Bailey, 1975) once suggested the natural order itself, which I no longer think is the correct basis for sequencing for acquisition or learning. Other proposals include frequency of occurrence, grammatical simplicity, and "utility" (see, for example, Larsen, 1975). (My impression is that despite the existence of these options, and the fairly widespread discussion of them in the professional literature, the vast majority of texts utilize some version of linguistic simplicity, going from formally less complex to more complex structures.)

Second language acquisition theory, as presented here, does not yet make predictions as to the exact learning sequence. It does predict, however, something about the set of rules that can be learned. First, if the goal of grammar teaching is in fact to provide students with a Monitor, as we discussed earlier in this chapter, simplicity will play a large role. We can only teach what is *learnable*, and, restricting the set even more, what is *portable*, what can be carried around in the students' heads. (These two requirements need to be distinguished— learning a rule does not always mean being able to use it in performance, even when conditions are favorable for Monitor use.) As we have seen above, in discussing cases of under-users and incompetent Monitor users, we have, as a profession, overestimated what most people can learn, and what they can retain and use in performance. Even optimal users, "good language learners" have limits that are far below many teachers' expectations.

Second, unless our goal is language appreciation (see below), we don't have to teach rules that our students have already acquired. How, then, do we know which items to teach? We could, conceivably, perform a detailed error analysis on each student, compare the results of tests that tap learning and acquisition, and determine those items that have been acquired, but have not yet been learned, and focus on just this set. This is possible, but probably unnecessary. The "natural order" studies can provide us with at least some of the information we need. While some individual variation exists among second language acquirers, we have a good idea of what is acquired "early" and what is acquired "late" for some structures. We can be fairly certain that beginners in ESL will not have acquired the third person singular /s/ or the possessive /s/, for example. I think that a very worthy goal of applied linguistics is to attempt to describe this set of what are typically late-acquired, but learnable rules, beyond the few morphemes and structures we know about now.

Rules to be learned should thus meet these three requirements:

1. Learnable
2. Portable
3. Not yet acquired

The sequencing issue then becomes, or reduces to, determining which of the rules meeting all three of these requirements should be presented first. This thus still remains an issue, but one we have contributed to by limiting the set of items that must be sequenced.

F. Notes on Error Correction

Another controversy related to conscious learning is the issue of error correction. Henrickson (1978) lists the "five fundamental questions" and reviews the literature that addresses them:

1. Should errors be corrected?
2. If so, when should errors be corrected?
3. Which learner errors should be corrected?
4. How should learner errors be corrected?
5. Who should correct learner errors?

Second language acquisition theory has "answers" to four of these questions, answers that are, as are all other implications in this book, themselves hypotheses. In this case, I am predicting that if error correction is done according to the principles described below, it will be effective.

1. Should errors be corrected?

According to the second language acquisition theory presented here, when error correction "works", it does so by helping the learner change his or her conscious mental representation of a rule. In other words, it affects learned competence by informing the learner that his or her current version of a conscious rule is wrong. Thus, second language acquisition theory implies that when the goal is learning, errors should indeed be corrected (but not at all times; see below; and not all rules, even if the goal is learning). The theory maintains however, that error correction is not of use for acquisition. Acquisition occurs, according to the input hypothesis, when acquirers understand input for its meaning, not when they produce output and focus on form.

2. When should errors be corrected?

Hendrickson, following Birckbichler (1977), suggests that in general error correction be limited to "manipulative grammar practice"— more errors may be tolerated during "communicative practice".

The implications of second language acquisition theory are similar. If error correction aims at learning, it is logical to suppose that the conditions for error correction should be identical to the conditions for utilizing learning—we should focus our students on form, and correct their errors, only when they have time and when such diversion of attention does not interfere with communication. This implies no error correction in free conversation, but allows for error correction on written work and grammar exercises. This is precisely Terrell's procedure in the Natural Approach (described in Chapter V).

3. Which errors should be corrected?

Hendrickson reviews three hypotheses and accepts them all as plausible.

(1) We should correct "global" errors, errors that interfere with communication or impede the intelligibility of a message (Burt and Kiparsky, 1972). Such errors deserve top priority in correction.

(2) Errors that are the most stigmatized, that cause the most unfavorable reactions, are the most important to correct.

(3) Errors that occur most frequently should be given top priority.

In the previous section, the linguistic domain of the Monitor was described. I recommended that we restrict the conscious learning of rules for Monitor use according to these characteristics: the rules to be learned should be (1) learnable, (2) portable, and (3) not yet acquired. These characteristics might also describe which errors should be corrected, if it is indeed the case that error correction affects only the conscious grammar. Perhaps we should only correct mistakes that reflect rules that can be used as part of the conscious Monitor.

This may appear to be a modest contribution to the issue of which errors are to be corrected. Many teachers, however, try to point out or correct *all* errors. This suggestion reduces the size of the task considerably. Within the small set defined by the three characteristics of learnable, portable, and not yet acquired, we still have to make decisions, and here considerations such as frequency, contributions to communication, and irritability may be relevant. The overall task, however, is reduced enormously.

4. How should errors be corrected?

Hendrickson reviews several methods of error correction, including the two most widely used:

(1) providing the correct form ("direct" correction).

(2) the discovery (inductive) approach.

He notes that little research is available that establishes the superiority of one method. Some research shows that direct correction is not particularly effective; students who have had direct correction of their oral and written output in instructional programs did not produce fewer errors (Hendrickson, 1976, 1977b, cited in Hendrickson, 1978; Cohen and Robbins, 1976). This may, notes Hendrickson, be due to the lack of consistent and systematic correction (Allwright, 1975; Cohen and Robbins, 1976).

Second language acquisition theory predicts that error correction will show positive results only if the following conditions are met:

(1) Errors corrected are limited to learnable and portable rules.
(2) Errors are corrected under conditions that allow Monitor use. This will give the learner time to reconsider the rule that was violated.
(3) Measures evaluating the efficacy of error correction are administered under conditions that allow Monitor use, to allow the learner time to refer to his or her conscious knowledge.
(4) Subjects used as known to be "Monitor-users" (i.e. they are not under-users of the Monitor).

Error correction that is not done under these conditions, I predict, will not "work"; I am also not optimistic about the efficacy of error correction even when all the above conditions are met. As is the case with conditions for Monitor use, they are necessary but not sufficient—even under the "best" conditions, correcting the simplest rules, with the most learning-oriented students, teacher corrections will not produce results that will live up to the expectations of many instructors.

B. Grammar as Subject Matter

As mentioned earlier (p. 88), "grammar" has another place in the pedagogical program, a place that is not always clearly distinguished from its use as a conscious Monitor. This is grammar as subject matter.

Many students (probably fewer than most of us think) are interested in the study of the structure of language *per se*. They may also be interested in language change, dialects, etc. Especially satisfying, for some students, is learning what has already been acquired, the Eureka phenomenon described earlier in this section (p. 88). My students who recognized that they had already acquired the three uses of the present progressive tense in English were very satisfied and pleased to have conscious knowledge corresponding to their subconscious knowledge. They also thought that I was an outstanding language teacher for providing them with this kind of insight!

Providing learning that corresponds with previous acquisition has its advantages, but I do not think it is language teaching—it is not input for acquisition (although the language of classroom discussion may be; see below), and it also does not provide useful learning that can be utilized as a supplement to acquisition, as a Monitor. It may serve one purpose, however: it can demonstrate to the language student that acquisition is real, and that it can be trusted. Pointing out what has been acquired may thus stimulate more faith in the acquisition process, and lower the affective filter. It may thus be a partial cure for over-use of the Monitor.

The study of the structure of language, how it varies over time (historical linguistics) and in society, has many general educational advantages and values that high school and university level language programs may want to include in a program. It should be clear, however, that teaching complex facts about the second language is not language teaching, but rather is "language appreciation" or linguistics.

Teaching grammar as subject-matter can result in language acquisition in one instance, however: when the target language is used as a medium of instruction. Acquisition occurs in these classes when students are interested in the subject matter, "grammar". Very often, when this occurs, both teachers and students are convinced that the study of formal grammar is essential for second language acquisition, and the teacher is skilled at presenting explanations in the target language so that the students understand. In other words, the teacher talk, in such classes, meets the requirements for input for acquisition, as presented in Chapter III: the input is comprehensible and considered to be relevant. The filter is low in regard to the language of explanation, as the students' conscious efforts are usually on the subject matter, *what* is being talked about, and not the medium.

This is a subtle point. In effect, both teachers and students are deceiving themselves. They believe that it is the subject matter itself, the study of grammar, that is responsible for the students' progress in second language acquisition, but in reality their progress is coming from the medium and not the message. Any subject matter that held their interest would do just as well, so far as second language acquisition is concerned, as long as it required extensive use of the target language.

This may underlie and explain the success of many grammar-based approaches. They are taught in the target language, and this provides comprehensible input for acquisition, input that is relevant and interesting as long as the student believes that conscious grammar is good for him. (For further discussion of such a class, see Krashen, 1980.)

Notes

[1] This is not, I should point out, Seliger's interpretation. See Note 2.

[2] Seliger interprets his results as being counter to the theory of second language acquisition presented in Chapter II. His interpretation of the test, and the theory, are both different from mine. He considers the test situation to be "formal", and "not a sample of language within a natural context" (p. 362). There is, I think, some truth to this analysis, as mentioned in the text. Subjects' performance, however, is consistent with the hypothesis that the test tapped primarily acquisition—this is supported by the data and is consistent with the hypothesis that Monitor use occurs only when several necessary conditions are met, as stated in Chapter II and repeated in this chapter. More strange is his interpretation of the acquisition–learning distinction and the Monitor hypothesis: his results are counter to "Monitor Theory", he claims, since Monitor Theory maintains that "learners do what they say they do", and his data shows this is not so. His data does indeed confirm that performers do not always do what they say they do, but "Monitor Theory" does not, and never has, made the claim that people do what they say they do.

Seliger outlines his own position in the same paper. Pedagogical rules, he asserts, "most likely serve as mechanisms to facilitate the learner's focussing on those criterial attributes of the real language concept that must be induced" (p. 368). They serve as "acquisition facilitators" and "make the inductive hypothesis testing process more efficient" (p. 368). Seliger provides, unfortunately, very little more than this by way of description of his hypothesis, which he presents as an alternative to Monitor Theory. He also presents nothing in the way of empirical support for his position. There is, moreover, a serious problem with this hypothesis: If rule learning is so often wrong (a point we agree on), how can it be useful as an acquisition focussing device? Also, as we have seen earlier in this section, acquisition need not be preceded by conscious learning. Rather, the available evidence supports the hypothesis that acquisition occurs only when the acquirer's attention is on the message, not on the form of the input. According to the Input Hypothesis, conscious rules do not facilitate acquisition. Acquisition occurs via a completely different route. An alternative hypothesis must deal with the evidence supporting the Input Hypothesis, and the arguments that acquisition does not require previous learning.

[3] Before we conclude that Eva and Ue-lin simply need more drill and learning, consider the possibility that they are among the better learners. Cohen and Robbins' subject Hung, an "under-user" of the Monitor, also made errors on the third person singular /s/ and /-ed/, consistent with the hypothesis that such items are typically late-acquired. In contrast to Ue-lin and Eva, Hung could not self-correct by rule, however. When confronted with a third person singular /s/ deletion he had made, he remarked: "I guess I just never learned the rule that well, so I just write down whatever I feel like it." (p. 52). Also, "When confronted with a sentence he had written where an *ed* deletion error occurred ('He got discourage'), Hung supplied *ed*, but he commented: 'I don't see

why'." (p. 53). Hung also noted that it was very hard for him to detect errors in his own output. Hung is quoted many times as saying he does not pay attention to form: "I don't care the grammar (p. 50) . . . I just never learned the rules that well. . . . I just write down what I feel like it (p. 59) . . . I get kind of bored when I study English" (p. 51). Again, many people, despite exposure in class, have practically no idea of rules that seem straightforward to us.

[4] In a recent study, J. Brown (1980) administered a grammar-type test whose format was quite similar to that of Larsen-Freeman. Subjects only had to supply one morpheme, as in:

I _____ (talk) to John yesterday.

The test was administered with no time limit to 66 ESL students with a variety of first languages at Marymount Palos Verdes College. Here is the difficulty order Brown reported:

Auxiliary	96% correct
Copula	94.2%
Regular past	92%
Plural	91.8%
The (def art)	88.2%
Irregular past	88%
a (indef art)	86.6%
Ø (art)	85.8%
Possessive	80.2%
ing	80.2%
Third person sing	77%

This order, Brown reports, correlates significantly with other second language morpheme orders (rho = 0.73, compared to Andersen, 1978). It is analyzed somewhat differently from other studies in that the allomorphs of article are presented separately; they are very close in rank order, however.

Brown's order is difficult to interpret due to the closely bunched scores. The order appears to be similar to other L2 orders in the literature with two exceptions: *ing* is unusually low, and *regular past* is unusually high (see Chapter II, Hypothesis 2). The high rank of regular past is consistent with my hypothesis that such formats encourage Monitor use, which results in a jump in accuracy of the rank of late-acquired but easy to learn morphemes. I have no handy explanation for *ing*'s relatively poor showing, nor can I account for the third person singular's low rank in this Monitored test. Brown's high correlation with other studies is counter to some of my claims, but the rise in regular past is not.

[5] It is very interesting to note that accuracy for the third person singular in other Monitor-free studies is very similar to the accuracy found in the composition study for the "free" condition. In Bailey, Madden, and Krashen (1974), using the BSM, third person singular accuracy was 0.41, while in Krashen, Houck, Giunchi, Bode, Birnbaum, and Strei (1977), using free speech, accuracy for this morpheme was 0.36. Compare to Table 4.3, where accuracy in the two free conditions is 0.54 and 0.32, going up to 0.61 and 0.65 in the edited condition, respectively. This similarity is consistent with the hypothesis that the edited condition involved light Monitor use, and that late-acquired, easy items are most apt to be affected.

[6] In focussing on the regular past and third person singular, I by no means wish to imply that these are the only points of grammar that can be consciously Monitored. They are,

rather, typical of what can be Monitored, and are convenient to follow through several studies since they are mentioned and analyzed so often.

[7] Several other studies also pertain to Monitoring ability but do not focus on self-correction. As described earlier, Krashen, Butler, Birnbaum and Robertson (1978) asked ESL students at USC to write "free" and "edited" compositions in English (conditions 1 and 2). In both cases, natural orders were found, with a slight increase in the third person singular morpheme in the edited condition. There also was a 6% overall increase for the edited condition for the six morphemes analyzed, for the group as a whole with some individual variation according to first language, Farsi speakers being the most efficient, showing a 16% gain in accuracy in the edited condition. This is a different measure than that described in the text, since subjects wrote completely new and different essays. Tucker and Sarofin (1979) presented 18 "advanced intermediate" Arabic speaking students at the American University at Cairo with 14 deviant sentences. Students were asked to "draw a line underneath the error and correct it if you can" (p. 32). This corresponds to condition (3). The range of the proportion of errors corrected was from 33% to 83%, depending on the error, with errors of "number" being easiest to correct (as in: * So, I took the advices of my parents).

Lightbown, Spada and Wallace (1980) also contributes to our knowledge of Monitor efficiency. They gave their subjects, grade 6, 8, and 10 students of EFL in Quebec a test of grammaticality judgments in English. Subjects were asked to circle the errors in a sentence and write the correct form. The study focussed on these structures:

Plural   /s/
Possessive   /s/
Third person singular   /s/
Contractable copula   /s/
Contractable auxiliary   /s/
Be, used for expressing age (e.g. I am six years old. This is considered a problem structure for French speakers.)
Prepositions of location (They are going *to* school.)

The test was given three times, the first two administrations being only two weeks apart, the third coming five months later, after summer vacation. In between administrations I and II, the rules used on the test were reviewed in class. Lightbown *et al.* report some improvement from time I to time II—the review in class resulted in a modest but noticeable 11% improvement for grades 8 and 10, compared to 3% for control students who simply retook the test without review, and a 7% increase for the 6th graders (no controls were run for the 6th grade). In the third administration, five months later, scores fell back to a level between administrations I and II.

The results of Lightbown *et al.* are consistent with those reported in the text, even though the task is not self-correction but is correction of errors presented to the student, as in Tucker and Sarafin. The students were only able to correct approximately $\frac{1}{4}$ to $\frac{1}{3}$ of these errors, despite two to six years of formal study and despite the fact that the structures involved were fairly straightforward. The task corresponds to condition (3) in Table 4.4.

Review of the rules in class also had a modest effect, much of which was lost after summer vacation. I concur with Lightbown *et al.*'s interpretation that "improvements on the second administration were based on the application of knowledge temporarily retained at a conscious level, but not fully acquired". The results of administration III show just how temporary learned knowledge is.

Lightbown *et al.* also provide an analysis of results for individual structures. They note that subjects made significant ("dramatic") improvement from time I to time II on the be/have rule and on the third person singular. This supports, they note, my hypothesis that simpler rules are easier to consciously learn, since the description of both of these rules is relatively straightforward. There was also a significant improvement of a much less transparent rule, the use of locative prepositions, and the plural, which appears to be "easy", did not, however, show large gains.

Difficulty orders for the /s/ morphemes conformed to the natural order presented in Chapter II, confirming both the reliability of the natural order itself, and the claim that it takes more than condition (3) to disturb the natural order significantly (i.e. condition (3) does not focus on form strongly enough). (See Lightbown, in press, for a discussion of the effect of classroom input on morpheme orders.)

[8] In an earlier paper (Krashen, Seliger and Hartnett, 1974), we suggest a compromise: teach rule-first, which will satisfy the deductive students. The inductive students can simply ignore the rule presentation. "Practice" can then serve as practice in rule application (Monitoring) for the deductive students, and as rule-searching for the inductive students. The rule can be (re)stated after the practice, a review for deductive students and confirmation for the inductive students' hypothesis.

Chapter V

Approaches to Language Teaching

Chapters III and IV were devoted to a discussion of the general implications of second language acquisition theory. Chapter III described the characteristics of optimal input for acquisition, hypothesizing that language acquisition takes place best when input is provided that is:

1. Comprehensible.
2. Interesting and/or relevant to the acquirer.
3. Not grammatically sequenced.
4. Provided in sufficient quantity.

The presentation of this input, moreover, should be done in a way that does not put the acquirer "on the defensive"; it should not raise or strengthen the affective filter. In addition, acquirers need to be provided with tools to help them obtain more input from the outside world.

Chapter IV tried to "put learning in its place". Conscious rules should be used only when they do not interfere with communication. In addition, only a small part of the grammar is both learnable and "portable" for most people. Rules that seem very transparent to professional linguists and language teachers may be quite opaque even to "good language learners". We also concluded that the effects of learning are quite modest in terms of syntactic accuracy, but that the application of conscious rules may provide a cosmetic effect that is important for some language students. Chapter IV also discussed the fact that conscious grammar can be taught as subject matter; acquisition results if such a course is taught in the target language. This "language appreciation" function, however, needs to be distinguished from the Monitor function for grammar.

The goal of the first part of this chapter is to analyze some current approaches to language teaching in terms of the conclusions of Chapters III and IV. The results of this analysis will then be compared with the results of what applied linguistics research has been done in the area of "method comparisons". My interpretation will be that in this case, current second language acquisition theory and applied linguistics research come to very similar conclusions.

The next section examines some alternatives to the traditional classroom, alternatives that seem to have the advantage of satisfying input requirement #2 (the "interesting/relevant" requirement) far better than any traditional classroom approach. Next, there is a brief discussion of the implications these ideas have for second language testing. I will suggest that we need to carefully consider what affects our achievement tests have on student and teacher behavior. Our goal in testing is this: when students "study for the test", they should be doing things that encourage or cause second language acquisition. The final sections of this chapter deal with what I perceive to be some gaps in materials, and some of the practical problems in implementing the suggestions made here.

A. Present-day Teaching Methods

The conclusions of Chapters III and IV can be summarized as the matrix in Fig. 5.1. We can simply ask, for each approach to classroom teaching, to what extent it satisfies the requirements for optimal input and to what extent it puts learning in its proper place. We will review what are surely the most widely used methods, grammar-translation, audio-lingualism, cognitive-code teaching, and one version of the direct method. We will then cover some new approaches, Asher's Total Physical Response method, Terrell's Natural Approach and Lozanov's Suggestopedia. (Several very interesting methods are not included, such as Gattegno's Silent Way and Curren's Counseling–Learning method. This is due to several factors, including my own lack of familiarity with these methods, the lack of empirical data comparing these methods to others, and the availability of Stevick's excellent analysis (Stevick, 1980).) The brief description supplied at the beginning of each analysis is not intended to be a full and adequate description of each method, but is intended to serve only to inform the reader

Fig. 5.1. Evaluation schema for methods and materials

Requirements for optimal input

1. Comprehensible
2. Interesting/relevant
3. Not grammatically sequenced
4. Quantity
5. Filter level ("off the defensive")
6. Provides tools for conversational management

Learning

Restricted to:
1. Certain rules; those that are
   a. learnable
   b. portable
   c. not yet acquired
2. Certain people ("Monitor users")
3. Certain situations
   a. time
   b. focus on form

what my understanding of each method is. It should also be pointed out that this analysis assumes that the methods are used in their pure forms, a situation which, I am sure, does not occur in every classroom.

1. GRAMMAR-TRANSLATION

While there is some variation, grammar-translation usually consists of the following activities:

1. Explanation of a grammar rule, with example sentences.
2. Vocabulary, presented in the form of a bilingual list.
3. A reading selection, emphasizing the rule presented in (1) above and the vocabulary presented in (2).
4. Exercises designed to provide practice on the grammar and vocabulary of the lesson. These exercises emphasize the conscious control of structure ("focus on", in the sense of Krashen and Seliger, 1975) and include translation in both directions, from L1 to L2 and L2 to L1.

Most grammar-translation classes are designed for foreign language instruction and are taught in the students' first language. We turn now to an analysis of grammar-translation in terms of the matrix in Fig. 5.1.

(a) Requirements for optimal input

(i)   *Comprehensible*. It can only be claimed that grammar-translation provides scraps of comprehensible input. The model sentences are usually understandable, but the focus is entirely on form, and not meaning. The reading selection is the primary source, but the selections provided are nearly always much too difficult, often requiring what Newmark (1966) calls "crytoanalytic decoding". Students are forced to read word by word, and consequently rarely focus completely on the message. The sentences used in the exercises may be comprehensible, but here again, as in the model sentences, they are designed to focus the students on form.

(ii)   *Interesting/relevant*. There is usually an attempt, especially in recent years, to provide topics of interest in the reading selection, but the usual topics fall far short of the Forgetting Principle (Chapter III). They clearly do not seize the students' attention to such an extent that they forget that it is written in another language—reports of a trip to France, even if it includes the Louvre, generally do not provide information that most high school and college students in the United States are eager to obtain.

(iii) *Not grammatically sequenced*. Grammar-translation is, of course, grammatically sequenced, the majority of texts attempting to proceed from what the author considers easy rules to more complex rules. Each lesson introduces certain rules, and these rules dominate the lesson.

(iv) *Quantity*. As discussed above, grammar-translation fails to provide a great deal of comprehensible input. The small amount of comprehensible input in the model sentences, the readings, and exercises is, moreover, rarely supplemented by teacher talk in the target language.

(v) *Affective filter level*. In Chapter III, it was hypothesized that one way to encourage a low filter was to be "true" to the Input Hypothesis.

Grammar-translation violates nearly every component of the Input Hypothesis, and it is therefore predicted that this method will have the effect of putting the student "on the defensive". Students are expected to be able to produce immediately, and are expected to be fully accurate (although in writing, and not usually in speaking). Anxiety level, it has been pointed out, is also raised for some students who are less inclined toward grammar study (under-users), as pointed out by Rivers, 1968.

(vi) *Tools for conversational management.* Grammar-translation makes no attempt, explicitly or implicitly, to help students manage conversations with native speakers.

(b) Learning

Grammar-translation implicitly assumes that conscious control of grammar is necessary for mastery. In other words, learning needs to precede acquisition. This assumption necessitates that all target structures be introduced and explained. There is, therefore, no limitation of the set of rules to be learned to those that are learnable, portable, and not yet acquired, as suggested in Chapter IV. There is no attempt to account for individual variation in Monitor use, nor is there any attempt to specify when rules are to be used, the implicit assumption being that all students will be able to use all the rules all the time!

(c) Summary

Grammar-translation, if the above analysis is correct, should result in very low amounts of acquired competence; what comprehensible input is available faces a high affective filter, and learning is vastly overemphasized.

2. AUDIO-LINGUALISM

Here are the common features of audio-lingual language teaching. Again, there may be substantial variation in practice. The lesson typically begins with a dialogue, which contains the structures and vocabulary of the lesson. The student is expected to *mimic* the dialogue and eventually *memorize* it (termed "mim-mem"). Often, the class practices the dialogue as a group, and then in smaller groups. The dialogue is followed by pattern drill on the structures introduced in the dialogue. The aim of the drill is to "strengthen habits", to make the pattern "automatic".

Lado (1964) notes that audio-lingual pattern drills focus the students' attention *away* from the new structure. For example, the student may think he is learning vocabulary in an exercise such as:

> That's a _____. (key, knife, pencil, etc.)
> (cued by pictures, as in Lado and Fries, 1958)

but in reality, according to audio-lingual theory, the student is making the pattern automatic.

There are four basic drill types: simple repetition, substitution (as in the example above), transformation (e.g. changing an affirmative sentence into a negative sentence), and translation.

Following pattern drill, some audio-lingual classes provide explanation. According to proponents of audio-lingualism, the explanation is a description of what was practiced, not a prescription of what to say. The "rules" presented are therefore not to be considered instructions on how to perform. The explanation section is considered optional, since, in our terms, it is "language appreciation".

(a) Requirements for optimal input

(i) *Comprehensible*. It can be maintained that audio-lingual methodology does provide comprehensible input. The dialogues and pattern practice are certainly understandable by most students, although some theorists have said that in early parts of a lesson actual comprehension is not necessary, that purely mechanical drill is useful.

(ii) *Interesting/relevant*. While Lado (1964) advises that the dialogue contain "useful" language, that it be age-appropriate and natural, most dialogues fall far short of the mark of true interest and relevance. Most pattern practice, of course, makes no attempt to meet this requirement.

(iii) *Not grammatically sequenced*. There is a clear sequence in audio-lingual teaching, based usually on linguistic simplicity, but also influenced by frequency and predictions of difficulty by contrastive analysis. As is the case with grammar-translation, the entire lesson is dominated by the "structure of the day".

(iv) *Quantity*. While audio-lingual teaching is capable of filling an entire class hour with aural–oral language, it is quite possible to argue that audio-lingualism does not meet this requirement as well as other methods (see below). While the presentation of a dialogue, for example, may take up a full period, students spend very little of this time focussing on the message, which is presented over and over. The goal is the memorization of the dialogue, not the comprehension of a message. Pattern practice may also be comprehensible in theory, but students probably do not attend to meaning after the first few repetitions (Lee, McCune and Patton, 1970). Indeed, according to some practitioners, the idea behind pattern practice is to avoid meaning altogether. For both dialogues and pattern practice, the entire hour might be spent with just a few sentences or patterns, as compared to the wide variety real communication gives.

(v) *Affective filter level*. Audio-lingual teaching violates several aspects of the Input Hypothesis: production is expected immediately, and is expected to be error-free. Over-use of drill and repetition, procedures such as not allowing students access to the written word in early stages may also add to anxiety (see, for example, Schumann and Schumann (1978) pp. 5–6).

(vi) *Tools for conversational management*. Audio-lingualism does a slightly better job in this category than does grammar-translation, as the dialogues do contain material that can be used to invite input and to control its quality. The applicability of dialogues to free conversation and to genuine conversational management may be limited, however. Most dialogues are actually scripts, and are not designed to be used to negotiate meaning.

(b) Learning

Theoretically, conscious learning is not an explicit goal of audio-lingualism. The goal, rather, is to have the student over-learn a variety of patterns to be used directly in performance. In practice, however, audio-lingual teaching often results in inductive learning, the student attempting to work out a conscious rule on the basis of the dialogue and pattern practice, with the explanation section serving to confirm or disconfirm his guess. There is thus no explicit attempt to restrict learning to rules that are learnable, portable and not yet acquired, nor is there any attempt to encourage rule use only in certain situations. Despite the fact that pattern practice attempts to focus students off rules, the requirement of complete correctness probably encourages Monitor use at all times.

(c) Summary

Some acquisition should result from the use of the audio-lingual method, but nowhere near what is obtainable with other methods that provide a larger amount of comprehensible and interesting/relevant input with a low filter. The diet of dialogues and patterns will occasionally be understood and be at $i + 1$, and may thus cause some acquisition. If learned according to plan, students will end up with a stock of sentences and patterns that will be of occasional use in conversation, and also serve the conversational management goal, to some extent. Inductive learning is implicitly encouraged (which may raise the filter for some deductive learners; see Chapter V), but no attempt is made to limit which rules are to be learned or when they are to be applied.

3. COGNITIVE-CODE

Cognitive-code bears some similarity to grammar-translation, but also differs in some ways. While the goal of grammar-translation is basically to help students read literature in the target language, cognitive code attempts to help the student in all four skills, speaking and listening in addition to reading and writing. The assumptions are similar, however, insofar as cognitive code posits that "competence precedes performance". In this case, "competence" is not the tacit knowledge of the native speaker, as originally defined by Chomsky (1965), but is conscious knowledge. Cognitive code assumes, as mentioned in Chapter III, that "once the student has a proper degree of cognitive control over the structures of a language, facility will develop automatically with the use of language in meaningful situations" (Carroll, 1966, p. 102). In other words, learning becomes acquisition.

As in grammar-translation, the lesson begins with an explanation of the rule, and this is often done, in foreign language situations, in the students' first language. Exercises follow, and these are meant to help the student practice the rule consciously. In other words, Monitor use is actively promoted. Exercises are followed by activities labelled "communicative competence". This term has been used in the literature in several ways; in cognitive-code literature it appears to be synonymous with "fluency". These activities provide the practice in meaningful situations referred to in the quote from Carroll above, and include dialogues, games, role playing activities, etc.

(a) Requirements for optimal input

(i) *Comprehensible*. The explanation and exercise section, as is the case with grammar-translation, will provide very little comprehensible input, as the focus, at all times, is on form and not meaning. The "communicative competence" section of cognitive-code promises to provide greater amounts of comprehensible input, but this potential is diminished if activities are limited by the desire to contextualize the "rule of the day". This practice, as claimed in Chapter III, limits the structures used (which may *deny* the student the $i + 1$ he needs), limits what can be discussed, and disturbs the naturalness of the communication.

(ii) *Interesting/relevant*. This depends, of course, on the activities chosen for the communicative competence section. Regardless of what is chosen, however, the goal remains the learning of a specific structure, and because of this it is nearly impossible to satisfy the Forgetting Principle.

(iii) *Not grammatically sequenced.* Cognitive-code, like grammar-translation, is sequenced, and the structure of the day dominates all parts of the lesson.

(iv) *Quantity.* Thanks to the communicative competence section, there is greater quantity of comprehensible input in cognitive-code, as compared to grammar-translation. It does not, however, live up to the ideal of a class full of comprehensible input with total focus on the message, since the communicative competence section is only a part of the program and even here, the focus is on form.

(v) *Affective filter level.* Error correction on all output is part of most cognitive-code classrooms, students are expected to produce right away, and it is expected that this production will be accurate. This predicts a high filter for many students.

(vi) *Tools for conversational management.* There is no announced attempt to provide this, but it is quite possible that some activities in the communicative competence section will provide some of these tools.

(b) Learning

As is the case with grammar-translation, the assumption of cognitive-code is that conscious learning can be accomplished by everyone, that all rules are learnable, and that conscious knowledge should be available at all times. We can only conclude that cognitive-code encourages over-use of the Monitor, unless all rules "fade away" as soon as the structures become automatic.

(c) Summary

Cognitive-code should provide greater quantities of comprehensible input than grammar-translation does, and hence more acquisition, but does not come near to fulfilling the potential of the classroom. As in grammar-translation, learning is overemphasized.

4. THE DIRECT METHOD

The term "direct method" has been used to refer to many different approaches to second language teaching. I will use it here to refer specifically to de Sauzé's method and its present day versions, namely Pucciani and Hamel's method for French (see *Langue et Langage*), and similar versions for Spanish developed by Barcia.

Here are the characteristics of the direct method, as I understand it. First, all discussion, all classroom language, is the target language. This includes the language of the exercises and teacher talk used for classroom management. The method focusses on inductive teaching of grammar. The goal of the instruction is for the students to guess, or work out, the rules of the language. To aid in induction, the teacher asks questions that are hopefully interesting and meaningful, and the students' response is then used to provide an example of the target structure. If this is well done, it can give a direct method session the mood of a conversation class. Let me repeat my favorite example from an earlier paper (Krashen, 1980), one that one of my teachers used in a direct method French class. The goal of this exercise was to teach the conjunction "bien que", and the fact that its presence requires the following verb to be subjunctive:

> *Teacher:* Fait-il beau aujour'dhui?
> *Student:* Non, il ne fait pas beau aujourd'hui.
> *Teacher:* Irez-vous cependent à la plage pendant le week-end?
> *Student:* Oui, j'irai cependent à la plage pendant le week-end.
> *Teacher:* Irez-vous à la plage bien qu'il ne fasse pas beau?
> *Student:* Oui, j'irai à la plage bien qu'il ne . . .

My teacher used this particular example on a determined beach-goer, and generally tried to tailor questions to students' interests.

The direct method insists on accuracy and errors are corrected in class. After several exchanges of the sort given above, when the teacher considers that enough examples have been given, the rule is discussed and explained in the target language.

(a) Requirements for optimal input

(i) *Comprehensible.* The direct method, with its insistence on the use of the target language at all times, provides a great deal of comprehensible input. As is the case with the Natural Approach, the entire period is filled with target language use with a variety of topics and structures utilized.

(ii) *Interesting/relevant*. As mentioned above, there is an attempt to make the language use in the classroom of some interest to the students. The goal of the lesson, however, is grammar teaching, and as discussed earlier, this puts heavy constraints on what can be discussed. Discussion is always meaningful, but is rarely genuinely communicative. According to Pucciani and Hamel's manual, sentences such as:

Est-ce que votre pantalon est vieux ou neuf? (198)
Mangez-vous des carottes? (236)
Qui prepare le diner dans votre famille? (237)
Est-ce que vous vous rasez tous les matins? (297)

are recommended to help the student induce various points of grammar. As with other methods that rely on contextualization (see e.g. discussion of the Silent Way), the requirement that all discussion embed a grammar point makes this requirement hard to meet.

(iii) *Not grammatically sequenced*. The direct method is strictly sequenced, which distorts efforts at real communication.

(iv) *Quantity*. As mentioned above, the direct method meets this requirement as well as any classroom method can, filling the entire hour with comprehensible input.

(v) *Affective filter level*. The insistence on grammatical accuracy at very early stages, the use of error correction, and the grammatical focus of the course may cause anxiety and a high filter for all but the most dedicated Monitor user.

(vi) *Tools for conversational management*. Students are given the tools for interaction in the classroom in the target language—they are soon able to initiate discussion with the teacher and ask questions about grammar. Some of this conversational, or better, "classroom competence" will be useful on the outside, but some will not. There is no explicit goal of providing tools for conversation with a more competent native speaker.

(b) Learning

The direct method presumes that conscious control is necessary for acquisition, that conscious knowledge of grammar can be accessed at all times, and by all students. It demands full control of late-acquired structures in oral production from the very beginning (e.g. gender), and may thus encourage over-use of the grammar.

(c) Summary

The direct method provides greater amounts of comprehensible input than many of its competitors. It remains, however, grammar-based, and this constrains its ability to provide truly interesting messages, and leads to over-use of the Monitor. The direct method, according to informal reports, has been very successful with certain populations, among students who have intrinsic motivation for language study and who believe that the study of conscious grammar is essential. For these students, the inductive study of grammar is in itself interesting, and provides all the interest necessary. In other words, grammar is subject matter. Acquisition, SLA theory predicts, comes from the teacher talk used to present the grammar. (See Chapter IV for discussion, and Krashen, 1980.)

5. THE NATURAL APPROACH

The Natural Approach was developed by Tracy Terrell at the University of California at Irvine for foreign language instruction at the university and high school levels. While originally developed independently of "Monitor Theory", its later development and articulation have been influenced by the second language acquisition theory presented in this volume. The method can be described by the following principles:

1. Classtime is devoted primarily to providing input for acquisition.
2. The teacher speaks only the target language in the classroom. Students may use either the first or second language. If they choose to respond in the second language, their errors are not corrected unless communication is seriously impaired.
3. Homework may include formal grammar work. Error correction is employed in correcting homework.
4. The goals of the course are "semantic"; activities may involve the use of a certain structure, but the goals are to enable students to talk about ideas, perform tasks, and solve problems.

(a) Requirements for optimal input

(i) *Comprehensible*. The entire goal of classroom practice in the Natural Approach is to provide comprehensible input. Natural Approach teachers utilize realia, pictures, and students' previous knowledge to make their speech comprehensible from the first day.

(ii) *Interesting/relevant*. This is a serious problem for a foreign language class. Natural Approach attempts to capture students' interest by using what Terrell terms "Affective Acquisition Activities", adapted from Christensen, that encourage discussion of topics of personal interest to the students (e.g. "Suppose you are a famous person, and there is a newspaper article about you. Tell at least one thing about yourself which is mentioned in the article . . ."). In the early stages of the Natural Approach, classroom discussion focusses on personal information, the goal being to establish a group feeling. Later, students discuss their past histories, and eventually they are able to talk about their hopes and plans for the future.

(iii) *Not grammatically sequenced*. The focus of the class is not on the presentation of grammar. There is a tendency for certain structures to be used more often in certain stages, but there is no deliberate sequencing.

(iv) *Quantity*. Since the entire class period is filled with comprehensible input, the Natural Approach meets this requirement as well as any foreign language teaching method can.

(v) *Affective filter level*. Since the Natural Approach attempts to remain "true" to the Input Hypothesis, many sources of anxiety are reduced or eliminated. Students do not have to produce in the second language until they feel they are ready. Error correction for form is not done in the classroom. Also, an attempt is made to discuss topics that are interesting to students. This predicts lower filter strength than most other methods.

(vi) *Tools for conversational management*. Some tools for conversational management are provided in the form of very short dialogues, designed to help students converse with native speakers on predictable and frequent topics. Also, students are introduced, right from the beginning, to phrases and expressions that will help them control the teacher's input (e.g. "I don't understand", "What does _____ mean?", etc.).

(b) Learning

The Natural Approach is designed to be consistent with what is known of Monitor functioning. The absence of error correction in the classroom is a recognition that there are constraints on when the conscious grammar is used: students are expected to utilize the Monitor only at home, when they have time, when they are focussed on form, and when they know, or are learning, a rule. At the university level, grammar homework is assigned to everyone, but it is conceivable that the Natural Approach can be adapted for variations in Monitor use, with varying amounts of homework, or different type homework assignments for under, or optimal users. While little experimentation has been done with children, SLA theory predicts that younger children would not profit from grammar homework, while older children and adolescents might be able to handle limited amounts. (For more detail, see Terrell, 1977.)

(c) Summary

The Natural Approach makes a deliberate effort to fit all requirements for both Learning and Acquisition. Its only weakness, according to SLA theory, is that it remains a classroom method, and for some students this prohibits the communication of interesting and relevant topics (see discussion below).

6. TOTAL PHYSICAL RESPONSE

This unique method was developed by James Asher, and is described in many of his journal papers and his book (Asher, 1977a). Total Physical Response, or TPR, consists basically of obeying commands given by the instructor that involve an overt physical response. The instructor, for example, says "stand up" and the class stands up. The commands become more complex as the class progresses, and Asher claims that it is quite possible to embed vast amounts of syntax into the form of a command. Students speak only when they are "ready", which usually occurs at around 10 hours of instruction, and consists of student commands. In the typical TPR class (as described by Asher, Kusudo, and de la Torre, 1974), the first few months (45 hours in this case) would consist of 70% listening comprehension (obeying commands), 20% speaking, and 10% reading and writing. Asher (1977b) lists the three principles of the TPR system:

(i) Delay speech from students until understanding of spoken language "has been extensively internalized" (p. 1041).

(ii) "Achieve understanding of spoken language through utterances by the instructor in the imperative" (p. 1041).

(iii) "Expect that, at some point in the understanding of spoken language, students will indicate a 'readiness' to talk" (p. 1041).[1] *

(a) Requirements for optimal input

(i) *Comprehensible*. TPR meets this requirement. The total physical response required of the student is, in effect, a manifestation of his comprehension of the teacher's utterance. It can, in fact, be argued that a TPR is not necessary for comprehension or for progress in sec-

* Superscript numbers refer to Notes at end of Chapter.

ond language acquisition, but merely shows that the input has been understood. Asher's own research supports the view that the use of the TPR is not essential. A series of studies using children (Asher, 1966; Asher and Price, 1967) and adults (Kunihira and Asher, 1965; Asher, 1965, 1969) shows that students who merely observe a TPR do as well as those who perform TPR's on tests that demand a TPR. Both groups, those who observed TPR's and those who performed them, outperformed students who wrote their answers on tests. This suggests that Asher's second principle may not be necessary, but may be simply an effective device to focus students on the input and to keep them actively involved.

(ii) *Interesting relevant*. The novelty and freshness of the TPR technique probably does a great deal to make the class experience interesting. It may be difficult to remain interesting if one holds to the requirement of producing imperatives 100% of the time, however (Asher nowhere recommends this).

(iii) *Not grammatically sequenced*. According to Asher's description, each lesson does have a grammatical focus in TPR. In other words, commands contextualize various points of grammar. As discussed earlier, this can hinder efforts to meet requirement 2 above. There is nothing inherent in the TPR approach that demands a grammatical focus, however.

(iv) *Quantity*. TPR can fill an entire class period with comprehensible input in the form of commands. It thus has the potential of meeting this requirement fully.

(v) *Affective filter level*. TPR makes one very important contribution to lowering student anxiety: students are not asked to produce in the second language until they themselves decide they are ready. They are, in other words, allowed a silent period. Asher does not state explicitly whether error correction on early student output is required in TPR; this may vary from teacher to teacher. It has been pointed out, however, that the necessity of producing overt physical responses right away may provoke anxiety in some students.

(vi) *Tools for conversational management.* There is no explicit mention of this in Asher's papers.

(b) Learning

The assumption of TPR is that grammar will be learned inductively, that is, students will work out the correct form of the rule during the class activity. In terms of the theory presented in this book, this can be interpreted as claiming that much of the grammar will be *acquired* and/or inductively *learned* in the technical sense of inductive learning. (See Chapter IV for discussion of the difference between inductive learning and acquisition.) The emphasis on listening comprehension and the delay of speech will, in itself, prevent much misuse of conscious learning: students will tend not to monitor their output for form in inappropriate circumstances and they will not use rules unsuited for Monitor use if there is less demand for production.

(c) Summary

Second Language Acquisition theory predicts that TPR should result in substantial language acquisition, and should not encourage overuse of the conscious Monitor. The use of TPR insures the active participation of students, helps the teacher know when utterances are understood, and also provides contexts to help students understand the language they hear. It may fail to completely satisfy the interesting/relevant requirement, first, since it is a classroom method, and second, because of constraints imposed by the continuous use of imperatives and the grammatical focus of lessons. It should, however, do far better than methods such as audio-lingual and grammar-translation.

7. SUGGESTOPEDIA

From what I have read in the sources available to me, the "classic" Suggestopedia class, as conducted in Lozanov's Institute of Suggestology in Sofia, Bulgaria, consists of the following. Courses are given to small groups, around 12 students at a time, and are intensive, meeting for four hours per day for one month. Each four-hour class, according to Bancroft (1978), consists of three parts:

1. Review, done via traditional conversations, games, plays, etc. It may include some exercises and error correction, but does not include the use of a language lab or pattern drill.
2. Presentation of new material. New material is introduced in the form of dialogues based on situations familiar to the students. Bancroft notes that "new material is presented in a somewhat traditional way, with the necessary grammar and translation" (p. 170). The dialogues are very long. According to Bushman and Madsen (1976), they run from 10 to 14 pages.
3. This portion is the "truly original feature" of Suggestopedia (Bancroft, p. 170), and is itself divided into two parts. In the first part, the active seance, the dialogue is read by the teacher, while students follow the text and engage in deep and rhythmic Yoga breathing. These activities are co-ordinated: "In accordance with the students' breathing, the teacher reads the language materials in the following order and with the following timing: Bulgarian (L1) translation (two seconds); foreign language phrase (four seconds); pause (two seconds). While the foreign language phrase is being read, the students retain their breath for four seconds, look at the appropriate part of the text, and mentally repeat to themselves the given phrase or word-group in the FL. Concentration is greatly promoted by the retention or suspension of breath" (Bancroft, p. 171).

The second part, labelled the passive or concert part of the seance, involves music. The central activity is the teacher's reading of the dialogue "with an emotional or artistic intonation" (Bancroft, p. 171). The students, "with eyes closed, meditate on the text" while baroque music is played. The musical selections are specifically chosen to contribute to a "state of relaxation and meditation . . . that is necessary for unconscious absorption of the language materials" (Bancroft, p. 172).

In discussing adaptions of the Sofia method, Bancroft notes that "three elements of the Lozanov Method are considered essential for the system to work effectively: (1) an attractive classroom (with soft lighting) and a pleasant classroom atmosphere; (2) a teacher with a dynamic personality who is able to act out the materials and motivate the students to learn; (3) a state of relaxed alertness in the students . . ." (p. 172).

In Suggestopedia, each member of the class is given a new name and role to play, "to overcome inhibitions" (p. 170). Other Suggestopedia techniques and attitudes will be discussed below, as we work through the analysis according to input requirements for acquisition.

(a) Requirements for optimal input

(i) *Comprehensible*. Several Suggestopedia procedures are specifically designed to aid comprehensibility of input. Initial dialogues are based on situations familar to the student, and the use of the students' first language in Part One is partly justified on the ground that it helps the student confirm that he has indeed understood the text presented in the target language (Racle, 1979, p. 100).

(ii) *Interesting/relevant*. The topics of the dialogues are designed not only to be of inherent interest, but also to be of some practical value and relevant to students' needs. In a Suggestopedia course designed to teach French to Anglophone public servants in Canada, at the Public Service Commission in Ottawa, the aim was to take into account both student interest and their communicative needs in the office situation (Public Service Commission, 1975). Also, Novakov, cited (and translated into French) by Racle, 1979, notes that "Les situations présentées sont typiques, réelles, contiennent un message et sont proches de l'expérience des élèves, ce qui facilite leur activité" (p. 99).

(iii) *Filter level*. While Suggestopedia attempts to meet the other goals discussed both above and below, its primary focus and greatest apparent success is here. Practically every feature of Suggestopedia is aimed at relaxing the student, reducing anxieties, removing mental blocks, and building confidence. Here are just a few more examples:

The design of the classroom is meant to produce "a pleasant and warm environment" (Public Service Commission, 1975, p. 29). Students are seated on comfortable chairs in a circle to "encourage informal contact and free natural communication" (Bushman and Madsen,

1976, p. 32). The traditional classroom, it is felt, "calls to mind the frustration, failure, and artificiality of many previous learning efforts" (Bushman and Madsen, p. 32).

The special breathing exercises have as their goal both increased mental alertness and reduction of tension. Bancroft reports that American adaptions of Suggestopedia also utilize physical exercises (stretching and bending), and "mind-calming exercises", in addition to Yogic breathing to help students achieve the desired state of relaxed alertness.

Music is also used as a means of lowering anxiety and diminishing tension, and inducing the state of relaxed alertness considered optimal for second language acquisition (see Racle, 1980, pp. 73–74).

Another key Suggestopedic idea aimed at lowering the filter is the behavior of the teacher. Suggestopedia considers the "authority" of the teacher to be very important ("an integral part of the method and not just a desirable characteristic of the teacher"; Stevick, 1980, p. 238). The teacher's behavior is meant to build the students' confidence both in their own potential for second language acquisition and in the method itself; the teacher should be confident, but not tyrannical, exercise firm over-all control but also encourage student initiative (for excellent discussion, see Stevick, 1980, Chapters 2 and 18).

(iv) *Not grammatically sequenced*. There is a deliberate attempt to include a certain amount of grammar during the first one month intensive course (Racle, 1979, p. 95 lists the structures covered for French). It does not appear to be the case, however, that a rigid sequence is followed. All writers on Suggestopedia I have read emphasize that the focus, from the very beginning, is on communication, and the dialogues do not seem to focus on specific points of grammar. According to Bushman and Madsen, "Dialogues are rambling conversations loosely aggregated around common themes, which cover a great deal of territory with considerable built-in redundancy" (p. 33). In our terms, Suggestopedia seems to depend on the net of grammatical structures provided by successful communication.

(v) *Quantity*. Suggestopedia seems to meet this requirement as well. While there is some explanation in the first language, the long and varied dialogue dominates the session, both as pure input (parts two and three) and as a basis for communicative use of the L2 (part one).

(vi) *Tools for conversational management*. This is not mentioned explicitly, but may be covered, since the dialogues attempt to be realistic. Texts used in the Public Service Commission course in Canada were apparently designed to allow and promote conversation in Public Service offices as well as elsewhere. There is no explicit mention, however, of giving students the tools they need to converse with more competent speakers.

(b) Learning

According to Bushman and Madsen (1976), "Content precedes form. Accurate pronunciation and grammar are to come in due course" (p. 32). While there is error correction and grammar explanation in part one of each lesson, grammar use in Suggestopedia apparently does not interfere with communication.

(c) Summary

While I have attempted to fit the Suggestopedia system, as I understand it, into my schema, and have omitted mention of several aspects of Suggestopedia philosophy that its practitioners would undoubtedly consider to be very important, it appears that Suggestopedia comes very close to completely matching the requirements for optimal input. Elements that Lozanov might consider to invoke hyper- or super-memory, or that "desuggest" limitations, are, in our terms, conditions that lower the affective filter and that allow the subconscious language acquisition system to operate at full, or near full capacity and efficiency. Suggestopedia also seems to put grammar in its proper place.

B. Applied Linguistics Research

We turn now to attempts to empirically test teaching methods via "applied linguistics research". I defined applied linguistics research in Chapter I as research aimed at solving a practical problem, with or without reference to an underlying theory. A portion of applied linguistics research has consisted of empirical comparisons of language teaching methods, and the purpose of this section is to review the major findings of these studies in order to make the following points:

1. When older methods such as grammar-translation, cognitive-code, and audio-lingual are compared with each other, we see small differences, or no differences in terms of efficacy. Cognitive-code, in some studies, shows a very slight superiority for adult students when compared to audio-lingual, and no differences are seen when adolescents are compared.

2. Data are not as plentiful as we would like them to be for newer methods, but the results we do have are quite consistent with our theoretical analysis of the previous section. Newer approaches, such as Total Physical Response, produce significantly better results than older approaches.

We will conclude that we see little difference between older methods since they all fail many of the requirements for optimal input and overemphasize conscious learning. The newer methods put to the method comparison test satisfy the requirements better, and are also shown to outperform their rivals.

1. REVIEW OF METHOD COMPARISON STUDIES

Before proceeding directly to the studies, it should be pointed out that classroom research, while it often produces valuable and interesting data, does not produce "definitive" data. This is because of the many "confounding variables" that prevent us, in nearly all cases, from concluding that it must have been a particular treatment or method that was responsible for the results obtained. It may be useful to list some of these potential confounds here.

If students in approach A did better in achievement tests than students in approach B, assuming they were equal to start with, it may be the *teacher* rather than the actual method that was responsible for the difference. Even if the same teacher taught both classes, the teacher may have preferred one approach to the other, or may have even liked the students in one class better! Class A might have been taught early in the morning, and class B right after lunch. Thus, students in class A

TABLE 5.1. *American studies comparing foreign language teaching methods*

Study	Methods	TL	n	Tests:	Speaking	LC	Reading	Write	Attitude toward method
Scherer & Wertheimer	GT, AL	German	130, 150	Year 1:	AL	AL	GT	GT	AL
				Year 2:	nd	AL	nd	GT	AL
Chastain & Woerdehoff[1]	CC, AL	Spanish	51, 48	Year 1:	AL	nd	CC	CC	
			35, 31	Year 2:	AL	nd	nd	nd	
Mueller	CC, AL	French			not given	CC	CC	CC	CC (fewer dropouts)

AL = audio-lingual
GT = grammar-translation
CC = cognitive-code
nd = no difference
[1] Includes both Chastain & Woerdehoff (1968) and Chastain (1970).

·might have been more alert. Class B might have been located near the athletic field, causing more distractions. Texts may have made a difference. There might also have been a selection bias on the part of the students; some may have deliberately enrolled in class A because they knew it was "special". The teacher can certainly add other potential confounds. (For more technical discussion, see Campbell and Stanley, 1963.)

Many of the methodological problems can be reduced. If approach A *consistently* does better in many studies, involving different classrooms with many students in different schools, that is, if A is reliably superior in a variety of conditions using a variety of measures, the results of classroom experiments are at least worth considering, especially if they are consistent with conclusions derived from other sources, e.g. second language acquisition theory.

(a) American studies of AL, GT, and CC

Table 5.1 summarizes several comparisons of teaching methods all of which lasted one or two years. These studies were all concerned with foreign language teaching in the United States, comparing the audio-lingual system with either grammar-translation (GT) or cognitive-code (CC).

Scherer and Wertheimer (1964) found some differences between audio-lingual (AL) and grammar-translation (GT) after year one, differences that appeared to reflect the modality each method emphasized. These differences were attenuated after the second year, and combined scores for sub-tests showed no significant differences between the two methods. It was concluded that students tend to do well in those areas emphasized in the teaching method.

Chastain and Woerdehoff (1968) and Chastain (1970) found similar results after comparing audio-lingual and cognitive-code teaching, finding some differences after year one, differences that could plausibly be traced to those skills emphasized in the method used, but no differences after year two. Chastain (1970) also noted that males tended to do better with AL, while females did better in CC sections. We return to these interesting findings later.

Mueller (1971) limited his study to one year, comparing AL and CC teaching. For those skills tested, CC was superior, while AL classes scored at national (MLA) norms. The results of previous studies force us to ask whether this advantage would have been maintained in the second year.

Table 5.2 gives us some idea as to the degree of superiority shown by one method over another. What is obvious is that both methods result in some progress; students do better at the end of the course than at the beginning. While differences are occasionally significant, they are certainly not huge.

TABLE 5.2
Degree of superiority shown in comparative method studies (American series)

MLA Cooperative Tests:	Reading[1]	Writing[1]	Listening comp.	Speaking[2]
AL	26	59	25	51
CC	30	64	26	49

1: Significant difference in favor of CC.
2: Significant difference in favor of AL.
From: Chastain and Woerdehoff (1968).
Tests administered after one year of university level study of Spanish.

(b) The GUME project

The first group of studies looked at language teaching efficacy over one or two years, using proficiency tests. Another group of studies focussed rather on specific structures over a shorter time span. These studies are the result of the GUME project, which dealt with English as a foreign language in Sweden. The GUME project studies are summarized in Table 5.3.

The GUME project aimed to compare AL type teaching with "cognitive" methods, the latter being quite similar to the cognitive-code system. I will not present their results study-by-study, but will attempt instead to summarize the overall results; the interested reader can refer to Table 5.3 for details, or to the studies themselves (see especially von Elek and Oskarsson, 1975, for a complete review of the adult studies).

Stated very simply, the GUME project found no overall differences between what they termed "implicit" methods (similar to AL) and "explicit" methods (similar to CC) for adolescent subjects. For adult subjects, explicit methods were found to be somewhat better. The difference for adults was statistically significant, but not very large.

To go into slightly more detail for the adolescents, despite the overall finding of no differences, some sub-groups did better using explicit methods: (1) an "accelerated" class in Levin's study, (2) females, in von Elek and Oskarsson, a finding similar to that of Chastain (1970). One class in von Elek and Oskarsson's study, described as being lower than the norm in "verbal intelligence" (von Elek and Oskarsson, 1975, p. 29) was reported to have had more trouble than other classes with the explicit method.

In addition to simple comparisons of explicit and implicit methods, von Elek and Oskarsson also compared various combinations of these methods. They found that IMEX (see Table 5.3) was superior to IM alone; in other words, adding some grammatical explanation to a method based totally on pattern drills was helpful (see footnote two on Table 5.3). However, EXIM was not superior to EX: adding pattern drills to a cognitive approach did not help.

Table 5.4 is included to give the reader an idea of the degree of superiority the explicit methods showed with adult subjects in the GUME studies. As is the case with American studies described in the previous section, the differences are not large. Clearly, both groups make progress.

2. SOME PRELIMINARY CONCLUSIONS TO METHOD COMPARISON STUDIES

Taken as a whole, American and Swedish studies show only small differences, if at all, between the methods they investigated. Students make at least some progress no matter what method is used, a result that had two different kinds of reactions in the field of language teaching. Stevick (1976) noted the implicit contradiction, which he stated in the form of a riddle:

"In the field of language teaching, Method A is the logical contradiction of Method B: if the assumptions from which A claims to be derived are correct, then B cannot work, and vice-versa. Yet one

TABLE 5.3. *GUME project research comparing teaching methods*

Study	Method	Students	Materials	Results
Olsson, 1969	Implicit[1] EX Swedish EX English	Age 14	One structure (passive)	No differences
Levin, 1972	Implicit EX English EX Swedish	Ages 14-15		No overall difference; "advanced" group excells in EX Swedish
Levin, 1972	Implicit EX Swedish EX English	Age 13		No overall difference; more "able" students do well with EX Swedish, but less able do worse
Von Elek & Oskarsson, 1975	IM[2] EX	Adults n = 125	Ten lessons	EXPLICIT significantly better
Von Elek & Oskarsson, 1975	IM EX	Adults n = 91	As above	EXPLICIT significantly better
Von Elek & Oskarsson, 1975	IM EX	Age 12	As above	No difference, due to low performance of one EXPLICIT class

TABLE 5.3.—*Continued*

Study	Method	Students	Materials	Results
Von Elek & Oskarsson, 1975	EX, IM, EXIM, IMEX[3]	Adults n = 277	4 lessons on 2 structures	EX superior to IM; IMEX better than IM, but not significant; EX superior to EXIM (not predicted)
Von Elek & Oskarsson, 1975	EX, IM, EXIM, IXEM	Age 12 n = 335	4 lessons on 2 structures	Girls tend to conform to the adult pattern (see above) but boys do not

[1] IM = "implicit" (pattern drills only). EX = "explicit" (patterns drills in combination with explanation). EX Swedish = explanation in Swedish. EX English = explanation in English.

[2] IM = "structured and graded pattern drills, performed on the basis of situational pictures projected on a screen in front of the class . . . no explicit explanations, comparisons with the source language, or translation exercises" (von Elek and Oskarsson, 1975, p. 16). EX = "students were given explicit information about the syntactic characteristics of the structures being practiced . . . comparisons were made with the corresponding structures in Swedish . . . grammar was taught deductively . . . explanations and directions were given before main practice with the structure under study . . . exercises were mostly of the fill-in type or translation . . . no pattern drills were performed" (von Elek and Oskarson, 1975, p. 16–17).

[3] IMEX = identical to IM with the addition of explanation. EXIM = identical to EX with addition of oral pattern drills.

TABLE 5.4
The degree of superiority shown in comparative method studies (GUME project)

Group	Test	Pre-test	SD	Post-test	SD	Progress
IM	A	26.94	8.61	33.00	9.31	6.06
	B	23.75	7.64	27.53	7.79	3.78
	C	5.86	3.40	9.40	4.16	3.54
EX	A	25.71	6.61	36.59	9.17	10.88
	B	21.82	5.19	29.18	8.14	7.36
	C	5.65	3.28	11.84	4.39	6.19

Description of tests:
A: 60 items; Students listen to oral conversation. They choose one of three alternatives to fill in missing part of last exchange (no more than two words).
B: 50 items: described as an "ordinary multiple choice test" (p. 66).
C: 20 items: written production test; students "fill in the crucial element in incomplete English sentences. The meaning of each sentence was clarified either by the complete Swedish equivalent, or by a cue word" (p. 66).

From: Von Elek and Oskarsson (1972).

colleague is getting excellent results with A and another is getting excellent results with B. How is this possible?" (p. 104).

To apply this riddle to the results of comparative method research, we can ask how the cognitive approach, which assumes that learning becomes acquisition, can give results comparable to audio-lingual teaching, which is based on the hypothesis that we learn languages by conditioning and habit-strengthening.

Before turning to a possible answer, it should be noted that there was a different reaction: not everyone saw the contradiction Stevick saw. Many methodologists and teachers simply assumed that the solution was simply to be eclectic, to choose parts of each system in the belief that the answer must be somewhere in the middle. As fair minded as this sounds, it often resulted, in my opinion, in teachers choosing the worst from each, the parts least likely to encourage language acquisition: pattern drill from the audio-lingual system, and rule explanation from the cognitive and grammar-translation approach!

In my interpretation, the results of method comparison studies using audio-lingual, grammar-translation, and cognitive code are quite consistent with the theoretical analysis of these methods presented in the previous section: according to this analysis, none of these methods does a particularly effective job in encouraging subconscious language acquisition, although each will provide at least some, and the cognitive methods will allow somewhat more learning. This predicts the close similarly in effectiveness, and the slight superiority cognitive systems show for older subjects and the more "verbal" adolescents. It also predicts that other methods should do much, much better. Unfortunately, we do not have detailed method comparison data on all the newer methods, but some is available, and the results are quite consistent with this prediction.

3. MORE RECENT METHOD COMPARISON STUDIES

We turn now to studies that involve the newer methods, methods with better report cards, according to second language acquisition theory, than grammar-translation, audio-lingual, or cognitive-code. We do not have detailed reports on every method compared to every other, and some of the newer approaches have never been tested. The studies that have been performed, however, indicate that those methods that provide more of the input necessary for acquisition, and that "put grammar in its place", are superior to older approaches.

(a) The TPR series

Asher has done a thorough job in putting his method to the empirical test. He has compared TPR to other methods using foreign language classes and second language classes, using children and using adults. Here is a brief survey.

The TPR series with adults begins with Asher (1972), which compared students in a TPR German course with controls in a "standard" college course. Asher reported that after only 32 hours of TPR instruction, TPR students outperformed controls, who had had 150 hours of classtime, in a test of listening comprehension, and equalled controls in tests of reading and writing. Asher's students progressed nearly five times faster! This is in contrast to the very small differences seen in older comparative method experiments comparing audio-lingual, cognitive-code, and grammar-translation.

Asher, Kusudo and de la Torre (1974) compared TPR students studying Spanish at the first year university level with AL controls. After 45 hours of TPR instruction, students outperformed controls who had had 150 hours in listening comprehension, and equaled controls' performance on a reading test (Pimsleur Spanish Proficiency Test).

After 45 additional hours of instruction, TPR students performed beyond the 50th percentile on a Spanish proficiency test designed for students with 150 hours on all skills.

Asher (1977a) compared 30 ESL students using TPR to controls using audio-lingual instruction, and reported that TPR students out-performed controls who had had the same amount of training (120 hours) but who had started at a higher level class.

TPR studies have also been done using children as subjects. Asher (1977b) is really three experiments in one, all involving Spanish as a foreign language in grades five through nine. In Experiment I, TPR classes in grade six, and a class consisting of seventh and eighth graders were compared to grade nine controls. The controls covered similar material, but their instruction focussed on repetition, and formal in-struction in reading and writing, "emphasizing Spanish grammar". All groups had a total of 40 hours of classtime. All TPR classes (seven dif-ferent classes in all) exceeded the controls on a test of written produc-tion (subjects were asked to write a short story based on a cartoon, and were graded on the number of meaningful expressions produced).

In Experiment II, nine elementary school TPR classes, from grades five through eight, and an adult education TPR class, were compared with two control classes from grades seven through nine. This time, TPR classes had only 20 hours of instruction while controls had 200 hours of instruction similar to that described in Experiment I. The test used was the "Spanish Picture Test for Listening", which asked stu-dents to judge whether a given sentence was true or false in relation to a picture. All TPR classes, with the exception of grade five, outper-formed controls after 100 hours, and the adult class, after only 20 hours, outperformed controls after 200 hours. Similar results were ob-tained using a reading test.

In Experiment III, fifth and sixth grade TPR and control classes were compared on tests that measured fluency (e.g. "Write as many Spanish orders or sentences as you can recall . . ."). Both groups had equal classtime. TPR students did significantly better than controls on both fluency tasks.

The TPR results are clear and consistent, and the magnitude of superiority of TPR is quite striking. Even the one sub-group that did not turn out to be superior (grade five in Experiment II above) can be explained: the TPR advantage was outweighed by the fact that the controls were older, and, as mentioned in Chapter II, older children are known to be faster acquirers (Krashen, Long and Scarcella, 1979).

(b) Other input methods compared

A variety of studies have been done examining the efficacy of methods that, like TPR, focus on providing comprehensible input and do not force early production. None of these methods has been analyzed in the previous section, since they are not "standard" or widely used, but they strengthen both the case for TPR and the hypothesis that methods allowing a silent period will do better than methods that do not, even when "speaking skills" are tested directly.

Gary (1975) examined children studying Spanish as a foreign language over a period of five months. Her experimental group did not speak at all for the first 14 weeks but, instead, had to produce "active responses" that demonstrated comprehension. Also, they were not forced to speak for much of the next seven weeks. The experimental group was shown to be superior to the control group in listening comprehension and equal in speaking, despite the fact that the controls had more "practice" in speaking.

Postovsky (1974) used students at the Defence Language Institute, studying Russian in an intensive 12 week course, six hours per day, in a fairly standard audio-lingual course. The "experimental" group did not speak for the first four weeks, but wrote their responses. The two groups were combined after four weeks. At mid-terms, the experimental group excelled in reading, writing, and speaking tests (especially with respect to "control of grammar" and "reading aloud"), and after 12 weeks, they were significantly better in listening comprehension.

Swaffer and Woodruff (1978) examined the effects of a first year college German course taught at the University of Texas. As is the case with the studies just cited, their approach was not exactly any of the standard ones described in the first part of this chapter, but it fits the requirements for providing optimal input for acquisition and for putting learning in its place very well. The first four weeks of the course were TPR based, with the emphasis switching to reading "for global meaning" (p. 28). Students were not required to speak at all in German for the first two weeks of the class, and "thereafter students were encouraged to speak on a voluntary basis" (p. 28). Also, "overt corrections of beginning students' production errors (was) kept at a minimum" (p. 28). Low filter strength was further encouraged by the use of relaxation exercises and yoga breathing. Also, "except for a brief (five-minute) question and answer period at the close of each hour, German was the exclusive language of instruction" (p. 28). No drill was used, and the only grammar taught was those features "considered essential for listening and reading comprehension" (p. 30). Swaffer and Woodruff's method thus appears to supply comprehensible input in quantity, using techniques that encourage a lower affective filter, and does not encourage the over-use of the Monitor.

The Swaffer and Woodruff program was evaluated in several ways, and all indicated clearly that the method was a huge improvement over other approaches. First, as compared to previous years, more students continued on to second semester German. Second, German courses taught the new way received much better evaluations from the students. Third, students completing the course performed well above the national norms on the Modern Language Association reading and listening tests (70th and 68th percentiles), and last, student self-report of their own abilities was, in my opinion, amazing: 78% of the students finishing the first year "expressed confidence that they could read German and grasp main ideas at least most of the time" (p. 32); 48% said they could understand spoken German at least most of the time. I do not know of control data for this last question, but from experience, these responses are quite unusual.[2]

(c) Suggestopedia research

While there have been reports of students learning 1000 words per day using Suggestopedia, in the normal one month intensive course, students cover about 2000 words. Lozanov is quoted as saying that "after completing the course, the students can express themselves freely within the framework of their lexical capacity, and can read newspapers and books." (Interview published in *Pravda*, reprinted in Ostrander and Schroeder, 1976, p. 74.) These are excellent results, but are not superhuman—the month's course, as noted earlier, is quite intensive, meeting four hours per day, six days a week, for a total of nearly 100 hours. In terms of classhours alone, this is equivalent to more than one year of study at the university level. If students can indeed "get by" in conversation in the target language and read many things in it as well, Lozanov's approach may be just about as successful as other "input methods", such as the method used by Swaffer and Woodruff, who report similar results.

Bushman and Madsen (1976) put Suggestopedia to the experimental test in a small scale study done at Brigham Young University. (Lozanov has carried out extensive experimentation which reportedly demonstrate the superiority of Suggestopedia over AL-type methods. Details of these studies are not available to me. For a very critical review, see Scovel, 1979.) Six different classes at BYU, teaching Finnish as a foreign language, with an average of seven students in each class were used. Two control classes were taught "with a modified audio-lingual approach" (p. 34). Two classes were taught using the "full" Suggestopedia treatment and two with a modified treatment. The modified Suggestopedia classes followed all aspects of Suggestopedia but lacked music, the easy chairs, and the "living room environment". They were held instead in ordinary classrooms. Each class received 10 hours of instruction and covered similar linguistic material. To control for teacher effect, two instructors taught all three treatments.

Suggestopedia students in both full and modified classes clearly out-performed controls in a vocabulary test and were "vastly superior" in a test of "communication". (In this test, students were rated on their success in conveying a message to a native speaker.) There were no significant differences between Suggestopedia classes and controls on a grammar test or in a pronunciation test; this result supports the hypothesis that Suggestopedia was superior to the control group, since control classes had far more work on pronunciation and grammar in the form of pattern drills and repetition exercises.

Bushman and Madsen also probed students' personal reactions to the different treatments, and reported no differences between groups: there was no difference in measured affect between Suggestopedic and control groups. This conflicts, to some extent, with reports from the Canadian Public Service Commission, in their report of a full one-month French course. They reported changed attitudes toward language learning ("learning" used here in the general sense), and even "a real and total change in the person himself" (p. 33). Just as Lozanov maintains happens in Suggestopedia, Canadian researchers report "the student discovered new capabilities in himself, became aware of what he was able to do, realized the extent of his creativity and his potential; he 'found himself', which gave him more self-confidence and self-assurance" (p. 33). In our terms, they became aware of the reality of their own second language acquisition capacity and the fact that it remains very powerful in the adult.

C. Alternatives to Methods

The previous section attempted to show several things. First, that we can analyze all commonly used approaches to classroom second language teaching in terms of the requirements for optimal input presented in Chapter III and the criteria for teaching conscious grammar rules, as presented in Chapter IV. Second, it was seen that certain methods satisfied these requirements and criteria better than others. Third, it was claimed that the available applied linguistics research reveals that those methods that are shown to be superior in method comparison research come closer to satisfying the criteria that derive from second language acquisition theory.

What we can conclude from this survey and review is that there is no one way to teach, no one method that is clearly the best. Some methods are clearly more effective than others, however, and the claim made here is that the same underlying principles will hold for any successful second language teaching program, the principles outlined in Chapters III and IV.

The purpose of this section is to explore ways of helping people acquire second languages that go beyond classroom methods. In the sections that follow, I will review what I consider the essential function of the classroom to be, and some limitations inherent in all classroom methods. Following this, I will discuss some possibilities in language teaching that are consistent with my views on the role of the classroom, and which, at the same time, bypass or avoid some problems that arise with classroom methods.

1. FUNCTION OF THE CLASSROOM

Quite simply, the role of the second or foreign language classroom is to bring a student to a point where he can begin to use the outside world for further second language acquisition. As expressed in Chapter II this means we have to provide students with enough comprehensible input to bring their second language competence to the point where they can begin to understand language heard "on the outside", read, and participate in conversations. Since they will be less than fully competent, we also need to provide them with tools for encouraging and regulating input.

In other words, all second language classes are transitional, and no second language class can be expected to do the entire job. As discussed in Chapter III, second language classes are best thought of as places to gain comprehensible input in early stages, when the acquirer does not yet have the competence to understand the input provided on the outside.

2. THE SECOND LANGUAGE CLASSROOM AND REQUIREMENT #2

As we have seen, many of the newer methods make valiant attempts to meet requirement #2 of Chapter III, to provide input that is genuinely interesting and relevant. The Natural Approach attempts to do this by focussing on personal topics, Community Language Learning by having the students generate their own input. The literature contains many other useful and interesting suggestions as to how to solve the problem of what to talk about: Stevick (1980) has an excellent discussion of the possibility of using poetry for second language students, and Winn-Bell Olsen (1977) has numerous other suggestions.

There are two fundamental problems with any attempt to meet requirement #2 in the second language classroom, however. The first is that what is of interest to some people may not be of interest to others. Stevick notes this in relation to his poetry experiment: one teacher who tried poetry noted that for her students, "poetry just isn't their thing; they prefer politics" (p. 225). Stevick also notes that some students may object to humanistic approaches, such as Community Language Learning, that promote personal growth along with second language acquisition: "Some (students) . . . will eagerly accept a 'humanistic' language course as an arena, or as a medium, in which to find new adventures in discovering themselves and other people, and in which they can go on to become more than they had been before. Others of them, however, may decide that the language class is not a place where they choose to confront issues of alienation, or of personal values . . . they may just want to be taught well. . . . We must respect this decision" (p. 293).

What is perhaps a more fundamental problem is that the second language classroom is seen, by many students and teachers, as an artificial linguistic environment regardless of attempts to promote "real" communication. The fact that it is a classroom, and the fact that the class is called "Spanish" or "English", of itself may subvert any effort to meet requirement two, and may prevent students from fully focussing on the meaning of what is said. In other words, the filter may always be "up", to some extent, and many students will never get so interested in what is being said that they forget it is in a second language.

There are other limitations of the classroom that are not related to its failure to fully satisfy requirement two. As mentioned in Chapter III, there is really no way the classroom can provide the variety of second language use necessary for real competence in a second language, no matter how varied the presentation, no matter how many different situations are used in role playing activities. There is also no way the classroom can provide the quantity of input required for truly advanced competence in a second language. These are not real problems, when we consider what the classroom is for. If the student can make the transition to the real world, if the student can begin to use the outside for comprehensible input, both quantity and variety will be provided.

3. THE ALTERNATIVES

We will examine a number of possible alternatives and supplements in the sections that follow, and, as we did with language teaching methods earlier, analyze them according to the predictions made by second language acquisition theory and survey what empirical evidence there is that confirms that these approaches are effective. We will first look at some very obvious supplementary activities to the second language classroom, conversation (the real thing, with native speakers of the target language) and pleasure reading, then move to some ideas and programs that have met with real success in some contexts and that could be extended to other contexts.

(a) Conversation

Before making the prediction that "conversation with native speakers" is good for second language acquisition, I need to define conversation in a limited way: conversation here refers only to interaction with a native speaker who is motivated to try to help the second language acquirer understand, and who is genuinely interested in the acquirer as a person. In other words, conversation with "foreigner talk", if it is necessary, and with a real or potential friend, business associate, etc.

There will be no attempt to demonstrate that this sort of conversation has any effect on conscious learning. It only could if the conversational partner were a language teacher and/or the acquirer were an extremely gifted inductive learner. It does appear to be the case, however, that conversation defined in this way has the maximum impact on subconscious acquisition. The following analysis demonstrates what to most lay people is completely obvious, that conversation with someone who is interested in interacting with you, and who is trying to help you understand what he is saying, is good for second language acquisition.

Requirements for optimal input

(i) *Comprehensible*. If meaning is successfully negotiated, if the conversational partner is able to adjust his speech, use extra-linguistic information and context, and if the acquirer has enough linguistic competence and can regulate the quality of input, the input provided in conversation will be comprehensible.

(ii) *Interesting/relevant*. Conversation has the best chance of meeting this requirement of all the methods we have considered. It has the best chance of achieving total focus on the message and of bringing the acquirer to the point of forgetting that the input is in another language.

(iii) *Not grammatically sequenced*. This requirement is clearly satisfied.

(iv) *Quantity*. Conversation certainly has the potential for satisfying this requirement, depending on the personal circumstances of the acquirer.

(v) *Filter strength*. In free conversation with a sympathetic native speaker, filter strength should be low. In general, there is little or no error correction for form and most people do not demand perfect accuracy or complete utterances, as do language teachers. The topic of conversation is of course unpredictable but is generally of far greater interest than anything that goes on in a classroom, and this also will contribute to a lower level of anxiety and a low filter. A possible tension-raiser in free conversation is the chance of the acquirer "getting in over his head", and not understanding what is said to him. If he is prepared, if he has tools for conversational management and is willing to use them, this is less of a problem.

(vi) *Tools for conversational management*. Conversation will give the acquirer a chance to practice the tools he has learned and give him perhaps the best opportunity to acquire new ones.

(b) Pleasure reading

As was the case with conversation, covered in the previous section, I will define "reading" in a special way. I do not mean intensive reading, analysis of written prose, reading and then answering questions for content, or reading as preparation for discussion or writing assignments. The sort of reading to be analyzed here is extensive, and concerns subject matter that the student would read in his first language for pleasure. It is completely voluntary. In doing pleasure reading, readers have the option of skipping whole sections they find either too difficult or less interesting (e.g. detailed descriptions in fiction). They even have the option of putting the book or story down and selecting another after reading a few pages. They can skip words they do not understand, if they think they are following the main point, and they have the option, of course, of looking up every word, if that is their style.

In other words, we are considering pure pleasure reading. What is read depends on the student and what is available to him. For some people, it may be mystery novels, for others, science fiction, and for others, comic books. The only requirement is that the story or main idea be comprehensible and that the topic be something the student is genuinely interested in, that he would read in his first language.

I will not try to show that pleasure reading has any effect on learning. The analysis, as done with conversation in the previous section, will be restricted to the effects of pleasure reading on acquisition.

Requirements for optimal input

(i) *Comprehensible*. We have defined pleasure reading as reading that is comprehensible, so there is no problem here. I would like to note, however, that pleasure reading is made comprehensible by the reader's own selection of passages and texts, and by the rejection of reading material that is too difficult. The success of pleasure reading thus depends on the reader's willingness to find material at his level and reject material that is beyond him.

(ii) *Interesting/relevant*. Reading as defined here is by definition interesting and relevant, since the student has the option (which must be exercised) of only reading things that are of personal interest.

(iii) *Not grammatically sequenced*. This requirement is met, unless the student insists on reading specially-prepared pedagogical materials.

(iv) *Quantity*. Reading certainly has the potential for satisfying this requirement. The only problems are practical: the availability of materials, their cost, and the students' time.

(v) *Filter level*. If the student is able to find materials that are comprehensible and that are interesting, this requirement is easily met. There is no frustration caused by incomprehensible messages, no early demands for output, no demands for premature grammatical accuracy. The pleasure reader should be completely off the defensive.

(vi) *Tools for conversational management*. Pleasure reading might even make a contribution toward meeting this requirement, if the texts read include some dialogue.

At this point I would like to include a personal observation about pleasure reading. I have been attempting, over the last few years, to improve my French, largely via pleasure reading, an attempt that has been successful. Mostly through input, I have increased my competence from "advanced beginner" to "high intermediate". I define the intermediate level in the following way: Requiring only some "downshifting" on the part of a native speaker to be able to converse easily, and being able to read most texts without a dictionary, without necessarily knowing every word. I can now read a great deal of French without a dictionary, and even derive real pleasure from it. Being a Monitor user and someone with an intrinsic interest in the structure of language, I occasionally look at grammar books (the ones that gave me so much trouble in high school). I have noticed, to my surprise, that the reading passages at the end of the elementary grammar book still give me trouble! I find them more difficult than "raw", unedited French, French written for native speakers. The reason "pedagogical" passages are more difficult for the intermediate is that they are packed full of subjunctives, conditionnel passé, futur anterieur, and all manner of infrequent vocabulary! In reading through these passages, I found them difficult to understand, and extremely frustrating: the topics were not even of mild interest, and I felt my affective filter going up, as I encountered word after word I did not know. My frustration was further aggravated by the fact that I realized that I was having trouble with a text designed for second year students!

What this experience suggests is that our intermediate students may find real texts, read for interest and pleasure, easier than our pedagogical materials. Moreover, if the above analysis is correct, it may be that free pleasure reading will result in more acquisition of the language.

For those who object on the grounds that reading in language courses should be restricted to the classics, to serious literature, I can only say that the ability to read "literature" will be facilitated by the development of a high level of competence in the second language. I personally *agree* with those who feel that a major goal of language instruction in the university is the study of the literature written in the second language. I do not think, however, that we need to start out with serious literature immediately. Devoting several months to free reading of easier material might be the fastest way to bring students to the point where they can read great literature in a second language without a serious language barrier.

Summary

Both conversation and pleasure reading have the potential of meeting the requirements for optimal input for acquisition very well. We have reached the conclusion that an interesting conversation in a second language, and reading something for pleasure, are excellent language lessons. This comes as no surprise to the millions of people who have acquired language using only these "methods", and have acquired them very well.

(c) Using subject matter for language teaching

Another class of alternatives to classroom teaching involves the use of subject matter in the second language classroom, using the second language as a vehicle, as a language of presentation and explanation. I do not mean by subject matter teaching what is known as submersion, mixing second language students in with native speakers. I do mean special classes for second language students, classes in which no native speakers participate as students, in which teachers make some linguistic and cultural adjustments in order to help their students understand.

In this section, we will first put subject matter teaching through the familiar analysis according to the predictions made by second language acquisition theory. As was the case with conversation and pleasure reading, there will be no attempt to claim that subject matter teaching helps conscious learning in any way. We will then turn to several concrete manifestations of subject matter teaching: the successful immersion programs underway in Canada and the United States, and some untried possibilities for the use of subject matter in second language situations.

Requirements for optimal input

(i) *Comprehensible*. Subject matter teaching will be of use for acquisition only to the extent it is comprehensible. What this means is that different subjects may be of more use to students at different levels. Cazden (1979) points out that one could make a case that mathematics is ideal for teaching in an imperfectly acquired L2. There is a limited vocabulary, less interactional demand than in some other subjects, and considerable extra-linguistic support to aid comprehension. (She points out, however, that complex "story problems" might be an obstacle for beginning level students.) Students with more second language proficiency could handle subject matter that is more displaced in time and space, that supply less concrete referents, such as history and literature. The point is not simply that second language students can survive in subject matter classes, but also that they will receive comprehensible input that will help them improve more in the second language.

The comprehensibility requirement argues against submersion, against mixing second language acquirers in with native speakers before the second language acquirers reach higher levels of proficiency: the presence of native speakers insures that a good proportion of the language heard by the intermediate acquirer will not be comprehensible.

(ii) *Interesting/relevant*. Subject matter may not always be interesting, but it is relevant. When students are focussed on the subject matter, there is a very good chance they will be focussed off the form of the language it is presented in. Subject matter affords a good chance of meeting the "forgetting principle", of the student being so focussed on what is said that he is not aware of how it is said.

(iii) *Not grammatically sequenced*. This requirement is also clearly met. In fact, it is hard to imagine subject matter teaching not meeting it. This would require contextualizing beyond our wildest dreams.

(iv) *Quantity*. Clearly, there is the potential of supplying great quantities of input this way. Subject matter teaching in the second language automatically reaches the pedagogical ideal of filling the entire class hour with comprehensible input.

(v) *Filter strength*. Subject matter teaching may invoke, and in fact require, some minimum amount of anxiety. This anxiety, however, is not directed at the language it is presented in, if the message is comprehensible. Subject matter teachers can keep the language portion relatively anxiety-free and the filter down by:

(1) insuring comprehensibility of the message;
(2) not demanding premature production;
(3) not demanding full grammatical accuracy from students.

Subject matter second language teachers might consider testing procedures that require less linguistic production (short answers instead of long essays), and class discussion procedures that take students' linguistic capacities into consideration (not correcting errors on form or even allowing use of the L1 where practical, as in the Natural Approach). The point to remember is that further language acquisition comes with more comprehensible input, from teacher talk and reading, and not from demands for production.

(vi) *Tools for conversational management.* Subject matter teaching may not provide the tools necessary to maintain conversations on the outside, but it can lead to the learning and acquisition of academic communicative competence in another culture. In a class composed entirely of immigrants and foreign students, teachers can be aware of cultural differences in academic behavior and teach classroom behavior, either via learning, for obvious aspects of classroom behavior (standing or not standing when the teacher enters the room; what sort of paper to hand in homework on, etc.) or acquisition, for more subtle aspects.

Summary

Subject matter teaching has, thus, the full potential for encouraging language acquisition. This may be a good place to point out that by subject matter teaching, I do not mean "English for Special Purposes" or for "Academic Purposes". ESP and EAP are, to my understanding, standard language teaching classes whose syllabi are based on an analysis of the tasks students will face and the language they will need (see, for example, Robinson, 1980). Subject matter teaching appears to me to be fundamentally different, although it may meet many of the goals ESP is designed for. While ESP requires a detailed analysis of the syntax, vocabulary, and discourse of a subfield, to be developed into a syllabus and presented bit by bit, subject matter teaching focusses only on the topic, the information or skill to be learned, the assumption being that much of the syntax, vocabulary, and discourse style will be *acquired* along with the subject matter. (This idea is not entirely foreign to ESP; several ESP courses emphasize "authentic activities". See, for example, Robinson, p. 39; Widdowson, cited in Robinson, p. 23.)

(d) Evidence for subject matter teaching: the immersion programs

Immersion bilingual programs have demonstrated what is possible in second language acquisition using subject matter. In immersion programs, initially monolingual majority children are schooled in a minority language (French in Anglophone Canada; Spanish in the United States). They are taught their academic subjects totally in the second language. In what is known as "total early immersion", input in the second language begins in kindergarten. Late immersion programs may begin later, after the children have had at least one year of instruction in the second language.

The immersion programs appear to be successful in many ways. The many reports that have been published confirm over and over that immersion students acquire high levels of competency in the second language (while they may not reach native-like levels, they outperform peers who have had standard foreign language classes), they make normal progress in school, doing as well in subject-matter as monolinguals, and they do not fall behind peers in first language development (for reviews, see Lambert and Tucker, 1972; Swain, 1974).

Cohen and Swain (1976) discuss these successes in light of the lack of success of many other types of bilingual programs. Among the differences between immersion and other programs, these characteristics of immersion may help to explain its success. Cohen and Swain point out that in early immersion "all kindergarten pupils are unilingual in L1. In essence, the successful program starts out as a *segregated* one linguistically" (p. 47). As mentioned above, this raises the students' chances of getting comprehensible input, since teachers cannot gauge their speech only to native speakers, leaving second language acquirers behind.

Cohen and Swain point out several other factors that, in our terms, lead to a lower affective filter in immersion programs. The linguistic segregation "eliminates the kind of ridicule that students exert on less proficient performers" (p. 47), teachers have positive expectations, and the program is voluntary. Also, "in kindergarten, the children are permitted to speak in the L1 until they are ready to speak in the L2" (p. 48). Thus, a Silent Period is allowed.

The immersion experience, it needs to be emphasized, does not bring these students to native speaker levels, and immersion students' second language competence may have gaps, especially when it comes to interaction abilities in casual conversation. (See Conners, Menard and Singh, 1978, who report problems immersion students have in this area; on the other hand, see Bruck, Lambert and Tucker, 1974, for a report on what immersion children can do in this area.) It is thought that these gaps exist only because the second language input does not include input from peers. Immersion children hear the second language only from the teacher and only in class. Considering this limitation, their achievements are remarkable.

The immersion programs show us what is possible linguistically from subject matter teaching, when social and psychological problems are eliminated or reduced. They provide strong empirical evidence that subject matter teaching can not only teach subject matter but the language it is taught in as well, as long as the input is made comprehensible.

(e) Other possibilities in subject matter teaching

There is no reason that subject matter teaching cannot be extended to other second language acquisition domains, and utilized to at least supplement the second language classroom and provide some help in the difficult transition from language class to real world. One such domain is the university. I will discuss here the situation in the American university, but the principles can be generalized to any higher education situation in which large numbers of second language speakers are enrolled.

Practically every large American university has an ESL program. They range in quality, of course, from excellent to sub-standard, but regardless of quality, it is my feeling that foreign students regard them as an obstacle. ESL is, moreover, perceived as irrelevant at just those levels that both theory and applied research conclude it is irrelevant: at the "intermediate" level. Many foreign students no longer feel they need ESL when they are able to survive in regular classes, yet well-meaning administrators feel that for the foreign students' own protection, their level of English competence should be higher.

Applied research confirms that intermediate ESL is not productive. The studies of Uphsur (1968) and Mason (1971), reviewed in Chapter II, which showed that extra ESL does not help when students are enrolled in regular classes, included only students at this level.

For some "good language learners" (acquirers), the answer to this problem may very well be the elimination of the "ESL" requirement or placing the level of required proficiency in English lower. For others, however, this would not be the best solution. The feelings of ESL administrators that some students need "more" is quite real and justified. All too often, students are able only to survive in classes where the language demand is very low, and/or they end up relying heavily on native language help, in the form of texts or classmates.

Subject matter teaching may be part of the answer to this "transition" problem. What I propose is that the university consider classes for international students in subject matter, classes in which international students are in fact "segregated", to be offered in all areas foreign students are likely to enroll, and to be made available on a voluntary basis. Such courses would give full academic credit and cover regular subject matter. The main differences would be the fact that the professor or instructor would be sensitive to the needs of international students and their linguistic deficiencies, and be aware of the fact that the students may be unfamiliar with American academic practices.[3]

The absence of native speakers in the class would help to insure that the input is comprehensible for the same reason immersion provides more comprehensible input than submersion. Both the level of complexity of the classroom presentation and the amount and complexity of outside reading would be regulated to the linguistic level of the class. Other modifications that would help comprehensibility are also possible: We would expect lower demands on student output, including a tolerance for errors (many of which will be eliminated by more comprehensible input over time) and tests requiring short answers in lieu of long essays.

International classes can not only take into account and help eliminate linguistic deficiencies, they can also help fill several other gaps in international students' knowledge. They can provide an anxiety-free, or at least anxiety-low, initial exposure to the American style of education. Students will be able to acquire the subtleties of American classroom style behavior, and learn many of the obvious differences that exist between what is acceptable behavior in a classroom in their country and what is expected in the American university. In other words, international classes can give students some of the tools for communicative competence in the context of the classroom.[4,5]

(i) *The New England problem*. International students can also fill foreign students in on cultural information that is presupposed in courses for native speakers and American students. Thomas Jablonski of the History Department at USC has been teaching an American history course exclusively for international students for the last three years, and he has pointed out to me that many international students lack information that American professors take for granted. A clear example is his finding that many of his students did not have a clear idea of where New England was, a point of information that was essential to a particular presentation. Information gaps such as this one are not obvious, and probably abound. They have a better chance of being filled in international classes, where students are encouraged to ask questions, and where instructors presuppose less.

(ii) *The role of ESL in subject matter teaching*. The establishment of international classes does not signal the end of ESL, although it may result in some modification, and hopefully improvement, of our ESL offerings.

First, while we can imagine pushing subject matter classes "down" to the lowest linguistic proficiency level possible, we may always have a need for the second language class at the beginning level. It is an empirical question just how much competence and instruction (i.e. comprehensible input) is necessary before students can begin special subject matter classes, but there will, in most cases, be a need for a general class at the beginning.[6]

Second, as discussed in Chapter IV there are many aspects of language that are consciously learnable, both in "grammar" (mostly morphology for the majority of students) and discourse (conscious rules for the fine points of writing, including punctuation and organization).

Also, a large percentage of foreign students may desire more English than they can get in the classroom situation in order to facilitate participation in American social life. Intermediate level classes that focus on providing the tools for communicative competence and conversational management would be very helpful for students with more integrative orientation and/or who plan to remain in the United States for extended periods of time.

In addition, ESL teachers might serve the useful function of assisting and consulting with the subject matter teachers who teach international sections.

Figure 5.2 presents a schema of the possible interaction between an ESL component and an academic component.

Fig. 5.2. ESL and academic components of international students'
program at the university level

Level	ESL component	Academic component
Beginning	Classroom language teaching, focussing on topics of general interest; introduction to University life	None
Intermediate	Optional course work on 1. English grammar (Monitor) 2. Stylistics (learnable) 3. Conversation (see text)	International sections of subject matter courses (optional)
Advanced	None	Regular sections of subject matter courses

See Note 6 for suggestions for a transition between the beginning and intermediate levels.

(iii) *The need for applied linguistics research*. If I were simply to assert that the International Students program as outlined above was "the answer" to our foreign student problems in the American university, I would be repeating the sins of the past, claiming that we need only consult theory in order to come to the correct form of practice. To return to the message of Chapter I, this is not sufficient. At least the following questions need to be asked and answered with empirical data:

1. Do students in international classes acquire more English?
2. Do they learn as much subject matter as those who elect to take standard courses?
3. Do they have more success in their studies over the long run?
4. Do they feel more comfortable in the academic environment?

Clearly, the answers to these questions will be of both theoretical and practical interest.

(iv) *Adult ESL and subject matter*. The ESL profession in the United States has already been experimenting with a form of subject matter teaching at the "adult education" level, in courses designed for adult immigrants to the United States. (This is another example of teachers and administrators not waiting for theory and research, but discovering "what works" on their own; see Chapter I for discussion.) S. Brown (1979) describes one experiment of this sort in Los Angeles.

While part of ESL instruction in Brown's school is "the more traditional grammar-oriented" style class, students also participate in units covering "life situations" topics that last from two to four weeks. Examples include the use of community services (post-office, library, etc.), consumer education, employment (covering classified ads, employment agencies, unions, etc.), family life (e.g. wedding invitations, birthday parties, etc.), citizenship (e.g. traffic and parking tickets, voting, taxes, etc.), and other "life situations". Teachers can use guest speakers, films, field trips, and commercial materials in helping students understand the "mechanics of life" in a new country.

Again, as is usually the case, no evidence is yet available confirming the utility of such a program. Two of the three sources of inspiration for programs presented in Chapter I, second language acquisition theory and teacher insight/intuition, predict, however, that such programs will be of great use for language acquisition, in addition to their obvious practical value, as long as the input is comprehensible.[7]

D. Comments on Achievement Testing

In this section, we will consider the implications of second language acquisition theory on testing. I will begin with a very short review of what we normally consider to be relevant in selecting tests for second language achievement, and the kinds of test options we choose from. As was the case in describing language teaching systems earlier, this is not done in an effort to supply new information, but to establish a common set of assumptions; I will assume, therefore, some familiarity with the standard literature in second language testing (e.g. Harris, 1969; Valette, 1977; Oller, 1979). I will then focus on one major consideration, what Oller (1979) terms the "instructional value" of a test, and suggest that if we take this property of tests seriously, second language acquisition theory severely limits our options in achievement test selection.

1. NORMAL CONSIDERATIONS IN TEST EVALUATION AND SELECTION

The standard literature on tests and measurements tells us that a good test needs to meet certain standards. It must be reliable, that is, it must consistently give the same results under different conditions. It must also be valid, that is, it should really measure what it is supposed to measure. Testing experts also advise us to make sure a test is practical, that it is economical, easy to score, and easy to interpret (Harris, 1969, pp. 21–22). Harris also suggests that we consider the face validity of a test, "the way the test *looks*—to the examinees, test administrators, educators, and the like" (p. 21), noting that if a test does not appear to be a valid measure, whether it is or not in reality, students and teachers will not take it seriously.

Teachers and administrators in second language programs now have a wide variety of tests to choose from. Tests are usually classified according to the modality they use (reading, writing, speaking, listening) and their place among the discrete point/integrative continuum. Discrete-point tests are tests that attempt "to focus attention on one point of grammar at a time" (Oller, 1979, p. 37). An extreme discrete point test requires a minimum of knowledge of context outside the sentence containing the item tested. Here is an example of a discrete-point item:

Mary _____ in New York since 1960.
   a. is living
   b. has lived
   c. lives

Integrative tests, on the other hand, make no attempt to focus on one aspect of language at a time; according to Oller (1979), "Whereas discrete items attempt to test knowledge of language one bit at a time, integrative tests attempt to assess a learner's capacity to use many bits all at the same time, and possibly while exercising several presumed components of a grammatical system, and perhaps more than one of the traditionally-recognized skills or aspects of skills" (p. 37). Examples of tests that are usually considered integrative include reading comprehension, cloze tests, dictation, compositions, and tests of oral communication.

2. INSTRUCTIONAL VALUE

I would like to focus here on only one aspect of one kind of testing, the instructional value of achievement tests, and make only one point. Tests have a huge impact on classroom behavior, and need to be selected to encourage students to engage in activities that will help them acquire more language. It may be that the instructional value criterion is possibly of more importance than the criterion listed above.

Stated simply, the sort of test selected has a huge impact on the class. If students know in advance what sort of test will be used to measure their achievement in a course, they will, naturally, tend to study for the test, and teachers will feel pressure to teach to the test. I suggest we harness this natural tendency and select tests that will encourage student preparation that in itself causes more second language acquisition.[8]

Jones (1979) gives a good example of the results of harnessing this tendency, which he calls the "backwash" effect. In teaching an elementary German course at the university level, he decided to give an oral midterm, a short (five minute) conversation done on a one-on-one basis. Jones noted on this test that few of his students were proficient in the area of social communication: "When I greeted them, asked how they were, or said good-bye, the majority of them had no response but awkward laughter, even though they had practiced these protocols in the classroom" (p. 56).

The effect of this midterm experience on the class was striking: "The teaching assistants told me shortly after the first oral test that students were begging for more oral practice in the classroom. The situation was much different on the second test. They were waiting for me. It was obvious that they had made a great effort to develop speaking proficiency in a very short period of time. The test not only gave me vital information about their ability to speak the language, but it also served as a motivating influence for them to spend more time developing this important skill" (pp. 56–57).

What if Jones' oral test had failed the usual standards for reliability? What if, for example, the rating had been made by several judges and their interrater reliability had not met the required level? The powerful backwash effect, I am suggesting, may, in certain situations, more than make up for this problem.

The basic problem I am speaking of here is the fact that practice in certain types of tests does not necessarily lead to more acquisition of the second language. This factor eliminates some tests with very fine track records when judged on the basis of reliability and validity. There is no evidence, for example, that practicing cloze tests in class helps the student acquire more of the language, or improves performance on cloze tests. There is very good evidence, on the other hand, that participating in conversation, and reading for content or pleasure, do help the student acquire language. Conversational practice provides comprehensible input and helps the student acquire the tools needed for conversation with native speakers, which in turn results in more input and more language acquisition. Reading for content is also an effective way of getting input that meets the requirements for optimal input for acquisition, as we saw earlier in this chapter.

Achievement tests, I am suggesting, should meet this requirement: preparation for the test, or studying for the test, should *obviously* encourage the student to do things that will provide more comprehensible input and the tools to gain even more input when the class is over. This drastically reduces our options, but also, in a real sense, simplifies the task of achievement testing. Let us first examine what the consequences of this philosophy might be in the area of foreign language testing.

Achievement testing in foreign language classes attempts to assess whether a student has met the requirements of a given course, and sometimes whether he has satisfied a language requirement at an institution. I will deal with each of these situations in turn.

For the foreign language class, I see only two options. One of them is fairly traditional: reading comprehension. If students know in advance that they will be given a reading comprehension test, a test in which they are asked to read several short passages and answer general questions about the content of what they have read, they will be encouraged to read. They will be encouraged to study for the test in the simplest and most obvious way, and will seek out reading opportunities in the second language. As long as they know they will be presented with a variety of passages (on different topics) and as long as the questions focus on the "gist" of the passage and do not rely on one specific word or structure, it certainly will be the case that general reading for pleasure and interest will prepare them for such a test. Teachers will be encouraged to provide comprehensible reading materials, and students will be encouraged to go outside the bounds of the classroom in search of supplementary materials. Most important, if they read, they will acquire more of the target language.

The reading comprehension test is especially useful, since there is generally no problem in purchasing or constructing tests that meet the statistical requirements mentioned above. The standard literature has many suggestions on constructing reading tests (see, for example, Harris, 1969, chapter 6), and reliability measures and various types of validity measures can easily be obtained. Reading tests can be constructed that are practical and that have obvious face validity.

A second kind of test is more complicated, but, at the moment, I see no other valid options. What is needed is a test that will encourage students to engage in conversations, that requires use of the tools of communicative competence. Many standard oral tests fail to do this. A test in which the student answers questions does not require interactional ability, nor does a test in which a student simply talks or even asks questions. What is needed is a true test of conversational management.

I will attempt to give a rough description of what a test of conversational management would look like: Ideally, it would involve both tester and student in a conversation about something real, a problem that has to be solved, a topic that needs to be discussed. Second, the student would be rated on his ability to manage the conversation and communicate, not on grammatical accuracy. If, for example, the student had word-finding difficulties that resulted only in an embarrassed silence on his part, he would be graded down. If the student were able to "cover" the problem with appropriate fillers (just a moment . . . what I want to say is . . . how do you say . . . ?), he would not only not be penalized but would be graded up for having the ability to keep the conversation going and not lose the floor! Students would also be given credit for politeness and appropriateness, since a minimum amount of this knowledge is absolutely necessary for successful conversation. Most important, they would be given credit for successful communication, for successfully completing the communicative exchange. Students who were able to get the examiner to help them would also be graded more highly, the assumption being that those who can elicit needed vocabulary and help the native speaker give them comprehensible input will have more success in second language acquisition in the long run.[9]

There are predictable objections one can make to such a testing plan. Most obviously, it can be argued that such tests, especially the second one, will do nothing for the development of grammatical accuracy, and will only encourage sloppy speech, a laissez-faire, "anything goes" attitude toward language, and the establishment of permanent bad habits. Second language acquisition theory, however, makes quite different predictions: if tests of this sort encourage students to participate in conversation and develop the skills to manage conversations, they will contribute a great deal to the development of grammatical accuracy. Indeed, they will develop, perhaps, more grammatical accuracy in the long run than any other kind of measure! They will give the student the tools he needs to obtain comprehensible input, and this in turn will result in subsequent language acquisition, improvement after the term ends.

The conversational management test promises to be very difficult to grade reliably, and thanks to this unreliability, it may fail to meet acceptable standards of validity. It will be hard to train raters and hard to invent topics to discuss. Nevertheless, it has the promise of stimulating students to developing conversational skills that will enable them to use the language despite their less than perfect proficiency, thus help-ing to insure continued progress in second language acquisition after the term has ended.

One could also argue that at least some grammar testing should be included. As emphasized in Chapter II, we have not rejected the teaching of formal grammar. It has its use as a Monitor, when using the Monitor does not interfere with communication. It is therefore a por-tion of the instructional program. Shouldn't we therefore test grammar as well, in the form of testing our students' abilities to Monitor their output under conditions conducive to the use of the Monitor?

This argument appeared plausible to me at one time. Tracy Terrell presented me with a counter-argument to testing grammar, and I think he is right: if we allow grammar testing, it will grow and soon dominate the testing program, and hence the curriculum. While limited gram-mar testing is consistent with the limited role of the grammar, there is a real danger that teachers and administrators will revert to their old ways and gradually return to testing grammar exclusively!

3. LANGUAGE REQUIREMENTS

Many universities and some high schools still have language require-ments. This is usually expressed as the necessity of studying a foreign language for a given period of time, two to four semesters. If, however, the goal of the classroom is to bring students to the point where they can continue to acquire the language by using the outside world, or re-sources outside the classroom, this suggests that we should consider testing students to see whether they have reached this level: can they continue to obtain comprehensible input? The tests that probe this could be the identical ones proposed to be of maximum educational value in the preceding section: Reading comprehension and conversa-tional management are not only the most appropriate for achievement tests given at the end of the semester, but may also be the most approp-riate leaving exams. The tests ask only these questions: can the student read well enough in the second language so that he can read texts with-out having to consult a dictionary excessively and without undue pain, i.e. without what Newmark calls "crytoanalytic decoding". Is he able to communicate effectively with a native speaker who is willing to help?

Of course, I have left many serious questions unsettled, such as the range of topics to be read and discussed, the problem of requiring equal levels of proficiency in cognate, and hence more comprehensible languages, and more exotic languages, and how the passing level is determined. Some applied research may eventually help to solve them; at the moment, however, the format seems clear.

4. UNIVERSITY LEVEL ESL

Second language acquisition theory, as presented in this volume, gives no magical and obvious answer to the difficult question of ESL testing at the university level. The goal of such testing is to determine whether students know enough English to study in English. As is well known, the "backwash" effect has been a problem in this area for years: many foreign students study for the TOEFL examination exclusively, and are helped to do so by special courses designed to do just this (see discussion in Wiggon, 1979).

Applying the same arguments here that we used earlier, emphasizing the instructional value of tests, we come to the conclusion that subject matter testing would be of benefit at this level as well. This is more easily said than done; it would be prohibitively expensive to design standardized subject matter tests in all disciplines for international students. International courses, as outlined in the previous sections, may be a step in this direction, as long as they use subject matter tests as finals; a students' release from the ESL requirement could be at least partially dependent on his ability to pass international courses.

E. Some Gaps in Materials

If the conclusions we have reached in this volume are correct, it implies that we have some fairly serious gaps in our materials. Before listing where I think these gaps are, let me first of all note that materials need to meet the same requirements that methods do, as listed in Chapters III and IV. If materials are supposed to help students in language acquisition, they should either supply input that is comprehensible, interesting/relevant, and not grammatically sequenced themselves, or they should provide students with the means of obtaining such input. If materials are meant to help language learning, they should focus on rules that are learnable, portable, etc. While learning materials can be criticized, it is my impression that there is no lack of materials for this purpose, and that current texts can be useful for the language learning component of second language and foreign language courses. We will therefore focus on what sorts of materials need to be developed to encourage acquisition.

The new materials will be designed, I hope, to fill a basic need, helping beginning and intermediate students obtain comprehensible input outside the classroom. This is an obvious problem for foreign language students, and is especially crucial for students of "exotic" languages. It is also a major problem for students of commonly spoken languages and second language students; students at beginning levels do not have the competence to engage native speakers in conversation, and cannot understand radio and TV or read easily. We need materials, in addition to the input provided by the classroom, to bring students to the point where they can utilize the outside world.

One obvious and convenient source of comprehensible input is reading. As discussed earlier in this chapter, pleasure reading meets the requirements to qualify as input for acquisition very well. The problem we have today is that readers designed for second language students do not meet these requirements. What is currently available is often not comprehensible; as mentioned earlier, the only reading many foreign language students encounter are paragraphs that are loaded up with complex vocabulary and syntax. It is nearly always grammatically sequenced; writers are careful only to include syntax that the student is supposed to have studied or is currently learning. Also, there is simply not enough reading available.

The second language student needs massive amounts of comprehensible, interesting reading material, enough so that he can read for pleasure and/or interest for an hour an evening, if he wants to, for several months.

Some current texts are in the right direction, but they are flawed in several ways:

(1) The use of exercises, questions that test students on content and drill them on the grammar and vocabulary used. Teachers are, of course, free to ignore these exercises, but they often take up most of the pages of the reader. While it can be argued that exercises provide

learning, while the text provides acquisition, I think it is a dangerous practice to try to combine the two in this way. First, the necessity of answering content questions can ruin the pleasure of reading. Second, they encourage reading more for form and less for content.

The assumption underlying many of the exercises found in readers seems to be that students need "review" and "practice" on new vocabulary and grammar, otherwise they will not retain it. This is, it seems to me, a self-fulfilling prophecy. With fewer exercises, students might read more, and have a better chance of encountering these items in texts. With excessive exercises, we may be destroying our students' desire to read for pleasure and interest in the second language, thus insuring that many will indeed never see the new structures and words again.

(2) Current readers simply do not provide enough. Part of the problem is the inclusion of exercises, which take up valuable space. The reader of the future will be thick, full of reading, and on varied topics. Students will be able to pick and choose their topics. To do this, they need a lot to choose from. Simply including one story about the Wine Country of France, another about sports, and one mystery story is not enough.

(3) Finally, writers of such readers need to rid themselves of the illusion that each line, each paragraph, must count, and introduce some new structure or vocabulary item. As emphasized many times in this book, such grammatical emphasis will seriously distort any attempt to write anything of interest. We need not worry about each line. If we provide enough comprehensible input, everything the student needs will be there.

1. THE LANGUAGE LABORATORY

As many readers know, there has been a great deal of discussion and debate in the applied linguistics literature over the virtues of the language lab. In my view, it is not a question of whether the lab is "good" or "bad", but simply whether it can be used to supply input that is useful for acquisition, and thereby supplement what we can provide in class and in reading.

Not only can the lab be used in this way, but it appears to be the case that it is far easier, technologically speaking, to use the lab as a means of supplying comprehensible input than for other purposes. The traditional use of the language lab puts a tremendous technological and pedagogical burden on the teacher: the teacher is expected to monitor student output, and correct their errors. Using the lab as a source of comprehensible input is easier. Here are some possibilities: taped stories, with pictures to aid comprehension and add to enjoyment, class-type lectures, supplemented with lecture notes (on real topics, designed to supplement international classes, *not* sample lectures on random aspects of chemistry or the history of a pretend kingdom), radio programs, commercials, etc. In other words, comprehensible input, with simple aids to comprehension.

In my view, the lab should be a resource, a place students can go to get input on a variety of subject matters whenever it is convenient for them. The old view of the lab, with the vigilant drill master, does not allow this.[10]

2. A COMMENT ON FIELD TESTING OF MATERIALS

This slightly new approach to materials might also necessitate a slightly new approach to field testing. I think I can best illustrate this by relating a conversation I had several years ago with a representative of a publishing house that is active in both ESL and foreign language materials. He had come to see me because of our work on the order of acquisition of grammatical structures (e.g. Bailey, Madden and Krashen, 1974; Krashen *et al.*, 1978; Krashen *et al.*, 1976; Houck, Robertson and Krashen, 1978a) feeling that our work, and similar work done by other researchers, might give his writers a better sequence to base their readers on. He accepted it as a given fact that readers designed for students needed to be controlled for structures, and that our natural order studies would provide a superior basis for this. Book one, for example, would contain only those structures found to be early acquired, book two would add those structures slightly farther down on the natural order, etc.

I have argued against this philosophy several times in this volume. As Stevick (1980) notes, it leads to a style "which is linguistically antiseptic and emotionally sterile" (p. 203; see also his excellent discussion, pp. 203–204). I presented my arguments against this approach to this publisher's representative, and asked him what form of field testing his readers underwent. His response was that the linguistic analysis was deemed sufficient: his publishing house provides writers with a guide, indicating which structures are to be included for different levels. If the proposed texts do indeed only contain these structures, they are considered worthy and have passed the test. His purpose in seeing me was to revise this guide according to the natural order.

Here is an alternative approach to developing and field testing readers, one that is consistent with the philosophy set forth in this book. The first step is to use writers who are genuinely interested in telling, or re-telling a story, and who are interested in and sympathetic with the audience. They simply write, focussing on the story, using what they intuitively feel they need to tell it and make it comprehensible (recall Brown's advice to parents, repeated on page 65). The field test is not a syntactic analysis. It is done in order to answer these questions: do members of the intended audience understand it? Do they enjoy it? Do they find it interesting? Would they read it on their own (not as an assignment)? If the answers to these questions are in the affirmative, second language acquisition theory tells us that $i + 1$ will be there, that the reading is linguistically appropriate and it will help the reader acquire more of the target language.

We may apply similar criteria to other kinds of materials, i.e. the lab materials recommended earlier, and materials designed to help teach subject matter (see Note 10). Are they comprehensible? Are they interesting/relevant? etc. Only the students and language acquirers can answer these questions.

Let us also not forget the obvious question that needs to be asked about all materials: do they actually result in more proficiency in the target language? The *theory* predicts that if materials satisfy our requirements, this will happen, but, as emphasized in Chapter I, this is not enough. Applied linguistics research needs to confirm it.

F. Some Problems

Even if the theory presented here is totally correct, and my suggestions for application are in fact the appropriate ones, there are some serious problems that need to be mentioned before concluding. These have to do with the acceptance, by teachers and students, of language *acquisition* as primary, and comprehensible input as the means of encouraging language acquisition. These problems are caused by the fact that acquisition differs from learning in two major ways: acquisition is *slow* and *subtle*, while learning is *fast* and, for some people, *obvious*.

Acquisition takes time; it takes far more than five hours per week over nine months to acquire the subjunctive. It may, in fact, take years. Good linguists, on the other hand, can consciously learn a great deal in a very short time. Also, when we have acquired something, we are hardly aware of it. In a sense, it feels as if it was always there, and something anyone can do. Learning is different. Some people derive great pleasure from the learning and use of conscious rules, and I am one of them! "Mastering" the subjunctive in French was very satisfying for me, and I rekindle this sense of victory every time I plan and say sentences such as "Il faut que j'aille". It is sometimes hard for people like us to understand that this sort of pleasurable activity is not real language acquisition.

This leads to one major problem. Language curriculum and texts are designed by people like us, people who learn quickly and who derive satisfaction from it (Stevick's "group G", p. 253; Stevick, 1980). The vast majority of our students, however, are not as interested in the structure of language as we are, and get their pleasures elsewhere!

But what about those students who believed us, and will only accept conscious grammar and drill as the core of a language class, and who expect all of their errors to be corrected (see e.g. Cathcart and Olsen, 1976)? I can only recommend two sorts of solution, one long term and one short term. If the essentials of this book are correct, in the long term, these students and their teachers will be educated. Ideas change slowly, however, and some short-term solutions are needed. One of these, suggested by Tony Pfannkuche, is to present a short course on language acquisition as part of the language teaching program, or just prior to it. I think this is justified, especially if we conceive of the language requirement in high schools and colleges as including skills and information about how to acquire any language, not just the one presented in class. Another approach, and one that I am personally not above using in my classes, is deception. We can teach vocabulary or grammar, and, as long as it is done in the target language, a great deal of acquisition will take place, the medium being the message. We can teach situationally, giving students useful, short dialogues that satisfy the craving for learning and memorized language, but, at the same time, present comprehensible input. Finally, the subject matter international classes will also provide comprehensible input for a student, whether he believes in subconscious acquisition or not.

I think that I have presented a conservative view of language acquisition theory and its applications, conservative in the sense that it attempts to be consistent with all empirical data that are known to me. It is consistent with the way thousands of people have acquired second languages throughout history, and in many cases acquired them very well. They acquired second languages while they were focussed on something else, while they were gaining interesting or needed information, or interacting with people they liked to be with.

Notes

[1] These principles derive from what Asher considers to be the three critical elements of child language acquisition:

> (1) listening in advance of speaking: "It may be that listening comprehension maps the blueprint for the future acquisition of speaking" (p. 1041).
> (2) ". . . the understanding of spoken language may be acquired when adults manipulate the physical behavior of the infant through commands . . ."
> (3) ". . . listening skill may produce a 'readiness' for the child to speak . . . As understanding develops, there is a point of readiness to speak in which the child spontaneously begins to produce utterances" (p. 1041).

[2] While not strictly a method comparison experiment, Newmark's Minimal Language Teaching Program for foreign language teaching at the University level, reported in Newmark (1971), is of great interest. Newmark's students spent their instructional week as follows: three hours in conversation sections with native speakers; two hours of extensive reading ("in order to encourage scanning and rapid reading, assignments are purposely longer (10–20 pages) than students can study crytoanalytically, and examinations on readings purposely encourage rapid sketchy reading", p. 16); three hours in the lab for work on dialogues; and four hours with "learning" type activities (study of a conventional grammar, reading and discussion in general linguistics). Clearly, the first three portions focus on acquisition, with the conversational sections and extensive reading assignments providing comprehensible input. Newmark reports that his students consistently reach the MLA norms for two years in reading after only one year in his program.

[3] In some cases, international classes are impractical or impossible. One example is the large lecture class in elementary sciences. A possibility is the international discussion section and/or "pre-lecture" section, in which difficult vocabulary is explained, and the topic of the lecture discussed in advance.

[4] Currently, some "studies skills" classes and texts attempt to do just this. There have been at least informal reports that they are successful, and the establishment of international classes does not rule out the studies skills class (the "ESL clinic" is the term used by Schwabe, 1978), but it may have some advantages. First, the teacher of the studies skills class needs to determine, in advance, which study skills to teach. There must be, in other words, a needs analysis. Some of the needs are obvious. Schwabe (1978) lists the following:

1. Ability to take notes in lectures.
2. Ability to take notes on written, textual materials.
3. Ability to organize essay type examination questions and write accurately under the pressure of time.
4. Ability to recognize and understand the thinking strategies implicit in objective type test questions (p. 79).

The international class, it can be argued, provides a natural syllabus for the acquisition of study skills; needs such as those listed above will be met, as well as others not predicted by the needs survey (see footnote five for an example). Second, international students may not regard "study skills" classes as essential to their needs and as contributing directly to their educational program (although Schwabe points out that her students at the University of California at Davis appear to be more motivated for and interested in her ESL clinic than regular ESL classes). They may simply be another obstacle to get through before students can pursue their major interest.

This argumentation and speculation needs to be supplemented with research on the applied level, to determine whether the best approach is the clinic alone, the international class alone, or some combination.

[5] To give a concrete example of an easily-learnable aspect of classroom/academic behavior, Gloria Heller has pointed out to me that several of her ESL students would hand in homework assignments on three ring notebook paper with the rings on the wrong (right) side (on what we consider to be the back of the paper). This trivial error might be interpreted as a sign of sloppiness in a regular class and might not be corrected. It would be anticipated or at least corrected in an international students' class, and is a good example of a simple, learnable rule that makes a real difference. Using the correct side of the paper may not make a student a better student or improve his grasp of subject matter, but it will affect his image in the eyes of the teacher. "Learning" small aspects of classroom and academic behavior may thus have similar function as learning late-acquired aspects of language (Chapter IV): they may not be essential for communication, but add "polish", giving an often important cosmetic effect.

[6] Here is a possible summer intensive program, meant for the international student with a few years of formal English instruction in his own country who is not yet ready for academic work in English. The goal of the program is to provide subject matter instruction in areas that are, at the same time, very relevant to the students' needs and interests, and that are linguistically comprehensible.

(1) Course work, taught by subject matter teachers. The student selects courses from a list consisting of courses such as these:

(i) Mathematics review, from algebra through calculus.
(ii) Computer operation (not programming).
(iii) American consumer economics ("Sylvia Porter"), including credit, banking, shopping strategies, etc.

    (iv) English grammar ("language appreciation", or linguistics).
    (v) English grammar for Monitor use.

(2) Once a degree of fluency is achieved, discussion groups with both more experienced foreign students (in English) and with native speakers who are interested in the same area of study can supplement the formal course offerings.

My prediction is that such a program would result in far more acquisition of English than the standard intensive program, would be perceived of as more relevant by international students, and would be of considerable value in furthering the students' educational progress in his speciality.

[7] In areas where there are enough students to support such classes, other forms of subject matter teaching should also work in adult ESL, including job related classes for immigrants or non-native speakers of English, and topics of interest, e.g. introduction to American literature, American sports, cooking, etc. The point is that any topic will work as long as the input is comprehensible and the students are genuinely interested in the subject matter.

[8] As Carroll (1980) notes: "It is only natural for students to shape their learning efforts so as to be maximally successful on tests, and if the tests measure objectives that are in some ways different from those of the instruction, students will work towards those objectives and pay less attention to achieving other objectives. The nature of external examinations will often shape the behavior of the teachers themselves. We sometimes complain that teachers do nothing but 'teach for the tests' " (p. 528).

[9] I have no totally satisfactory topics to suggest that are "real" and that present real problems to be solved. In a consulting session with Karl Scheville's "PEFL" project at the University of California at Berkeley (Department of Education), I feel we came close to developing some. Here is one example. Examiner and student are given the following situation: they are siblings, and live in a small apartment with a large family. All the children share bedrooms. The oldest brother has decided that he wants a room of his own. A family meeting needs to take place to decide what to do, because if the brother gets his way, there will be intolerable space constraints on the rest of the family. The examiner and student discuss the situation, with the goal of recommending to the family what the possible solutions are. The topic is not "real", since it is a contrived situation, but in our rehearsals, we found that it was possible to stimulate some interesting back and forth discussion.

[10] The international classes I proposed earlier, special sections of subject matter classes for international students, might also profit from special materials. These might include texts in areas where slightly easier reading is not available, supplements to existing texts, and, as just mentioned, taped lectures supplemented with notes.

Bibliography

ALLWRIGHT, R. (1975) Problems in the study of the language teacher's treatment of error. In M. Burt and H. Dulay (Eds.) *New Directions in Second Language Learning, Teaching, and Bilingual Education*. Washington, D.C.: TESOL. pp. 96–109.

ANDERSEN, R. (1976) A functional acquisition hierarchy study in Puerto Rico. Paper presented at the 10th annual TESOL conference, New York, New York. March, 1976.

ANDERSEN, R. (1978) An implicational model for second language research. *Language Learning* 28: 221–282.

ASHER, J. (1965) The strategy of the total physical response: an application to learning Russian. *International Review of Applied Linguistics* 3: 291–300.

ASHER, J. (1966) The learning strategy of the total physical response: a review. *Modern Language Journal* 50: 79–84.

ASHER, J. (1969) The total physical response approach to second language learning. *Modern Language Journal* 53: 3–17.

ASHER, J. (1972) Children's first language as a model for second language learning. *Modern Language Journal* 56: 133–139.

ASHER, J. (1977a) *Learning Another Language Through Actions: The Complete Teacher's Guidebook*. Los Gatos, Calif.: Sky Oaks Productions.

ASHER, J. (1977b) Children learning another language: a developmental hypothesis. *Child Development* 48: 1040–1048.

ASHER, J. and PRICE, B. (1967) The learning strategy of the total physical response: some age differences. *Child Development* 38: 1219–1227.

ASHER, J., KUSUDO, J. and DE LA TORRE, R. (1974) Learning a second language through commands: the second field test. *Modern Language Journal* 58: 24–32.

BAILEY, N., MADDEN, C. and KRASHEN, S. (1974) Is there a "natural sequence" in adult second language learning? *Language Learning* 21: 235–243.

BANCROFT, J. (1978) The Lozanov method and its American adaptations. *Modern Language Journal* 62: 167–174.

BIALYSTOCK, E. and FROHLICH, M. (1977) Aspects of second language learning in classroom settings. *Working Papers on Bilingualism* 13: 1–26.

BIALYSTOCK, E. and FROHLICH, M. (1978a) The aural grammar test: description and implications. *Working Papers on Bilingualism* 15: 15–35.

BIALYSTOCK, E. and FROHLICH, M. (1978b) Variables of classroom achievement in second language learning. *Modern Language Journal* 62: 327–335.

BIRKBICHLER, D. (1977) Communication and beyond. In J. Phillips (Ed.) *The Language Connection: From the Classroom to the World*. Skokie, Ill.: National Textbook. pp. 53–94.

BRIERE, E. (1978) Variables affecting native Mexican children's learning Spanish as a second language. *Language Learning* 28: 159–174.

BROWN, J. (1980) An explanation of morpheme-group interactions. Paper presented at the Los Angeles Second Language Acquisition Research Forum, UCLA, February, 1980.

BROWN, R. (1973) *A First Language*. Cambridge: Harvard Press.

BROWN, R. (1977) Introduction. In C. Snow and C. Ferguson (Eds.) *Talking to Children*. New York: Cambridge University Press. pp. 1–27.

BROWN, R., CAZDEN, C. and BELLUGI, U. (1973) The child's grammar from I to III. In C. Ferguson and D. Slobin (Eds.) *Studies of Child Language Development*. New York: Holt Rinehart and Winston. pp. 295–333.

BROWN, S. (1979) Life situations: incorporating community resources into the adult ESL curriculum. *CATESOL Occasional Papers* 5: 48–65.

BRUCE, L. (1979) The acquisition of grammatical morphemes by adult students of Russian as a foreign language. MA Paper, Department of Linguistics, USC.

BRUCK, M., LAMBERT, W. and TUCKER, G. R. (1974) Bilingual schooling through the elementary grades: the St. Lambert Project and grade seven. *Language Learning* 24: 183–204.

BURT, M. and KIPARSKY, C. (1972) *The Gooficon: A Repair Manual for English*. Rowley, Ma: Newbury House.

BUSHMAN, R. and MADSEN, H. (1976) A description and evaluation of Suggestopedia—a new teaching methodology. In J. Fanselow and R. Crymes (Eds.) *On TESOL '76*. Washington: TESOL. pp. 29–38.

CAMPBELL, D. and STANLEY, J. (1963) *Experimental and Quasi-Experimental Designs for Research*. New York: Rand McNally.

CANCINO, H., ROSANSKY, E. and SCHUMANN, J. (1975) The acquisition of the English auxiliary by native Spanish speakers. *TESOL Quarterly* 9: 421–430

CARROLL, J. (1966) The contributions of psychological theory and educational research to the teaching of foreign languages. In A. Valdman (Ed.) *Trends in Language Teaching*. New York: McGraw-Hill. pp. 93–106.

CARROLL, J. (1967) Foreign language proficiency levels attained by language majors near graduation from college. *Foreign Language Annals* 1: 131–151.

CARROLL, J. (1980) Foreign language testing: persistent problems. In K. Croft (Ed.) *Readings on English as a Second Language*. Cambridge, Ma: Winthrop. pp. 518–530.

CATHCART, R. and OLSEN, J. (1976) Teachers' and students' preference for correction of classroom conversation errors. In J. Fanselow and R. Crymes (Eds.) *On TESOL '76*. Washington; TESOL. pp. 41–53.

CAZDEN, C. (1979) Curriculum/language contexts for bilingual education. In E. Briere (Ed.) *Language Development in a Bilingual Setting*. Pomona, California: National Multilingual Multicultural Materials Development Center. pp. 129–138.

CELCE-MURCIA, M. and ROSENZWEIG, F. (1979) Teaching vocabulary in the ESL classroom. In M. Celce-Murcia and L. McIntosh (Eds.) *Teaching English as a Second or Foreign Language*. Rowley, Ma.: Newbury House. pp. 241–257.

CHASTAIN, K. (1970) A methodological study comparing the audio-lingual habit theory and the cognitive code learning theory: a continuation. *Modern Language Journal* 54: 257–266.

CHASTAIN, K. and WOERDEHOFF, F. (1968) A methodological study comparing the audio-lingual habit theory and the cognitive code-learning theory. *Modern Language Journal* 52: 268–279.

CHIHARA, T. and OLLER, J. (1978) Attitudes and attained proficiency in EFL: a sociolinguistic study of adult Japanese speakers. *Language Learning* 28: 55–68.

CHOMSKY, N. (1965) *Aspects of the Theory of Syntax*. Cambridge: MIT Press.

CHRISTISON, M. (1979) Natural sequencing in adult second language acquisition. *TESOL Quarterly* 13: 122.

CLARK, E. and ANDERSEN, E. (1980) Spontaneous repairs: awareness in the process of acquiring language. *Papers and Reports in Child Language Dev.* **16**: 1–12.

CLARK, H. and CLARK, E. (1977) *Psychology and Language*. New York: Harcourt Brace Jovanovich.

COHEN, A. and ROBBINS, M. (1976) Towards assessing interlanguage performance: the relationship between selected errors, learner's characteristics, and learner's explanations. *Language Learning* **26**: 45–66.

COHEN, A. and SWAIN, M. (1976) Bilingual Education: the "Immersion" model in the North American context. *TESOL Quarterly* **10**: 45–53.

CORDER, S. P. (1967) The significance of learner's errors. *International Review of Applied Linguistics* **5**: 161–170.

CROSS, T. (1977) Mother's speech adjustments: the contributions of selected child listener variables. In C. Snow and C. Ferguson, *Talking to Children*. New York: Cambridge University Press. pp. 151–188.

d'ANGLEJAN, A. (1978) Language learning in and out of classrooms. In J. Richards (Ed.) *Understanding Second and Foreign Language Learning*. Rowley, Ma: Newbury House. pp. 218–236.

DE VILLIERS, P. and DE VILLIERS, J. (1973) A cross-sectional study of the acquisition of grammatical morphemes in child speech. *Journal of Psycholinguistic Research* **2**: 267–278.

DILLER, K. (1978) *The Language Teaching Controversy*. Rowley, Ma.: Newbury House.

DULAY, H. and BURT, M. (1974) Natural sequences in child second language acquisition. *Language Learning* **24**: 37–53.

DULAY, H. and BURT, M. (1975) A new approach to discovering universal strategies of child second language acquisition. In D. Dato (Eds.) *Developmental Psycholinguistics: Theory and Applications*. Georgetown University Round Table on Languages and Linguistics. Washington: Georgetown University Press. pp. 209–233.

DULAY, H. and BURT, M. (1977) Remarks on creativity in language acquisition. In M. Burt, H. Dulay and M. Finnochiaro (Eds.) *Viewpoints on English as a Second Language*. New York: Regents. pp. 95–126.

DULAY, H. and BURT, M. (1978) Some guidelines for the assessment of oral language proficiency and dominance. *TESOL Quarterly* **12**: 177–192.

DULAY, H., BURT, M. and KRASHEN, S. *Language Two*. New York: Oxford. In press.

DUSKOVA, L. (1969) On sources of error in foreign language learning. *International Review of Applied Linguistics* **4**: 11–36.

EKSTRAND, L. (1976) Age and length of residence as variables related to the adjustment of migrant children, with special reference to second language learning. In G. Nickel (Ed.) *Proceedings of the Fourth International Congress of Applied Linguistics*. Vol. 3. Stuttgart: Hochschul Verlag, pp. 179–197.

ERVIN-TRIPP, S. (1973) Some strategies for the first and second years. In A. Dil (Ed.) *Language Acquisition and Communicative Choice*. Stanford: Stanford University Press. pp. 204–238.

ERVIN-TRIPP, S. (1974) Is second language learning like the first? *TESOL Quarterly* **8**: 111–127.

FABRIS, M. (1978) The acquisition of English grammatical functors by child second language learners. *TESOL Quarterly* **12**: 482.

FANSELOW, J. (1977) The treatment of error in oral work. *Foreign Language Annals* **10**: 583–593.

FATHMAN, A. (1975) The relationship between age and second language productive ability. *Language Learning* **25**: 245–266.

FATHMAN, A. (1979) The value of morpheme order studies for second language learning. *Working Papers on Bilingualism* **18**: 179–199.

FATHMAN, A. (1980) Influences of age and setting on second language oral proficiency. Paper presented at Los Angeles Second Language Research Forum, UCLA, February, 1980.

FELIX, S. (1980) The effect of formal instruction on second language learning. Paper presented at Los Angeles Second Language Research Forum, UCLA, February, 1980.

FREED, B. (1980) Talking to foreigners versus talking to children: similarities and differences. In R. Scarcella and S. Krashen (Eds.) *Research in Second Language Acquisition.* Rowley, Ma.: Newbury House. pp. 19–27.

GAIES, S. (1977) The nature of linguistic input in formal language learning: linguistic and communicative strategies in ESL teachers' classroom language. In H. D. Brown, C. Yorio and R. Crymes (Eds.) *Teaching and Learning English as a Second Language: Trends in Research and Practice.* Washington: TESOL. pp. 204–212.

GARDNER, R. and LAMBERT, W. (1972) *Attitudes and Motivation in Second-Language Learning.* Rowley, Ma.: Newbury House.

GARY, J. O. (1975) Delayed oral practice in initial stages of second language learning. In M. Burt and M. Dulay (Eds.) *On TESOL '75: New Directions in Second Language Learning, Teaching and Bilingual Education.* Washington: TESOL. pp. 89–95.

GILLIS, M. and WEBER, R. (1976) The emergence of sentence modalities in the English of Japanese-speaking children. *Language Learning* **26**: 77–94.

HAKUTA, K. (1974) A preliminary report of the development of grammatical morphemes in a Japanese girl learning English as a second language. *Working Papers on Bilingualism* **3**: 18–43.

HALE, T. and BUDAR, E. (1970) Are TESOL classes the only answer? *Modern Language Journal* **54**: 487–492.

HALL, E. (1959) *The Silent Language.* Greenwich, Conn.: Fawcett.

HAMMARBERG, B. (1979) On intralingual, interlingual and developmental solutions in interlanguage. Paper presented at the Fifth Scandinavian Conference of Linguistics, Frostvallen, April, 1979.

HAMMERLY, H. (1975) The deduction/induction controversy. *Modern Language Journal* **LIX**: 15–18.

HANANIA, E. and GRADMAN, H. (1977) Acquisition of English structures: a case study of an adult native speaker in an English-speaking environment. *Language Learning* **27**: 75–92.

HARRIS, D. (1969) *Testing English as a Second Language.* New York: McGraw Hill.

HARTNETT, D. (1974) *The Relation of Cognitive Style and Hemispheric Preference to Deductive and Inductive Second Language Learning.* MA Thesis, Department of English (TESL), UCLA.

HATCH, E. (1972) Some studies in second language learning. *UCLA Workpapers in Teaching English as a Second Language* **6**: 29–36.

HATCH, E. (1976) Language in outer space. Paper presented at the UCLA–USC Second Language Acquisition Forum, Fall, 1976.

HATCH, E. (1978a) Discourse analysis and second language acquisition. In E. Hatch (Ed.) *Second Language Acquisition.* Rowley, Ma.: Newbury House. pp. 401–435.

HATCH, E. (1978b) Introduction. In E. Hatch (Ed.) *Second Language Acquisition.* Rowley, Ma.: Newbury House. pp. 1–18.

HATCH, E. (1979) Apply with caution. *Studies in Second Language Acquisition* **2**: 123–143.

HATCH, E., SHAPIRA, R. and GOUGH, J. (1978) "Foreigner-talk" discourse. *ITL: Review of Applied Linguistics* **39–40**: 39–60.

HAWKINS, J. (1978) *Definiteness and Indefiniteness: A Study in Reference and Grammaticality Prediction.* London: Croom Helm.

HENDRICKSON, J. (1978) Error correction in foreign language teaching: recent theory, research, and practice. In K. Croft (Ed.) *Readings on English as a Second Language.* Cambridge, Ma.: Winthrop. pp. 153–175.

HOUCK, N., ROBERTSON, J. and KRASHEN, S. (1978) On the domain of the conscious grammar: morpheme orders for corrected and uncorrected ESL student transcriptions. *TESOL Quarterly* **12**: 335–339.

HOUCK, N., ROBERTSON, J. and KRASHEN, S. (1978b) What happens in error correction. Abstract submitted to 1978 TESOL Conference.

HYLTENSTAM, K. (1977) Implicational patterns in interlanguage syntax variation. *Language Learning* **27**: 383–411.

INHELDER, B. and PIAGET, J. (1958) *The Growth of Logical Thinking from Childhood to Adolescence.* New York: Basic Books.

JOHNSON, T. and KRUG, K. (1980) Integrative and instrumental motivations: in search of a measure. In J. Oller and K. Perkins (Eds.) *Research in Language Testing.* Rowley, Ma.: Newbury House. pp. 241–249.

JONES, R. (1979) Performance testing of second language proficiency. In E. Briere and F. Hinofotis (Eds.) *Concepts in Language Testing.* Washington: TESOL. pp. 50–57.

JORDENS, P. and KELLERMAN, E. (1978) Investigation into the strategy of transfer in second language learning. Paper presented at AILA conference, Montreal, August, 1978.

KAYFETZ, J. (Fuller) (1978) *Natural and Monitored Sequences by Adult Learners of English as a Second Language.* Ph.D. dissertation, Florida State University.

KELLERMAN, E. (1978) Giving learners a break: native language intuitions as a source of predictions about transferability. *Working Papers on Bilingualism* **15**: 59–92.

KESSLER, C. and IDAR, I. (1977) The acquisition of English syntactic structures by a Vietnamese child. Paper presented at the Los Angeles Second Language Acquisition Forum, UCLA, 1977.

KLEINMAN, H. (1977) Avoidance behavior in adult second language acquisition. *Language Learning* **27**: 93–107.

KLIMA, E. and BELLUGI, U. (1966) Syntactic regularities in the speech of children. In J. Lyons and R. Wales (Eds.) *Psycholinguistic Papers.* Edinburgh: Edinburgh University Press. pp. 183–208.

KOUNIN, T. and KRASHEN, S. (1978) Approaching native speaker competence from two different directions. In C. Blatchford and J. Schachter (Eds.) *On TESOL '78: EFL Policies, Programs, Practices.* Washington: TESOL. pp. 205–212.

KRASHEN, S. (1976) Formal and informal linguistic environments in language learning and language acquisition. *TESOL Quarterly* 157–168.

KRASHEN, S. (1977) Some issues relating to the Monitor Model. In H. D. Brown, C. Yorio and R. Crymes (Eds.) *On TESOL '77: Teaching and Learning English as a Second Language: Trends in Research and Practice.* Washington: TESOL. pp. 144–158.

KRASHEN, S. (1978) Individual variation in the use of the Monitor. In W. Ritchie (Ed.) *Principles of Second Language Learning.* New York: Academic Press. pp. 175–183.

KRASHEN, S. (1980) The theoretical and practical relevance of simple codes in second language acquisition. In R. Scarcella and S. Krashen (Eds.) *Research in Second Language Acquisition*. Rowley, Ma.: Newbury House. pp. 7–18.

KRASHEN, S. (1981) *Second Language Acquisition and Second Language Learning*. Oxford: Pergamon Press.

KRASHEN, S. (1982) Newmark's "Ignorance Hypothesis" and current second language acquisition theory. Unpublished manuscript.

KRASHEN, S., SELIGER, H. and HARTNETT, D. (1974) Two studies in second language learning. *Kritikon Litterarum* 3: 220–228.

KRASHEN, S. and PON, P. (1975) An error analysis of an advanced ESL learner. *Working Papers on Bilingualism* 7: 125–129.

KRASHEN, S., MADDEN, C. and BAILEY, N. (1975) Theoretical aspects of grammatical sequencing. In M. Burt and H. Dulay (Eds.) *Second language Learning, Teaching, and Bilingual Education*. Washington: TESOL. pp. 44–54.

KRASHEN, S. and SELIGER, H. (1975) The essential characteristics of formal instruction. *TESOL Quarterly* 9: 173–183.

KRASHEN, S. and SELIGER, H. (1976) The role of formal and informal linguistic environments in adult second language learning. *International Journal of Psycholinguistics* 3: 15–21.

KRASHEN, S., SFERLAZZA, V., FELDMAN, L. and FATHMAN, A. (1976) Adult performance on the SLOPE test: more evidence for a natural sequence in adult second language acquisition. *Language Learning* 26: 145–151.

KRASHEN, S., HOUCK, N., GIUNCHI, P., BODE, S., BIRNBAUM, R. and STREI, J. (1977) Difficulty order for grammatical morphemes for adult second language performers using free speech. *TESOL Quarterly* 11: 338–341.

KRASHEN, S., BUTLER, J., BIRNBAUM, R. and ROBERTSON, J. (1978) Two studies in language acquisition and language learning. *ITL: Review of Applied Linguistics* 39–40: 73–92.

KRASHEN, S. and SCARCELLA, R. (1978) On routines and patterns in language acquisition and performance. *Language Learning* 28: 283–300.

KRASHEN, S., ZELINSKI, S., JONES, C. and USPRICH, C. (1978) How important is instruction? *English Language Teaching Journal* 32: 257–261.

KRASHEN, S., LONG, M. and SCARCELLA, R. (1979) Age, rate and eventual attainment in second language acquisition. *TESOL Quarterly* 13: 573–582.

KUNIHARA, S. and ASHER, J. (1965) The strategy of the total physical response: an application to learning Japanese. *International Review of Applied Linguistics* 4: 277–289.

LADO, R. (1964) *Language Teaching: A Scientific Approach*. New York: McGraw Hill.

LADO, R. and FRIES, C. (1958) *An Intensive Course in English*. Ann Arbor: University of Michigan Press.

LAMBERT, W. and TUCKER, G. R. (1972) *The Bilingual Education of Children*. Rowley, Ma.: Newbury House.

LAMENDELLA, J. (1979) Lectures presented at the 1979 TESOL Summer Institute, UCLA, English 272K.

LARSEN, D. (1975) A re-evaluation of grammatical structure sequencing. *On TESOL '74*. Washington: TESOL.

LARSEN-FREEMAN, D. (1975) The Acquisition of Grammatical Morphemes by Adult Learners of English as a Second Language. Ph.D. dissertation, University of Michigan.

LARSEN-FREEMAN, D. (1979) The importance of input in second language acquisition. Paper presented at the Linguistic Society of America, Los Angeles, December, 1979.

LAWLER, J. and SELINKER, L. (1971) On paradoxes, rules, and research in second language acquisition. *Language Learning* 21: 27–43.

LEE, R., MCCUNE, L. and PATTON, L. (1970) Physiological responses to different modes of feedback in pronunciation testing. *TESOL Quarterly* 4: 117–122.

LENNEBERG, E. (1962) Understanding language without ability to speak: a case report. *Journal of Abnormal and Social Psychology* 65: 419–425.

LEVIN, L. (1972) *Comparative Studies in Foreign-Language Teaching*. Stockholm: Almqvist & Wiksell.

LIGHTBOWN, P., SPADA, N. and WALLACE, R. (1980) Some effects of instruction on child and adolescent ESL learners. In R. Scarcella and S. Krashen (Eds.) *Research in Second Language Acquisition*. Rowley, Ma.: Newbury House. pp. 162–172.

LIGHTBOWN, P. Exploring the relationships between developmental and instructional sequences in second language acquisition. In H. Seliger and M. Long (Eds.) *Classroom Language Acquisition and Use: New Perspectives*. Rowley, Ma.: Newbury House. In press.

LoCoco, V. (1975) An analysis of Spanish and German learner's errors. *Working Papers on Bilingualism* 7: 96–124.

LONG, M. (1980) *Input, Interaction, and Second Language Acquisition*. Ph.D. dissertation, UCLA.

LUKMANI, Y. (1972) Motivation to learn and language proficiency. *Language Learning* 22: 261–273.

MACHA, D. (1979) Reading comprehension of non-native students in English composition at the freshman level. *TESOL Quarterly* 13: 425–427.

MACNAMARA, J. (1972) Cognitive basis of language learning in infants. *Psychological Review* 79: 1–14.

MAKINO, T. (1980) *Acquisition Order of English Morphemes by Japanese Adolescents*. Tokyo: Shinozaki Shorin Press.

MASON, C. (1971) The relevance of intensive training in English as a foreign language for university students. *Language Learning* 21: 197–204.

MILON, J. (1974) The development of negation in English by a second language learner. *TESOL Quarterly* 8: 137–143.

MINOURA, Y. (1979) An examination of the role of acculturation in second language acquisition through multivariate analysis. Paper presented at TESOL summer meeting, UCLA, July, 1979.

MUELLER, T. (1971) The effectiveness of two learning models: the audio-lingual habit theory and the cognitive code-learning theory. In P. Pimsleur and T. Quinn (Eds.) *The Psychology of Second Language Learning*. Cambridge: Cambridge University Press, pp. 113–122.

MURAKAMI, M. (1980) Behavioral and attitudinal correlates of progress in ESL by native speakers of Japanese. In J. Oller and K. Perkins (Eds.) *Research in Language Testing*. Rowley, Ma.: Newbury House. pp. 227–232.

NELSON, J. (1980) *Language Systems in Adult Informal Second Language Learners*. Ph.D. dissertation, McGill University.

NEWMARK, L. (1966) How not to interfere with language learning. *Language Learning: The Individual and the Process. International Journal of American Linguistics* 40: 77–83.

NEWMARK, L. (1971) A minimal language teaching program. In P. Pimsleur and T. Quinn (Eds.) *The Psychology of Second Language Learning.* Cambridge: Cambridge University Press. pp. 11–18.

NEWMARK, L. and REIBEL, D. (1973) Necessity and sufficiency in language learning. In M. Lester (Ed.) *Readings in Applied Transformational Grammar.* New York: Holt Rinehart Winston. pp. 220–244.

NEWPORT, E., GLEITMAN, H. and GLEITMAN, L. (1977) Mother, I'd rather do it myself: some effects and non-effects of maternal speech style. In C. Snow and C. Ferguson (Eds.) *Talking to Children.* Cambridge: Cambridge University Press. pp. 109–149.

OLLER, J. (1979) *Language Tests at School.* London: Longmans.

OLLER, J., BACA, L. and VIGIL, A. (1977) Attitudes and attained proficiency in ESL: a sociolinguistic study of Mexican-Americans in the southwest. *TESOL Quarterly* 11: 173–183.

OLLER, J. and PERKINS, K. (1978) Intelligence and language proficiency as sources of variance in self reported affective variables. In J. Oller and K. Perkins (Eds.) *Language in Education: Testing the Tests.* Rowley, Ma.: Newbury House. pp. 103–122.

OLLER, J., PERKINS, K. and MURAKAMI, M. (1980) Seven types of learner variables in relation to ESL learning. In J. Oller and K. Perkins (Eds.) *Research in Language Testing.* Rowley, Ma.: Newbury House. pp. 233–240.

OLSSON, M. (1969) Implicit and explicit: an experiment in applied psycholinguistics, assessing different methods of teaching grammatical structures in English as a foreign language. GUME Report #3, Gothenburg School of Education. Sweden.

OSTRANDER, S. and SCHROEDER, L. (Eds.) (1976) *The ESP Papers.* New York: Bantam Books.

OYAMA, S. (1976) A sensitive period for the acquisition of a non-native phonological system. *Journal of Psycholinguistic Research* 5: 261–285.

OYAMA, S. (1978) The sensitive period and comprehension of speech. *Working Papers on Bilingualism* 16: 1–17.

PATKOWSKI, M. (1980) The sensitive period for the acquisition of syntax in a second language. *Language Learning* 30: 449–472.

PAULSTON, C. (1972) Structural pattern drills: a classification. *Foreign Language Annals* 4: 187–193.

POSTOVSKY, V. (1974) Effects of delay in oral practice at the beginning of second language learning. *Modern Language Journal* 58: 229–239.

Public Service Commission of Canada, Staff Development Branch, Studies Division, Suggestopedia Program (1975) A teaching experience with the Suggestopedic Method. Ottawa, Canada.

PURCELL, E. and SUTER, R. (1980) Predictors of pronunciation accuracy: a re-examination. *Language Learning* 30: 271–287.

RACLE, G. (1979) Psychopédagogie profonde en enseignement des langes. *Medium* 4: 91–110.

RACLE, R. (1980) Psychopédagogie profonde en enseignement des langes. (suite). *Medium* 5: 73–83.

RAMSEY, C. and WRIGHT, E. (1974) Age and second language learning. *Journal of Social Psychology* 94: 115–121.

RAVEM, R. (1974) The development of wh-questions in first and second language learners. In J. Richards (Ed.) *Error Analysis: Perspectives on Second Language Learning.* London: Longman. pp. 134–155.

REBER, A. (1976) Implicit learning of synthetic languages: the role of instructional set. *Journal of Experimental Psychology: Human Memory and Learning.* **2**: 88–95.

RIVERS, W. (1968) *Teaching Foreign Language Skills.* Chicago: University of Chicago Press.

RIVERS, W. (1979) Foreign language acquisition: where the real problems lie. *Applied Linguistics* **1**: 48–57.

ROBINSON, P. (1980) *ESP: English for Specific Purposes.* Oxford: Pergamon Press.

SCARCELLA, R. Developing conversational competence in a second language. Forthcoming.

SCARCELLA, R. and HIGA, C. Input and age differences in second language acquisition. In S. Krashen, R. Scarcella and M. Long (Eds.) *Child-Adult Differences in Second Language Acquisition.* Rowley, Ma.: Newbury House. Forthcoming.

SCHACHTER, J. (1974) An error in error analysis. *Language Learning* **24**: 205–214.

SCHACHTER, J., TYSON, A. and DIFFLEY, F. (1976) Learner intuitions of grammaticality. *Language Learning* **26**: 67–76.

SCHERER, G. and WERTHEIMER, M. (1964) *A Psycholinguistic Experiment in Foreign Language Teaching.* New York: McGraw Hill.

SCHLUE, K. (1977) An inside view of interlanguage. In C. Henning (Ed.) *Proceedings of the Los Angeles Second Language Research Forum.* UCLA TESL Department. pp. 342–348.

SCHUMANN, J. (1978a) *The Pidginization Process.* Rowley, Ma.: Newbury House.

SCHUMANN, J. (1978b) The acculturation model for second-language acquisition. In R. Gingras (Ed.) *Second-Language Acquisition and Foreign Language Teaching.* Arlington, Virginia: Center for Applied Linguistics. pp. 27–50.

SCHUMANN, J. (1979) The acquisition of English negation by speakers of Spanish: a review of the literature. In R. Andersen (Ed.) *The Acquisition and Use of Spanish and English as First and Second Languages.* Washington: TESOL.

SCHUMANN, J. (1980) The acquisition of English relative clauses by second language learners. In R. Scarcella and S. Krashen (Eds.) *Research in Second Language Acquisition.* Rowley, Ma.: Newbury House. pp. 118–131.

SCHUMANN, J. and SCHUMANN, F. (1977) Diary of a language learner: an introspective study of second language learning. In H. D. Brown, C. Yorio and R. Crymes (Eds.) *On TESOL '77: Teaching and Learning English as a Second Language, Trends in Research and Practice.* Washington: TESOL. pp. 209–249.

SCHWABE, T. (1978) Survival English for ESL students in American educational institutions. *CATESOL Occasional Papers* **4**: 79–87.

SCOVEL, T. (1979) Georgi Lozanov: Suggestology and outlines of Suggestology. *TESOL Quarterly* **13**: 255–266.

SELIGER, H. (1975) Inductive method and deductive method in language teaching: a reexamination. *International Review of Applied Linguistics* **13**: 1–18.

SELIGER, H. (1979) On the nature and function of language rules in language teaching. *TESOL Quarterly* **13**: 359–369.

SELIGER, H., KRASHEN, S. and LADEFOGED, P. (1975) Maturational constraints in the acquisition of a native-like accent in second language learning. *Language Sciences* **36**: 209–231.

SELINKER, L. (1972) Interlanguage *International Review of Applied Linguistics* **10**: 209–231.

SHIPLEY, E., SMITH, C. and GLEITMAN, L. (1969) A study in the acquisition of language: free responses to commands. *Language* **45**: 322–342.

STAFFORD, C. and COVITT, G. (1978) Monitor use in adult second language production. *ITL: Review of Applied Linguistics* **39–40**: 103–125.

STAUBLE, A. (1978) The process of decreolization: a model for second language development. *Language Learning* **28**: 29–54.

STEVICK, E. (1976) *Memory, Meaning, and Method.* Rowley, Ma.: Newbury House.

STEVICK, E. (1980) *Teaching Languages: A Way and Ways.* Rowley, Ma.: Newbury House.

SWAFFER, J. and WOODRUFF, M. (1978) Language for comprehension: focus on reading. *Modern Language Journal* **62**: 27–32.

SWAIN, M. (1974) French immersion programs across Canada: research findings. *Canadian Modern Language Review* **31**: 117–129.

TERRELL, T. (1977) A natural approach to second language acquisition and learning. *Modern Language Journal* **6**: 325–337.

TUCKER, G. R. and SAROFIM, M. (1979) Investigating linguistic acceptability with Egyptian EFL students. *TESOL Quarterly* **13**: 29–39.

ULIJN, J. and KEMPEN, G. (1976) The role of the first language in second language reading comprehension—some experimental evidence. *Proceedings of the Fourth International Congress of Applied Linguistics.* Stuttgart: HochschulVerlag. pp. 495–507.

UPSHUR, J. (1968) Four experiments on the relation between foreign language teaching and learning. *Language Learning* **18**: 111–124.

VALETTE, R. (1977) *Modern Language Testing.* New York: Harcourt Brace Jovanovich.

VAN NAERSSEN, M. (1981) Ph.D. dissertation, Department of Linguistics, University of Southern California.

VARVEL, T. (1979) The Silent Way: panacea or pipedream? *TESOL Quarterly* **13**: 483–494.

VON ELEK, T. and OSKARSSON, M. (1975) *Comparative Method Experiments in Foreign Language Teaching.* Department of Educational Research. Mölndal (Gothenburg) School of Education. Sweden.

WAGNER-GOUGH, J. and HATCH, E. (1975) The importance of input data in second language acquisition studies. *Language Learning* **25**: 297–308.

WALBURG, H., HASE, K. and PINZUR RASHER, S. (1978) English acquisition as a diminishing function of experience rather than age. *TESOL Quarterly* **12**: 427–437.

WHITE, L. (1977) Error analysis and error correction in adult learners of English as a second language. *Working Papers on Bilingualism* **13**: 42–58.

WIDDOWSON, H. (1977) The significance of simplification. *Studies in Second Language Acquisition* 1.

WIGGIN, B. (1979) Comments on the TOEFL test. *TESOL Quarterly* **13**: 292–294.

WINN-BELL OLSEN, J. (1977) *Communication Starters and Other Activities for the ESL Classroom.* San Francisco: Alemeny Press.

WODE, H. (1976) Developmental sequences in naturalistic L2 acquisition. In E. Hatch (Ed.) *Second Language Acquisition.* Rowley, Ma.: Newbury House. pp. 101–117.

YORIO, C. (1978) Confessions of a second language speaker/learner. Paper presented at 12th annual TESOL convention, Mexico City, April, 1978.

ZOBL, H. (1980a) Developmental and transfer errors; their common bases and (possibly) differential effects on subsequent learning. *TESOL Quarterly* **14**: 469–479.

ZOBL, H. (1980b) Contact-induced language change, learner-language, and the potentials of a modified CA. Paper presented at the Los Angeles Second Language Acquisition Research Forum, UCLA.

ZOBL, H. (1980c) The formal and developmental selectivity of L1 influence on L2 acquisition. *Language Learning* **30**: 43–57.

Index